C 027344 II R

JSCSC Library

Date: -9 JUL 2004

Accession no:

Class Mark: 953.5 OWT

1 86 0646 74

Hobson Library

404856

Books Express
Specialist suppliers of Military History and Defence Studies
P.O. Box 10, Saffron Walden, Essex, CB11 4EW. U.K.
Tel: 01799 513726, Fax: 01799 513248
info@books-express.co.uk / www.books-express.co.uk

A Modern History of Oman

To Corinne and Carey and my parents

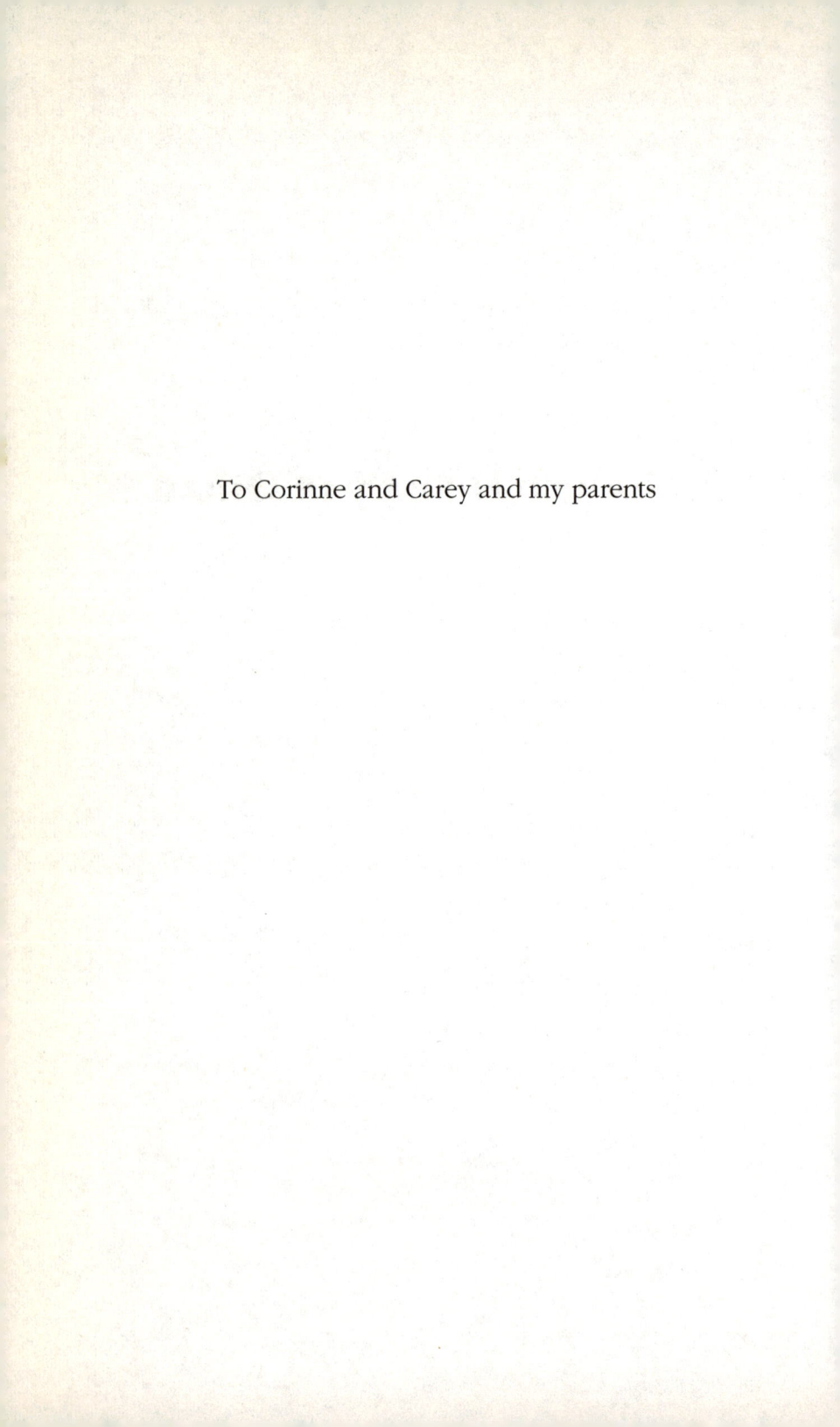

A Modern History of Oman
Formation of the State since 1920

Francis Owtram

Published in 2004 by I.B Tauris & Co Ltd
6 Salem Road, London, W2 4BU
175 Fifth Avenue, New York NY 10010
www.ibtauris.com

In the United States of America and in Canada distributed by
St Martins Press, 175 Fifth Avenue, New York NY 10010

Copyright © Francis Owtram, 2004

The right of Francis Owtram to identified as the author of this work has been asserted by the author in accordance with the Copyright, Designs and Patents Act 1988.

All rights reserved. Except for brief quotations in a review, this book, or any part thereof, may not be reproduced, stored in or introduced into a retrieval system, or transmitted, in any form or by any means, electronic, mechanical, photocopying, recording or otherwise, without the prior written permission of the publisher.

Library of Modern Middle East Studies 30

ISBN 1 86064 617 4
EAN 978 1 86064 617 1

A full CIP record for this book is available from the British Library
A full CIP record for this book is available from the Library of Congress

Library of Congress catalog card: available

Printed and bound in Great Britain by MPG Books, Bodmin from camera-ready copy edited and supplied by the author.

Thanks also to Dr Lester Crook and Claire Dubois at IB Tauris Publishers and to Catherine Warwick for preparing the camera-ready copy.

Table of Contents

Acknowledgements	vi
Abbreviations	vii
Introduction	1
Chapter 1 The Theoretical Context	9
Chapter 2 Oman and British Imperial Expansion 1798- 1920	29
Chapter 3 Informal Empire in Oman 1921 - 1931	51
Chapter 4 The Expansion of the Sultanate 1932 - 1955	69
Chapter 5 The Consolidation of the Omani State 1956 - 1977	97
Chapter 6 Western Strategic Interests in the Contemporary Omani State	143
Conclusions	193
Notes to the Reader	208
Bibliography	221
Index	229

Acknowledgements

It is a pleasure to thank people who have helped me with this book in various ways. I first discussed the topic of Oman and the West with Dr David Pool at the University of Manchester. At the London School of Economics Professor Fred Halliday supervised the thesis on which this book is based with interest and encouragement and I benefited from his incisive comments. I valued my conversations on Oman and Aden with my fellow PhD students at the LSE, Abdul Malik al-Hinawi and Christian Lekon. The input from the examiners of the thesis, Dr Charles Tripp and Professor Tim Niblock, considerably sharpened various aspects of the study.

Abbreviations

AOC	Air Officer Commanding
AWAC	Airborne Warning and Control System
BATT	British Army Training Team
BFAP	British Forces Aden Protectorate
CID	Committee of Imperial Defence
DLF	Dhofar Liberation Front
EEIC	English East Indian Company
FO	Foreign Office; Foreign Office Records in the PRO
GCC	Gulf Cooperation Council
IPC	Iraq Petroleum Company
MOFF	Muscat and Oman Field Regiment
MR	Muscat Regiment
MT$	Maria Theresa Dollar
NCO	Non-Commissioned Officer
NLF	National Liberation Front
NFR	Northern Frontier Regiment
ORM	Oman Revolutionary Movement
PDO	Petroleum Development (Oman) Ltd
PFLO/AG	Popular Front for the Liberation of Oman; previously Popular Front for the Liberation of Oman and the Arabian Gulf or Popular Front for the Liberation of the Occupied Arabian Gulf
PGSC	Persian Gulf Sub-Committee of the CID
PRO	Public Records Office (London)
RAF	Royal Air Force
RDF	Rapid Deployment Force
SAF	Sultan's Armed Forces (Oman)
SAS	Special Air Services (British)
SOCAL	Standard Oil of California
SOAF	Sultan of Oman's Air Force
SGRF	State General Reserve Fund
UAE	United Arab Emirates
USAAF	US Army Air Force
USCENTCOM	US Central Command

Introduction

The origins of this book was in an interest in the reasons for the military involvement of Western powers, particularly Britain and the United States, in the Persian Gulf area since World War Two. Oman provided an interesting country for an examination of one particular case in depth. Thus the main focus of the book is the development of Western strategic interests and military involvement in Oman in the 20th century. Engagement with Oman on this basis led to an exploration of the historical origins and context for this Western involvement and its impact on Omani society. Study followed of the way in which Omani society had developed, given its ecology and geographical position, and of concepts and theorisation which could explain the relationship between Oman, Britain and the United States. Theories of state formation and informal imperialism provide the theoretical framework of the book. The attention paid to Western strategic interests and military involvement is justified with regards to its relevance to the analysis of state formation as military support to the Sultanate has been the most significant support given by the West; without it the Sultanate would most likely not exist. The book addresses, therefore, the external and internal influences on the process of state formation in Oman in the period since 1920 during which Oman developed from part of Britain's informal empire to a state in the contemporary international system.

This book aims to address three central questions on informal empire and state formation in the case of Oman. (1) What factors have been most significant in the process of state formation in Oman in the era of modern Middle East politics?

(2) In comparative perspective, what is it about state formation in Oman that makes Oman different from the other GCC states: Saudi Arabia, Kuwait, Bahrain, Qatar and the United Arab Emirates? (3) To what extent are the concepts of informal empire and collaboration useful in analysing the relationship between Oman and the West?

With regard to the first question the argument advanced is that the modern Omani state has been produced by the process of interaction between imperialism, that is, external domination or intervention in some form, and anti-imperialism, that is, the internal resistance, as expressed in the repeated rebellions of Omanis. The external intervention at every stage in the process of state formation in the modern era was based not on economic interests intrinsic to Oman but for strategic and foreign policy reasons relating to economic interests external to Oman. Thus it has been Western strategic interests and Oman's geopolitical strategic importance in the broad context of Persian Gulf policy which have most influenced the evolution of Oman's contemporary state from the pattern of Oman's 'traditional' political dynamics - those pertaining prior to the impact of the West and the incorporation of Oman into the world capitalist market. The impact of capitalism on the Omani political system was mediated twofold, externally and internally. Externally it was mediated by British imperial strategic interests in the Indian Ocean and Persian Gulf area. Internally it was mediated by the pre-existing economic, social and political institutions of Oman. These external and internal influences on state formation in Oman and the interaction between them are the analytical themes of this study.

In comparative perspective state formation in Oman, whilst sharing a number of similarities to the rest of the oil monarchies of the Gulf, also displays a number of distinct differences. These are in the nature of Oman's political identity, geographical diversity and at the level of the ruling family. Sultan Qabus is alone at the apex of the political system far more than is the case in the other GCC states. With regard to the third question it would be hard to find a better example of informal empire than Oman - it represents an interesting case of the relationship between an imperial power and a peripheral society and the crises of collaboration that constituted this relationship. The relationship between Oman and Britain between 1798 and 1977 can be seen as divided into a number of historical stages, each representing a particular type of collaborative alliance between Muscat and Britain; each of these periods was marked off by particular crises of collaboration. Around 1800 Britain became more than just one of the European powers operating in the Indian Ocean. The Sultan of Muscat formed an alliance with the British to advance his own aims although the British were wary of becoming drawn into internal Arabian conflicts. Over the course of the 19th century this alliance turned into a relationship of domination as the actions of the British undermined the political and economic basis of the Sultans' rule (see chapter two). The British-sponsored separation of the African and Arabian Al Bu Sa'id Sultanates indicated increasingly direct British arbitration in Omani affairs. Following the Imamate's taking of Muscat in 1868 the British helped to restore the Sultan to power in 1871 and Muscat became a *de facto* protectorate; there followed a number of armed interventions by British warships in defence of their client Sultans against attacking tribal forces (Halliday 1974:272). In 1886 a formal guarantee was given to Sultan Turki to uphold him against unprovoked aggression. From the 1890s the British instituted a 'forward policy' in the Gulf which ever more tightly controlled the foreign relations of the Sultanate. This was signified by the 1891 British-Muscat treaty in which the Sultans promised never to cede any territory to a third power. This was the closest Oman came to being formally a part of the British empire (Peterson 1978: 141). In the 1920s the British became more involved in the running of internal government as well as the control of the external relations of Muscat. This constituted informal empire which was maintained, Sa'id bin Taimur's efforts notwithstanding, until 1970. The ending of informal empire is by definition not as distinct as formal colonial withdrawal. The returning of the airbases at Salalah and Masirah to the Omani government in 1977 can be designated as the final end of British informal empire in Oman. At this point the British, having prevented another Aden, withdrew and turned to other means to secure their interests, namely, by means of influence in the Omani 'post-colonial' state which the British had helped to construct.

These arguments on the process of state formation in Oman will be advanced using a historical narrative structured by three interrelated themes: the international context of external involvement, the nature of that involvement and its impact on Omani society.

Theme One
The context of the relationship is identified as the world wide expansion of the capitalism and its accompanying social relations and state system. The impact of capitalism on the Middle East and specifically Oman was mediated by the agency of British imperial expansion. Part of this broad historical process has been the ascendancy of Britain followed by imperial decline and de-colonisation, the rise of the United States and the Cold War, the development of Arab nationalism, and the collapse of the Soviet Union and the end of the Cold War.

In terms of Oman's relationship with the West since 1920 three inter-related developments have been of most importance. Firstly, the change in the basis of Western interest in the Arabian peninsula from its place in the security of the British Raj to the oil reserves lying in the strata of the peninsula itself; secondly, the gradual replacement of Britain by the United States as the predominant Western power in the Middle East; and thirdly, the resulting change in responsibility for the security of the Gulf.

However, there has been an underlying constant in Oman's place in this changing context: Oman's key importance to the West has always been strategic (Halliday 1974: 265); specifically, its role in protecting an economic interest external to Oman - be it the Raj or the vast oil reserves of the Saudi Arabia - described by American diplomats in 1945 as 'one of the greatest material prizes in history' (quoted in Stork 1980c: 24). This is not to underestimate the considerable Western economic interests in Oman but rather to emphasise that placed within the overall context they are relatively less significant.

Theme Two
This wider context of economic interest, foreign policy and defence strategy has created strategic interests in Oman and an ensuing involvement to protect those interests. In 1920 these strategic interests were such that Oman was a 'safe and static link' in British schemes for Indian Ocean security (Halliday 1974: 265). By the 1990s these interests had developed so that

Oman had played a vital role in Western military intervention to protect the oil reserves of Saudi Arabia and Kuwait. Not surprisingly, first Britain and then the United States have been concerned that there should be a social order in Oman conducive to the maintenance of these interests. Essentially, this was achieved through the creation and maintenance of a client relationship with the Al Bu Sa'id dynasty until the 1970s. This necessitated periodic interventions to either support Al Bu Sa'id rulers or, alternatively, to depose or undermine individual rulers when required.

Theme Three
The third theme is the consequences of Western involvement for Oman. The pattern of economy, social order, government and external relations have all been fundamentally affected by the impact of the West. For this describes the consequences for Oman of its integration in the modern state system that has resulted from the world wide expansion of capitalism.

The period since 1920, while it has sub-divisions in it, forms a distinct period in the relationship between Oman and the West in terms of the three narrative themes employed. (1) From the 1800s to the First World War British strategic interests in Oman were defined by the place it held in the British perception of the security of the Raj. With the discovery of oil in significant quantities in and around the Persian Gulf just prior to World War One came the realisation that the Arabian Peninsula could hold oil bearing strata. It was the subsequent development of these vast oil reserves that was to replace the British Raj as the economic interest framing Western strategic interests in Oman. (2) The development of air routes along the Arabian littoral in the 1920s to facilitate air communications and the application of air power led to the creation of important new strategic interests in Oman. (3) The granting of oil concessions by Sultan Taimur in the 1920s marked the beginning of a new phase in the incorporation of Oman into the world capitalist market and state system. It started with the first prospecting for oil and concomitant need to define the form and boundaries of the state, through to the first exports of oil and subsequent development of a *rentier* state.

Phases of state formation in Oman since 1920

From 1798 to 1920 state formation in Oman is defined by the requirements of the British link with India. State formation in Oman in the period since 1920 can be divided into the following stages: 1920 – 1931, 1932 – 1955, 1956 – 1977 and 1978 to the present. The period 1920 –1977 is the era of British informal empire in Oman which saw a particular form of British imperial influence. It will be argued that in each of these stages up to 1977, the decisive factor was British strategic interest in the context of an international environment that was subject to continuous change.

British informal empire in Oman 1921 – 1931

This phase is defined by the outcome of the First World War. Britain's greater involvement in the Middle East required a greater degree of supervision and control in the Arabian Peninsula. Thus, the period immediately after the 1920 Treaty of Sib represents the high point of British supervision of the government of Oman. Sultan Taymur bin Faisal (r.1913 – 1932) as we shall see later, was unwilling to 'rule' in the situation Britain presented him with and absented himself from Muscat. Therefore a Council of Ministers (1920 – 1932) 'governed' with British advisers and effectively British control of the customs revenue. Also during this time the development of new Western strategic interests in Oman in the form of air routes and oil prospecting began to increase the strategic importance of Oman.

The expansion of the Sultanate 1932 – 1955

The next chronological phase can be termed the expansion of the Sultanate; this phase is defined by the impact of the oil leases following the discovery of oil in Bahrain in 1932 and the development of air routes around the Arabian peninsula. Sultan Sa'id bin Taimur (r.1932 – 1970) sought to take an active part in the government of Oman; his interest in obtaining any revenues from oil coincided with the interest of the British government and oil companies to gain access to that resource rather than allow American companies this opportunity. The outcome was the overturning of the de facto division of the coast and the interior. This was achieved by the British financing and staffing of armed forces which occupied Nizwa and ousted the Imamate in 1955.

The consolidation of the Omani state 1956 – 1977

This phase of state formation in Oman is marked by the impact of Arab nationalism and radicalism on the British position in the Arabian peninsula. The Suez crisis of 1956 marked the end of European attempts to act in the Middle East in opposition to the United States and was followed by ineluctable British withdrawal from the region. In Oman this finally took place in 1977 when the British vacated their bases at Masirah Island and Salalah having defeated the left-wing rebellion in Dhofar and secured a political order Oman conducive to Western strategic interests. Sa'id bin Taimur had retreated to Salalah following his triumphant tour of the interior in 1955 and absented himself from Muscat. The Dhofari rebellion against his regime and the threat this posed to British interests meant that the modernising Qabus was allowed to become Sultan in 1970. The reforms undertaken then with the benefit of oil revenues signalled the consolidation of the Omani state into its newest form: the Sultanate of Oman.

Western strategic interests in the contemporary Omani state

The final stage is that of the contemporary *rentier* state. The development of significant oil revenues enabled Qabus to embark on a vast development programme for Oman which enable important groups to be co-opted. Qabus and the Royal Family and associates were able to keep a close grip on power whilst initiating various institutions of consultation. In terms of Western strategic involvement, whilst British personnel and influence remained significant in military matters there followed far greater American financial and political involvement following the 1980 US-Oman Access Agreement on military facilities. This reflected the Western strategic interest in Oman in planning for the deployment of military forces to secure Western access to Gulf oil; these planning arrangements were put into practice in the Kuwait War 1990-1991 and subsequent policies of dual containment and then regime change in Iraq.

Structure of the book

The structure of the book is as follows. Chapter one sets the historical narrative of state formation in Oman in the context of historical and theoretical work on the relationship between Oman and the West. State formation is a historical process.

Therefore, five empirical chapters organised chronologically then follow on each stage of state formation identified. The book concludes on the most significant factors in the process of state formation in Oman and how this compares with the other GCC states. It also considers the usefulness and applicability of theories of informal imperialism in understanding the relationship between Oman and the West.

CHAPTER ONE
The Theoretical Context

The historical narrative of this book is placed within a framework of comparative enquiry to examine the historical process of state formation in the case of Oman. This chapter examines various theoretical approaches which have been applied to Oman and state formation in the Middle East.

G. Lawrence Timpe (Timpe 1991) has analysed the relationship between British officialdom and the Omani Sultans, particularly Sa'id bin Taimur, using the theoretical framework of 'clientelism'. This framework, which is developed from psychology, anthropology and sociology, is characterised by Timpe as a 'middle-level theory'[1] which has traditionally been employed in the study of partisan politics and landowners/landlord - peasant relationships. Three fundamental characteristics of such a relationship are identified: dependence, reciprocity and personalisation. Timpe seeks to generalise the characteristics of clientelism as defined in the literature relating to peasants/landlords and apply them to the discipline of International Relations (1991: 76). Timpe identifies the following features of clientelism that apply in both the 'traditional' application of this concept identified above and that of an International Relations context, in this case Britain and Oman. In a traditional patron/client (landlord/peasant) relationship the client lacks capital, is educationally ill-equipped, and endures arbitrary injustice. The patron acts as a moderator and gatekeeper and the client goes to the patron for problem resolution. A face-to-face presence is maintained between the client and the patron. Timpe identifies a number of parallels in the British-Oman relationship where the client is Oman or specifically the Sultan and the patron is the

British or specifically Whitehall. Firstly, Britain fostered economic dependence whilst the client's general population (the Sultan's 'subjects') were uneducated. The Sultans suffered many British actions in silence and went to the British for military assistance as a form of problem resolution; Sa'id bin Taimur used Britain to moderate the Buraimi dispute at the United Nations. The way the British decided how Oman's military forces and economy were to be developed parallels the 'gatekeeping' function. The British maintained the Political Agent system as a form of face-to-face contact. A final similarity identified by Timpe is that a traditional clients engages in anxiety reduction behaviour and in the same way the Ibadhis have the concept of *kitman* which refers to the concealment of the Imamate (1991: 306).

Timpe also identifies three further characteristics of the relationship of Britain and Oman that differ in this international relations context from that pertaining in the context of landlord and peasant (1991: 307). Firstly, in the 'traditional' relationship, if the client wants the patron to resolve a problem, the problem can remain localised. In contrast, Britain's decision making process was multi-layered and framed in the wider context of Britain's interests in the Gulf as a whole and not just Oman. If the resolution of the problem in Britain's interest coincided with that of the client then that was good but not 'paramount'. Following from this was the possibility that if the British believed that the resolution of the problem required the deposition of a ruler (perhaps the client who brought the problem to the patron in the first place) that was acceptable, if it contributed to the maintenance of the British position in the region and furthered British interests (1991: 308). The third additional aspect is the need for secrecy in many aspects of the patron's dealing with the client. Timpe believes that this transfer of the theory of clientelism to the discipline of International Relations may be able to be applied to other relationships between industrialised nations and their various clients in the Arab Gulf region, Africa, South East Asia and even to the Pacific Trust Territories (1991:78-79).

It is useful to consider how this framework of clientelism contrasts with that of Robinson's concept of collaboration (1972) which we will examine shortly. Timpe uses the term collaboration noting that 'the patron-client relationship is at once an offensive and defensive attempt to improve one's condition in life. A mutual interest in collaboration is necessary for this voluntary association to be successful' (1991: 76). A slightly different emphasis is to be found in the work of Robinson, with its focus on 'collaborating or mediating elites' (1972: 120) with the recognition of the threat of force, either direct or implied that brought about such 'voluntary association'. Clientelism and collaboration both address the interaction between expanding European powers and peripheral societies but at different levels. In some senses clientelism is 'micro' theory: it throws light on the psychological process of the client-patron relationship with its reference to anxiety reduction behaviour. Collaboration is clearly a middle-range or partial theory. It focuses on the interaction between the metropole and peripheral societies and its relation to politics, taking an expanding Western or capitalist economy as a given variable. The work of Bromley (1994), which we will examine shortly, is an attempt at grand theory - it seeks to explain the motor of expansion within Europe and also the insertion of capitalist economic and social relations in the periphery and their subsequent development, and how this can be related to strategic policy.

Bierschenk and 'world systems analysis'

Bierschenk (1984, 1989) has produced important work on state formation in Oman. Of greatest relevance for this study is the evidence he marshals from oil company archives and British government official records to support his view that it was British strategic interests in the Gulf as a whole which prevailed over the essential indifference of the oil company as to with whom it signed oil concessions. Referring to the Imamate/Sultanate conflict of the 1950s he concludes:

> Thus the British and American oil companies can be seen to be moving forces behind the international conflict in the Gulf region as well as the vehicles of the USA's and Great Britain's imperial interests. However, the precise political structures and institutions which emerged did not necessarily correspond directly to the economic interests of the international oil companies. Rather, the changes in world market conditions initiated by the rise of oil, created a general need for new political structures, the definite institutional forms of which were also determined by the strategic

interests of the USA and Great Britain. The international border conflicts and the internal civil wars in Southeast Arabia after World War II were to decide who of several potential aspirants - the Sultan in Muscat or the Imam in Oman (or possibly also the ruler of Saudi Arabia) – would take over the political function of controlling the potential oil production areas in Oman. The oil companies were essentially indifferent towards the result of the conflict, provided oil prospecting and production were not interfered with. In fact, the Petroleum Concessions oil company at one point entertained serious thoughts of coming to a separate agreement with the Imam, and tried to gain the British Government's permission to do so. (1989:219)

The central thrust of Bierschenk's analysis is convincing in respect to the significance of British strategic interests in the Gulf as mediating the impact of capitalism on Oman. In his article in 1989 he explicitly places his analysis of the impact of world market forces on Oman in the context of Wallerstein's framework of 'world systems', something which he does not do in his earlier book-length work.[2] A number of problems can be found with Wallerstein's analysis – perhaps most notably its determinism (Brown 1997: 57); indeed Bierschenk uses the word determinism in the above extract. Thus, in this thesis, while Bierschenk's argument and evidence on the relative importance of various factors in state formation in Oman is accepted, the impact of the West on Oman is placed in a different theoretical framework, that of Bromley (1994) which will be examined in the review of the literature on state formation. First, we turn to the review of the literature on imperialism and informal empire.

Informal empire and collaboration: Robinson and Gallagher's theory of imperialism
The concept of 'informal empire'[3] was developed in modern times initially by Ronald Robinson and John Gallagher in their celebrated article 'The Imperialism of Free Trade' (1953). The central thrust of this article, on which all their subsequent work (1961, 1972, 1986, 1994) was based, was their argument emphasising the continuity of British imperial policy in the nineteenth century in contrast to the sharp break that had been identified by the proponents of

the 'New Imperialism'thesis (see Doyle 1986: 141). The 'New Imperialism' thesis was first developed by Hobson at the turn of the century and held sway until the World War Two. Hobson defined imperialism in terms of the seizure by the European powers of formal political control in territories in Asia and Africa, which took place in the last part of the nineteenth century due to financial developments in Europe. As H.L. Wesseling comments: 'with Hobson, we have a definition, a periodisation and an explanation' (1986: 1). Of fundamental importance was the seizure of territory in the last quarter of the nineteenth century which was deemed a fundamentally new development. For Lenin, imperialism was a particular stage in the development of capitalism: the monopoly stage. Notably, all proponents of the thesis shared a perception that the causes of the extension of empire in the last three decades of the 19th century were to be found within Europe itself - either politically, economically or socially.

In contrast, Robinson and Gallagher attacked what they saw as the artificial watershed imposed by the 'New Imperialism' thesis between a Mid-Victorian era of anti-imperialism and a late Victorian era of 'New Imperialism' including the 'scramble for Africa'. Instead, they posited a continuity in British imperialism from its heyday of mid-Victorian economic and commercial hegemony (Wesseling 1986: 2). This continuity was to be explained by the central dynamic they identified in Britain's empire, which they characterised as a 'free trade empire'. The adage they coined to characterize British imperial policy in terms of a free trade empire was 'trade with informal control if possible; trade with rule when necessary' in contrast to the previously accepted dictum of 'trade not rule' (Gallagher 1980: 15). Thus formal and informal empire were not entirely different phenomena but were rather two sides of the same coin. To illustrate their central argument on imperialism and to identify the mistake they believed the advocates of the 'New Imperialism' had made they used the metaphor of an iceberg to depict the relationship between 'formal' and 'informal' empire.[4] Just as you should not measure the size of an iceberg by equating it with that which is visible above the surface so should no-one equate the extent of the 19th century British empire with the area of world maps of the time coloured red to indicate British colonies. In *Africa and the Victorians* (1961) they further criticised the idea that all colonisation could be directly accounted for by processes in European society. They argued that the scramble for Africa had been precipitated not by economic developments within Europe but for strategic reasons issuing from a local crisis in Egypt that was due to a failure of collaborative arrangements between Britain and her local allies in Egypt.

Robinson and Gallagher had given their redefinition of the nature and period of imperialism but the question remained of how they were to account for the timing of the seizure by the European powers of vast swathes of territory in Africa and Asia in the later part of the nineteenth century - most famously the 'scramble for Africa'. In an attempt to answer this Robinson further developed his views on the essence of imperialism in his article 'Non-European Foundations of European Imperialism: Sketch for a theory of collaboration' (1972).

The Concept of Collaboration

Robinson argued that European imperialism and empire depended on collaborating or mediating elites in the societies of Africa and Asia . Without the voluntary or enforced cooperation of their governing elites, economic resources could not be transferred, strategic interests protected or traditional resistance to change contained. In most Afro-Asian countries this process of collaboration went through three stages. First, Europe attempted to lever local regimes into the collaboration necessary to open their countries to trade and commerce. Secondly, the breakdown of indigenous collaboration necessitated deeper imperial intervention though still using native collaborators to see that its policies were carried out. The choice of indigenous collaboration - whether it was a Sultan, Imam, Emir or King - determined the organisation and character of imperial rule. Thirdly, as the imperial rulers ran out of indigenous collaborators they either chose to leave or were made to go. A key point to note is that these transitions in imperialism were governed by the need to reconstruct and uphold a collaborative system that was breaking down. Robinson further developed his ideas on imperialism in the article 'The Excentric Idea of Imperialism, with or without Empire' (1986). H.L. Wesseling contends that in contrast to earlier versions of Robinson's thought on imperialism the 'excentric idea' is a general model of power relations which can be applied to all periods of history. Wesseling believes it is better to leave the terms imperialism and empire to that of a particular period - the expansion of Europe (1986: 9).

In summary, for Robinson and Gallagher empire could be formal or informal. In both these forms imperial rule depended on maintaining a collaborative system voluntarily or through coercion. The shifts in the relationship between the West and what were to become known as 'Third World' countries could be accounted for by the changes in collaborative alliances which produced a transition from powerful ally to imperial rule, formal or informal and then to independence.

Defining informal empire

One problem here is that Robinson and Gallagher did not offer a detailed definition or description of informal empire. Juergen Osterhammel (1986) has identified the key features of 'informal empire' as a classification or ideal type. In a situation of power differentials a strong country (S) possesses an effective veto over a weaker country (W) whilst avoiding direct rule. The stronger country has the capacity to impose basic guidelines on the foreign policy of the weaker country. S maintains a substantial military presence in W and brings influence to bear through aid and advisers. In the economic and financial realm W is entrenched in those sectors of the economy of S which shows above average rates of growth. W is a net recipient of capital and investment. The hold of S over W is aided by the collaboration of indigenous rulers and 'comprador' groups (Osterhammel 1986: 297-298).

All these characteristics are found in the relations between Britain and the Sultans of Muscat and Oman from 1920 - 1970. It is important to note that in this book the definition of informal empire employed excludes the Aden Protectorate and the Trucial States from that category. Rather they are placed in the category of formal empire. In legal terms Al-Baharna (1967: 80) notes that under British constitutional law protectorates differed from colonies in that they did not constitute part of the 'British Dominions'. In all British protectorates foreign relations were controlled by the 'British Crown'; however the amount of power reserved internally differed between 'Colonial Protectorates' and 'Protected States'. In 'Colonial Protectorates' the amount of power exercised by the 'Crown' was not that much different from that exercised in colonies. Powers of the 'Crown' in them were obtained through tribal chiefs agreeing to place themselves under the sovereignty of the British monarch. The Aden protectorate was of this type. Under the Aden Protectorate Order in Council, 1937, the British Governor of the Aden Colony was at the same time Governor of the Aden Protectorate. In British 'Protected States' the British government recognised the sovereignty of the local rulers who retained their independence with regard to internal administration. In legal terms the powers reserved to the 'Crown' in external affairs were based on treaty obligations. The first official reference to the Trucial States as 'British Protected States' was in the British Protectorates, Protected States and Protected Persons Order in Council, 1949. The 'Persian Gulf States' were, together with the states of Malay, Tonga and the Maldive Islands classified in the Second Schedule as 'British Protected States.' The First Schedule of the Order named all the African territories under British protection, including the Aden Protectorate and Zanzibar as 'Protectorates' (al-Baharna 1967: 82). In contrast, in legal terms a case could be made out that the Sultanate of Muscat and Oman was a fully independent and sovereign state which had accepted some limitations on its external relations (such as the 1891 agreement on non-cessation of territory) through treaty arrangements with Britain.

Ultimately, however, this legalistic approach does not explain anything (Halliday 1974: 271). It was power and the dynamic of the collaborative process which was enabling and forcing the British to became more involved in the internal, as well as the external affairs of its areas of influence in Arabia regardless of the constitutional position. Thus the same process took place in the Aden Protectorate, the Trucial States (British control of foreign relations through treaty) and the Sultanate of Muscat and Oman (legally fully sovereign in both internal and external affairs). In examining this process we need to pay attention to a number of factors involved in influencing the particular form of imperial influence and empire that took shape, be it formal or informal.

Doyle on empire and imperialism

Michael Doyle's study *Empires* (1986) argues that to explain empires and understand imperialism we need to combine insights from several sources. Both the opportunities that give rise to imperialism and the motives that drive it are to be found in a fourfold interaction among metropoles, peripheries, transnational forces, and international systemic incentives (1986: 19). In a multipolar system empire tends to be formal, in a bipolar system it tends to be informal. It is possible to highlight three useful distinctions made by Doyle. Firstly, he offers a succinct definition of empire, formal and informal and its connection with imperialism. He adheres to a behavioural definition of empire which he defines as effective control whether informal or informal in which one state, that of the imperial society, controls the effective political sovereignty of the subordinated society. Imperialism, he contends, is simply the process of establishing or maintaining an empire (1986:30). Informal imperialism can thus have the same results as formal imperialism: the difference lies in the process of control, which informal imperialism achieves through the collaboration of a legally independent (but actually subordinate) government in the periphery (1986: 38). These definitions, he argues, have considerable significance. They distinguish empires from the rest of world politics by the actual foreign control of who or what rules a subordinate polity. They imply that to explain the existence of a particular empire the existence of control must first be demonstrated, and also why one party expanded and the other submits or fails to resist effectively (1986: 45-46). Secondly, this allows him to distinguish between an era of empire and imperialism and an era of international inequality. Thirdly, Doyle draws a distinction between the impact of European imperial expansion on tribal and patrimonial societies in the periphery. In the first the interaction leads to formal empire, in the second to informal empire. This is because in a tribal society the effect of the metropolitan impact is far more disruptive of local political structures which tend to lack an organised hierarchy with which networks of collaboration can be established. In contrast patrimonial society is more differentiated socially and there are more opportunities for metropolitan commercial enterprise to engage with the peripheral society without automatically conflicting with religious ritual, social hierarchy or political procedure as is the case with tribal societies (Doyle 1986: 204). Of particular relevance to this thesis Doyle examines the case of Zanzibar as an example of the interaction of a patrimonial society with British imperial power. Over the course of the 19th century this relationship changed from alliance to one of dominance (this will be examined in more detail in chapter two). This was because when the British forced Sayyid Sa'id bin Sultan (r. 1806–1856) to ban the slave trade they undermined the political and economic basis of Sultan Sa'id's patrimonial authority. In the case of the Sultanate of Zanzibar this eventually led to it becoming absorbed into Britain's formal empire through the declaration of a British protectorate in 1890:

> British aims, both during and for a while after the protectorate was formally announced in 1890, were to control Zanzibar's foreign relations, leaving domestic politics intact. The British planned a hegemony to avoid Zanzibar's falling to another European state. But a hands-off policy proved impossible, and inevitably the sultan's regime became more unstable and British power in Zanzibar grew. When Britain changed its international relationship with Zanzibar from alliance to hegemony, it began to change the relationship of the ruler of Zanzibar to his people, from autocratic patrimon to foreign-supported puppet. Before this new relationship could become informal empire, however, a more reliable mechanism of influence was needed to supplement British naval power and commercial influence. (Doyle 1986: 359)

Where does the Sultanate of Muscat and Oman figure in this process? The British interaction with the rulers of Muscat (who until the splitting of the Zanzibar and Muscat Sultanates was the same ruler) comes in the same category: the interaction of a patrimon with an imperial power. Muscat society in the 19th century was a patrimonial one in contrast to the tribal society of the interior. Why was the Sultanate of Muscat and Oman not absorbed into the British formal empire as a protectorate? This thesis proposes that it was because of great power competition (international systemic factors) and will be examined in more detail in chapter two. At this point suffice it to comment that ultimately the proposal in 1896 to create a Muscat protectorate was not followed through because of the legalities of the 1862 Anglo-French agreement to maintain the independence of the

Arabian sultanate following the British-arranged separation of the sultanates of Muscat and Zanzibar. Instead British concern to control the foreign relations of the Sultan of Muscat were reflected in a number of treaties culminating in the 1891 commitment by the Sultan never to cede any territory to any other power apart from Britain. This followed French interest in the Sultanate in the 1890s (see Busch 1967) and was enforced with threats of naval bombardment of the Sultan's palace; thus the granting of a coaling station to the French was revoked. There was at this point no British interest or necessity in becoming involved in the domestic government. The Sultanate of Muscat and Oman (with its power limited to the coast) remained an unofficial protectorate until 1920. However, as with the sultanate in Zanzibar, British actions undermined the political and economic bases of the Sultan's patrimonial authority leading to ever greater crises. To use Robinson's term these were crises of collaboration, requiring greater imperial intervention and involvement in domestic government. Informal empire is concerned with control of both foreign relations and domestic government and can result from the interaction of an imperial power and a patrimonial society. In the case of Muscat informal empire came about with the British instigated reforms in government of the 1920s. The Sultans' authority had been so undermined by the British that a deepening involvement in Muscati government was required to prevent the coming to power of forces hostile to British influence, such as the Imamate forces of the tribal interior, and thus safeguard British strategic interests. It could be argued that this may apply to the 1920s but not to the relations between Sa'id bin Taimur (r.1932 – 1970) and the British.[5] Did he not abolish the British-created Council of Ministers when he became Sultan in 1932 and otherwise not accept any British advice or involvement in what he regarded as his affairs? In other words can British-Muscati relations 1932-1970 be termed informal empire? It will be argued that they can - Sultan Sa'id had a limited amount of room for manoeuvre but in the end his regime depended on the British who allowed him to rule as he liked providing their interests were not threatened (Halliday 1974: 271). Ultimately it was this threat to their interests that pushed the British to remove Sa'id bin Taimur in 1970. It has been seen that the category of informal empire and the process of collaboration are potentially useful in understanding the relations between Britain and Oman. However, as Doyle has indicated it cannot fully explain the dynamics of the relationship. In order to do this we must look elsewhere for an understanding of the expansion of the international capitalist system. One candidate explanation lies in that tradition of thought situated in Marx's idea of historical materialism.

Informal empire and collaboration: a partial theory in need of a context

In his survey of Marxist theories of imperialism, Brewer, whilst identifying Robinson and Gallagher as being non-Marxist theorists, finds nothing in their work that is incompatible with Marxist interpretations and considers that Marxists can learn from their work (1990: 256-259). He criticises the distinction between explanations of imperialism in economic or non-economic terms. Rather he argues that what is required is to trace the interconnections between economic and political development and to account for different forms of economic and political domination in history. Such an explanation would be a theory of the capitalist world system, a theory which in the mid-1980s Brewer felt did not exist (1986: 325). If it could be developed Brewer believed such a theory would usefully augment Robinson and Gallagher's ideas on forms of political control in the periphery. This political control has to be placed in a context of political, economic and social structures in both the centre and the periphery (1986: 330-331). As Robinson and Gallagher would concede, their theory is a partial theory - indeed for this reason it has been made use of by both Marxist and non-Marxist scholars. It is no surprise therefore, that we must look elsewhere for theories which avail of greater explanatory potential to supplement their framework. One such candidate theoretical framework is that of the historical materialist account of the expansion of the capitalism and its state system developed recently by Rosenberg (1994), Halliday (1994) and Bromley (1994). Thus Bromley in discussing the thesis advanced by L. Carl Brown and Fromkin of a Middle Eastern Question within the Middle East argues that such a thesis overlooks the continuities in the forms of imperialist control and notes the contribution of Robinson and Gallagher in identifying imperialism as the political moment of the process of incorporating new regions into the expanding international capitalist economy (Bromley 1994: 85).

Informal empire and collaboration: conclusion

From this review of the literature on informal imperialism it is clear that we must distinguish between relations in an era of imperialism and an era of international inequality between states. With this distinction in mind we can thus integrate the insights of informal empire and collaboration into the broader theoretical framework of the historical materialist perspective on state formation in the Middle East provided by Bromley which will be examined next. Furthermore we need to be aware that although the concept of collaboration and the typology of informal empire give an adequate account of the interaction between the metropole power and the peripheral society they do not address the dynamic of the context in which this interaction took place. This was the development of the imperialist construction of the capitalist world market and its linked sovereign state system (Bromley 1994: 85). We can now turn to the review of the literature on state formation.

Theoretical perspective on state formation

The central focus of this thesis is the process of state formation in Oman in the era of modern Middle East politics, since the end of the First World War.[6] It will examine the external and internal influences on the formation of the modern Omani state and assess their relative weight and the specific nature of their interaction in that process.

The broad perspective[7] from which this thesis is written is that of 'world capitalism', specifically that form of historical materialist analysis of international relations developed by Halliday (1994), Rosenberg (1994) and most specifically with reference to the Middle East that of Simon Bromley in his work *Rethinking Middle East Politics* (1994).

It is first necessary to make explicit what is meant by the term 'state' and thus with what an analysis of the process of state formation is concerned. Accordingly this section reviews selected writings which have addressed differing conceptions of the state employed in the discipline of International Relations (IR) (Halliday 1994), discussed the question of the relationship between state and society (Owen 1992) and formulated a theory of state formation (Bromley 1994). It concludes with a summary of the particular aspects of state formation to be examined in this study of the case of Oman.

Malcom Yapp (1996: 35) has noted that differing conceptions and usage of the terms 'state' and 'regime' have led to much confusion in writing on the Middle East and the same point can be made for IR in general. Fred Halliday has highlighted, in identifying two conceptions of state commonly used in IR, that much discussion of the state has ignored other theoretical development on the state in sociology and within Marxism. This work has centred on the historical and contemporary centrality of the state and instead of examining its supercession has sought to uncover its relations to social classes (Halliday 1994: 76). The question of the relationship between state and society is also alluded to in Roger Owen's succinct treatment of definitions of state in his *State, Power and Politics in the Making of the Modern Middle East* (1992). He first asserts the applicability of ideas of state derived from Western political thought and considers two definitions: 'the notion of the state as a sovereign political entity with international recognition, its own boundaries, its own flag and so on; and the notion of the state as the supreme coercive and rule making body' (Owen 1992: 3). He argues that these two definitions are essentially about claims to sovereignty and authority which first have to be established and then constantly re-justified and that the success of such a project would be dependent largely on the resources available to those controlling the central administration. He further adds that the claims made by any state have to be examined in concrete historical situations and at various levels.

Turning to the question of how to analyse the relationship between state and society Owen offers three broad points of departure for analysis (Owen 1992: 5-6). Firstly the modern Middle Eastern state was being created at a time when Middle Eastern society was itself subject to many of the same processes of transformation to be found at work throughout the non-European world. These involved a type of capitalist development which was dissolving old social solidarities and led to the formation of new kinds of solidarities based on class. Secondly he notes that the separation between state and society often described as the distinction between the public (sphere of the state) and private (sphere of society) is a modern characteristic. His third point is that the construction of the relationship between state and society takes place at the same time as the creation of the national consciousness.

Bromley commends the analyses of writers such as Owen (1992) and Halliday (see 1996: chapter one) which locate the development of states in the Middle East in terms of processes which took place throughout the Third World, in contrast to those accounts of political development which identify a particularity of the Middle East in terms of ideology (Islam) or geology (oil). However, commenting on the work of Halliday, Owen and Zubaida (1989) he contends that they do not address the basic theoretical questions involved in giving an adequate account of dependent state formation and hence political change in the Middle East. Merely to shift analytical attention to the process of state formation does not of itself solve substantive problems of explanation. He argues that many accounts of state formation, for example Owen's to a large extent, note the imposition of Western state forms in the colonial and mandate era, and then proceed to argue that subsequent political activity is patterned largely by this fact. Although this is useful as a generalisation Bromley submits that the variation in social forms found in the non-European world prior to the colonial impact tend to be relegated to a relatively minor role. These forms, often themselves products of an earlier encounter between local pre-capitalist arrangements and European informal imperialism, have been very diverse and often influence the subsequent process of state formation (Bromley 1994: 99).

Bromley seeks to develop some determinate qualitative criteria concerning the character of modern state formation. He notes that much recent theorising on state formation in the Middle East and elsewhere is based on the influential essay by Michael Mann 'The Autonomous Power of the State' (1984) which identifies the means by which a state could potentially act autonomously from its society. Bromley perceives a major problem with the formulation of Mann, and the work of Giddens (1985) which, from a similar standpoint, criticises realist and neo-Weberian views of the state. He argues that their project of constructing a general theory of the state in terms of its infrastructural (or administrative) power is bound to involve a reification similar to that identified by Marx in attempts to derive the forms of capitalist production from the feature of 'production in general' (Bromley 1994: 102). For this reason Bromley contends that an analysis of the process of state formation must also examine the establishment of new social relations which facilitate the form of surplus appropriation which is dominant in any given society (1994: 102-103).

Bromley then outlines how the nature of dependent state formation in the Middle East allowed of two models which both provided only a social basis for authoritarian rule in contrast to the possibility of liberal capitalist democracy. In the first model, preemptive state formation in a pro-Western fashion necessitated the repression of nationalist and Leftist groups in the domestic sphere. In the second, nationalist mobilisation against foreign influence made it difficult to sustain open competition between domestic forces. Thus, dependent development, whether for or against the grain of the international system supported an authoritarian form of state (Bromley 1994: 104).

Following on from these considerations Bromley offers three guidelines for investigating the process of state formation in order to avoid the polarity of external 'imperialist' or internal 'Islamic' determinations which characterises much analysis of Middle Eastern political development (Halliday 1996: 219). Firstly, it must relate the development of state apparatus to the changing nature of social relations. This is not to diminish the importance of the state apparatus but to place institutions of administration and coercion in their social context. Secondly, it must relate the process of state formation to the position of the state in the world market and the indigenous response to this. This also involves the relationship of the state with the dominant powers in the international system. Thirdly, if the process of state formation is to be understood in historical terms attention must be paid to the conflict of social forces involved in the struggle to reproduce and control the relations of appropriation and command (Bromley 1994: 105). Bromley uses these guidelines to sketch out the main trends of external involvement with the Middle East since the end of the First World War and the way in which the external involvement related to political and social development within the region; within this context he tests his hypotheses against his selected case studies (Bromley 1994: 106-114). This study of state formation in Oman utilises the second and third of the guidelines which Bromley identifies. We now turn to review literature which has focused exclusively on state formation in the Arabian peninsula.

Monarchy, imperialism and oil: state formation in the GCC states

Two recent works by Gause (1994) and Jill Crystal (1990) have provided comparative studies of state formation in the GCC states. Gause argues that the American conventional wisdom - that the basis of politics in the Gulf monarchies is characterised by the unchanging characteristics of Islam and tribalism - is not so much incorrect as outdated (1994: 10). He finds that these factors are significant but not in the way which is commonly attributed to them. They are significant in the way in which the symbols and rhetoric of Islam and tribalism have been used as legitimising ideologies for the rule of these regimes. He identifies the political characteristics that these monarchies share as a result of their *rentier* character which is the central concern of Crystal's work *Oil and Politics in the Gulf: Rulers and Merchants in Kuwait and Qatar*, (1990).

In a focused study of Kuwait and Qatar Crystal (1990) identifies the process in which the historical relationship between ruling families and merchants is transformed by the impact of oil revenues. Before oil, politics was dominated by a ruling coalition between the ruler, or shaikh, and the trading families. The ruler depended on these merchants for revenues in the form of customs dues, and personal loans. The merchants entered the realm of politics in order to protect their economic interests. After the advent of oil the merchants withdraw from the formal political realm to protect those economic interests in a compact with the ruling families which sees them relinquish participation in the decision making process in return for the rulers non intrusion on business activities. This represents a tacit arrangement - a trade of wealth for formal power (1990: 1). The merchants' withdrawal was accompanied by new relationships between the ruler and members of the ruling family through new political and bureaucratic roles and between the ruler and the population through the provision of social services. As oil revenues decline the rulers' ability to keep the original bargain with the merchants diminishes and the merchants begin to question the original arrangements. With growing dissatisfaction the merchants return to political life through the back door of the bureaucracy. She argues that this process is found in all the oil dependent states which, apart from Kuwait and Qatar, she names as Bahrain, Saudi Arabia and the United Arab Emirates, thus curiously omitting the Sultanate of Oman (1990: 2).

Both these studies focus on the key feature common to all the GCC states - their distributive character. These are states whose prime role, in contrast to the historical development of the state in Europe and the United States, is to expend rather than extract revenue. This is due to the nature of the oil industry in which external rent is paid for a commodity - oil - which in contrast to other Third World commodities, such as cotton and coffee, involves very few linkages to the society where the substance is found in order to facilitate its development. Rather it results in the payment of external rent first in the form of concession payments from multinational corporations and then in revenues derived from direct integration into the world oil market. Hence they are *rentier* states of an extreme kind.

Al-Naqeeb (1990) develops an analysis based on economic dependency arguments to explain the process of state formation in the GCC states that has led to authoritarianism. Linking pre- and post-oil eras he identifies three periods (Crystal 1997: 308). The first, which lasted until the end of the 17th century was based on speculative trade which linked cities and tribal hinterlands to trade networks outside the Gulf. Central political power in the form of the Ottoman state was weak and locally power was shared by tribal and urban settled leaders who were balanced in their power by merchant groups. The economy on which this system was based was destroyed in the imperial period when Britain, in the guise of eliminating piracy and the slave trade, imposed a European dominated economy and fragmented the region into distinct familial states kept in place by British force. Resistance to this came from the hinterland in the form of, for example the Wahhabi movement and the Ibadhi Imamate. The third era is that of contemporary authoritarianism and began with oil. Oil revenues concentrated power in the state which was at first benignly bureaucratic but increasingly expanded to absorb independent social institutions. This created opposition from the old labour force of bedouin and pearl divers who had become educated middle class bureaucrats. Initially, the state sought to buy these groups off but al-Naqeeb contends that as oil revenues increasingly will not be able to postpone the day of reckoning the state will resort to Western supplied instruments of force to contain this pressure. According to al-Naqeeb modern authoritarianism in the GCC states belongs to a group of authoritarian outcomes resulting from colonialism but in the GCC are distinct in that they also are characteristic of oil economies. On this last point Crystall comments that al-Naqeeb:

> links the older dependency-based writing to the new and growing body of literature on the rentier state, a literature which argues that oil, by freeing rulers from their dependence on domestic revenue sources, frees them from the demands for democratic participation that accompany the provision of taxes. The result is a movement away from democracy: no taxation, hence no representation. (Crystal 1997: 308)

Summary

Following from this survey of selected writings on state formation it is possible to summarise and restate three points of particular relevance for state formation in Oman which will shape the study to follow. Firstly the need to pay particular attention to the pre-colonial society prior to the encounter with the West and the way in which indigenous social and political forms in Oman prior to the modern era of Middle East politics since World War One were very much the outcome of their interaction with informal imperial influence. Secondly, whilst much of the process of state formation in Oman is concerned with territorial delimitation it is important to relate this to the economic changes of the period, principally but not exclusively the prospecting for and development of oil resources in Oman, and the change in social and political relations that ensued. A final point is to relate the existence of a 'sultanistic regime'[8] to the social basis of authoritarianism rather than by reference to any concepts such as 'traditional' and 'modern' states. We now turn to examine the nature of Omani society prior to its encounter with the West and the outcome of its interaction with the expanding capitalist powers up to 1920.

CHAPTER TWO
Oman and British Imperial Expansion 1798-1920

Introduction
The phase of state formation in Oman from 1798 to 1920 is defined by the impact of the British links with India which required British maritime supremacy in the Indian Ocean. After 1798 the British started to become something more than another foreign trading partner with the Omanis: during the nineteenth century the British relationship with the Omanis changed from important ally to dominant imperial power. This change manifested itself in increasing involvement with the Omanis and influence over the Omani position in the Indian Ocean. Through the arbitration which led to the separation of the Zanzibar and Arabian sultanates, the banning of significant Omani trading activities in slaves and guns and their financial and military support of the Muscat sultans the British reduced the Al Bu Sa'id rulers of Muscat from a significant maritime power to foreign-suported clients. This culminated in the British defence of Muscat from 1913 to 1920 without which the Imamate would have been restored. The British links with India required only a residual interest on the Arabian peninsula, mainly to exclude rival imperial powers and contain regional threats; it was not until the developments that followed World War One that the British were to become more directly involved in Omani internal affairs; this will be examined in chapter three. This chapter is structured by the three narrative themes that are to be used to examine the external and internal influences on the process of state formation in Oman in the period 1798 – 1920: (1) the international context of external involvement, (2) the nature of that involvement and (3) its impact on Omani society.

2.1: The international context 1798-1920

The Sultanate of Oman lies on the south-eastern corner of the Arabian Peninsula. The northern part of the Sultanate has two main geographical features: a mountain range and a coastal plain. The range of mountains of the interior extend from the Musandam Peninsula in the north, running in an arc until finally petering out on the coast of the Indian Ocean at Ras al-Hadd, the eastern most point of the Arabian Peninsula. Lying inside the arc of the mountains is the Batinah coastal plain which extends from Shinas in the north to al-Seeb, just before Matrah and Muscat, in the south. Together they form an 'island' - bounded on one side by the Indian Ocean and on the other by the trackless 'Empty Quarter'. Lying a thousand kilometres across the Jiddat al-Harasis, a gravel plain, is the southern province of Dhofar.

The word Oman has been used to describe different areas in different times reflecting the historical development of the Omani state and indeed those of the lower Gulf. One meaning has been the reference to the core area in the mountainous interior centering on Nizwa and Rustaq. This meaning was reflected in the name of the Sultanate until 1970: the Sultanate of Muscat and Oman. The process of state formation in the area has meant paradoxically that what had been known as coastal Oman (*sahel Oman*) developed into Trucial Oman or the Trucial States and subsequently the United Arab Emirates. In contrast, Dhofar, an area always considered separate from Oman, both geographically and culturally, has been incorporated (although not without difficulty) into the contemporary state - since 1970, the Sultanate of Oman.

The origins of British involvement in Oman and the Gulf as a whole lie in trade which commenced in the early seventeenth century through the activities of the English East India Company (EEIC). At this point in time the maritime outlets of the Indian Ocean were controlled by the Portuguese although they were now having their maritime supremacy and their control of trading challenged by the British, Dutch and French (Peterson 1978: 137). The Portuguese ran a 'protective costs system' for trade in the Gulf and Oman similar in essence to that operated by the previous Omani and Persian powers when they had controlled the area (see Bhacker 1992: 214 and Wilkinson 1977: 9). With the expulsion of the Portuguese the form of European influence on Oman, the Gulf and the Indian Ocean was to take a new form, different in nature to that of military conquest and the exacting of 'tribute'.

This new conduit of influence was the East India Companies of Britain, France and Holland; these companies were the means of the expansion of capitalism in the Indian Ocean. The Portuguese brought to the east new arms, ship designs and navigational skills (Risso 1986: 11-13). However, they failed to restructure Asian trade - 60 to 80 per cent of Asian exports to Europe continued to come overland in 1600 - and ultimately Portugal was unable to sustain its Eastern investment. The restructuring of Asian trade was undertaken by the English and Dutch East India Companies and the overland route for trade became insignificant thereafter. Although during this time Europe still ran a trade deficit with the east, the East India Companies were becoming involved in the inner Asian trade and ultimately a growing penetration was to create these areas as markets for European manufacturing goods (Bromley 1994: 57). The East India Companies were the bearers of new innovation:

> The organisation of the English and the Dutch East India Companies into joint-stock companies exercising separation between the ownership of capital and management by a professional class of merchants and salaried administrators, was a new and unique phenomenon in commercial organisation.
> Trans-continental trade was no longer the exclusive preserve either of royal monopoly, as had been the case of the Portuguese-Spanish crown or of individual merchants or partnerships operating as separate entities and covering vast trading areas such as that between the Italian ports and the ports of India. (Bhacker 1992:28)

The establishment of the East India Companies and their emerging patterns of long distance trade can be regarded as the beginning of a 'world economy' and preceded the dominant role of industrial capital and the social transformations of the early nineteenth century (Bhacker 1992:28). The English East India Company was granted a charter by Parliament in 1600; it made treaties, organised armies and fought wars: an interesting case of the franchising by government of political authority (Brown

1994: 49). Initially, it was in the shadow of the Dutch East India Company but gradually surpassed it in the latter part of the seventeenth century. Thereafter the main challenge came from the French East India Company until its collapse in bankruptcy due to massive war debts in 1769 (Wolf 1982: 129). The English East India Company was abolished after the Indian Mutiny of 1857 and the resulting reorganisation of British rule in India.

Britain, India and the Gulf
The value of Gulf trade declined gradually in the seventeenth and eighteenth centuries and by the end of the eighteenth century it had virtually disappeared (Peterson 1986: 9). The continued presence of the Bombay marine could only be justified by the protection of the minor 'country trade' from India. It was not until the end of the eighteenth century that an interest developed that was to remain a key Western interest in Oman to the present day: Oman's strategic importance to an external economic interest. In 1798 Napoleon invaded Egypt and easily defeated the Mamluk rulers. In British eyes his goal was India; this suspicion was confirmed by the interception of letters from Napoleon to the rulers of Muscat and Mysore. The ensuing defeat of Tipu Sultan and expulsion of the French from Cairo in 1801 by a British-Ottoman alliance made impossible any attempt by Napoleon to threaten India and also established British supremacy on the subcontinent. It also had the effect of making the Arabian littoral an extension of the security frontier of British economic interests in India. The British plunder of India allowed Britain to buy back the national debt from the Dutch and in the nineteenth century Indian surpluses allowed Britain to create and upkeep a global system of free trade (Wolf 1982: 261). After the EEIC acquisition of extensive territorial holdings in India at the end of the eighteenth century the British did everything they could to prevent any local, regional or Western power from challenging either their political or commercial hegemony in the Indian Ocean area (Bromley 1994: 67). The protection of British interests in India was the underlying factor in the evolution of British security policy in the Indian Ocean until the earlier part of the 20th century:

> ...British actions in the eighteenth century, designed to exclude other European states from activity in the Indian

Ocean were based on different priorities than those of the nineteenth century, when the predominant need was to protect the lines of communication to India, or the twentieth century with the necessity of a secure cordon around the subcontinent. (Peterson 1978:137)

Consequently, until 1947 British policy in the Gulf was decided in India rather than London. The British Governor (Viceroy) of India appointed British representatives in the Gulf who reported to the British Resident Persian Gulf (PRPG). For example, at the end of the nineteenth century the government of India initiated a 'forward policy' of Indian defence as a result of Lord Curzon's view of the strategic importance of the Gulf (Peterson 1986:9). A British commentator of the late 19th century, T. Bent, stated this clearly: 'like all the rest of the Persian Gulf, Masqat is really an outlying province of our Indian empire...as long as you are on the shores of the Gulf you are, so to speak, in India' (quoted in Bierschenk 1989:207). It was not until the emergence of oil as a key factor in the world market just before and during the First World War that India's place in defining British policy in the Gulf began to change (Biershenk 1989: 206).

2.1: Conclusion

Britain's overriding interest in the Gulf and Oman from 1798 to 1920 can therefore be described as 'maritime peace', that is unchallenged British supremacy of the seas and the exclusion of rival Western powers from significant influence on the Arabian coastline. To achieve this required action against local and competing Western powers. Local trading powers were subjugated economically and as part of this process certain Arab maritime activities were curtailed. The traditional protective costs trade system and competition thereafter was termed piracy,[1] and sea war and slave trading were progressively eliminated. Whilst there were some 'humanitarian' factors involved in the campaign against slave trading the most significant motivation was to undermine this source of Arab wealth (Halliday 1974: 269). British paramountcy was also challenged by Western rivals, principally France, and Britain had to guard against attempts to undermine her position. This was only finally achieved for a couple of decades after World War One when all challenges receded and the Gulf became in effect, a British lake. The specific impact of this broad context for British involvement in Oman will be considered next.

2.2: British involvement in Oman 1798 -1920

The nature of Britain's involvement with Oman that followed from this context can be divided into three broad periods up to 1920 in which Britain's dominance of the rulers of Muscat became progressively greater: 1798-1856, 1857-1871, and 1872-1920. Within these periods there were often sharp changes in British attitude towards the Muscat rulers which reflected shifts in the British perception of their commercial and political interests in the area. Before we consider these three broad periods it is necessary to examine the specific origins of British involvement with Oman.

Origins of involvement: the East India Company and the rulers of Muscat

In 1624 the port of Muscat, which at that point was under Portuguese control, came to feature in the commercial policies of the English East India Company (Bhacker 1992: 31). Following the expulsion of the Portuguese from Sohar in 1643 contacts between the Omanis and the EEIC were initiated in 1645 by Imam Nasir bin Murshid al-Ya'aribah who formally invited the Company to trade at Sohar and Sib, though not at Muscat which still remained under the Portuguese. Imam Nasir was keen to develop contacts with European traders other than his Portuguese enemies and in 1646 a treaty was made between the Imam and the EEIC representative, Philip Wylde. One writer has commented that the Wylde Treaty embodies, albeit in a tentative form, the concepts of currency convertibility (clause one), exemption from customs duty (clause three), anti-trust and retail price maintenance (clause four), religious toleration (clause five), and extraterritorial jurisdiction (clause six) (Skeet 1974: 211). It can also be added that clause eight seeks to exclude other European competitors.

Following this agreement contacts further developed between the Ya'aribah and the EEIC which clearly appreciated Muscat's strategic location, both commercially and militarily (Bhacker 1992: 32-33). In 1651 the Ya'aribah offered a house in

Muscat to the Company as a factory (in this context a trading post). During the Dutch Wars Muscat was perceived by the English as 'a port in these parts as that wee might call our owne...as wee are at present and are like to bee if these wars continue.' In 1659 negotiations were started for the establishment of a factory at Muscat but which came to nothing due to the death of the English negotiator. In the 1660s the EEIC came to consider the possession of a fort at Muscat as desirable from a military strategic point of view: 'Twill be a very beneficial place and keepe both India and Persia in awe.' However the EEIC was to actually obtain neither a factory nor a fort at Muscat, complaining that the 'King [who at that time must have been Imam Sultan bin Sayf al-Ya'aribah] had gone back on his word.' M. Reda Bhacker (1992) speculates that for the Ya'aribah 'the memory of their great struggle and the eventual expulsion of the Portuguese after more than a century of occupation must have been too fresh in their minds.' Although trade actually increased between Oman and the EEIC the Al Bu Sa'id maintained the Ya'aribah's wariness and it was not until 1798 that a treaty was signed giving the Company extensive trading rights but still no factory or fort. What was the change of circumstances that led to the Muscat rulers to sign a new treaty and what motivation did Britain have for securing this? M. Reda Bhacker contends that the signing of the treaty was 'the first nail in the coffin of Omani independence.' It is with an examination of the context of this treaty that we start our consideration of the first broad period that has been identified in British-Omani relations.

1798-1856: British limitations on Oman

It is clear that the EEIC had always appreciated the strategic benefits of the port of Muscat to themselves or other powers. In 1798 an Anglo-Omani treaty (Persian: *qalnamah*) was signed by the Persian representative of the EEIC and Sayyid Sultan bin Ahmad in response to apparent French interest with the ruler of Muscat. The British ignored the extent of Oman's association with France in East Africa; Bhacker contends that the British perhaps conjectured that Sultan bin Ahmad would never put his commercial dealings with India at risk. In 1800 this treaty was confirmed and British representation was established in Muscat; the ratifying agreement declared that the friendship of the

British and Omanis would 'remain unshook till the end of time, and till the sun and moon have finished their revolving career' (Risso 1986: 220). However, the realities of relations were somewhat less poetic. In 1803, in the words of the British chronicler Lorrimer 'it was directly intimated to Sultan more than once, that, were he to throw in his lot with the French, the British government would have no alternative but to place his dominions under a commercial blockade from the side of India' (quoted in Bhacker 1992: 41). In the same year, with the end for the time being of the French threat to India, the British agency in Muscat was closed down although it was reopened in 1805 when there was a renewed threat from the Qawasim of the Gulf to British shipping. This British ambivalence to the cultivation of an enduring relationship with the Al Bu Sa'id continued. In the ongoing struggle for power at Muscat following Sultan bin Ahmad's death, the British were compelled to take into account internal Omani disputes in their dealings with the Arab power for the first time in the history of British-Omani relations. At the beginning of Sa'id bin Sultan's rule (r.1806 – 1856) the British, in the absence of any direct threat from a Western power to their position, refused to become involved in his internal disputes. Indeed, in 1806 Britain even rejected Sa'id's offer of an alliance which, until then, had been sought for over a hundred years. Renewed French activity (an alliance was concluded with Persia in 1807) meant that Britain reluctantly moved closer to Sa'id as it recognised the value of his port to the defence of British interests in India; however, the loss of Ile de France (Mauritius) in 1810 meant the final demise of Napoleonic ambitions in the Indian Ocean. At this point, however, a further threat to British naval supremacy allowed a continuation of the British-Muscat alliance in the furtherance of a mutual interest.

Britain, Oman and the Saudi-Qasimi threat
Following Sultan bin Ahmad's death Britain began to take on the role hitherto played by Oman: the control of the high seas against depredations on cargo-laden shipping or 'piracy' as the British now termed it. In the early years of Sa'id bin Sultan's rule a British-Muscat alliance developed through a coincidence of interest: a shared opposition to the actions of the Qasimi seafarers. Sa'id had long sought to involve the British in his battles with the

newly expanding power of the Saudis and their militant doctrine of Wahhabism but the British had no particular interest in his fate in internal Arabian struggles.[2] However, the maritime activities of the Qawasim in the lower Gulf did threaten British interests and it was this that led to the joint Muscati-British expedition to Ras al-Khayma in 1809-10. For Sa'id it was a chance to enforce his authority on outlying parts of geographical Oman. After a number of campaigns against the Qawasim culminating in the 1819-1820 expedition the British imposed a General Treaty of Maritime Peace in 1820 which was renewed at intervals until a Perpetual Treaty of Maritime Peace was signed in 1853.

British actions and the subordination of the Al Bu Sa'id rulers
In the late seventeenth century the ruler of Muscat was the dominant political and commercial power in the west Indian ocean area (Boxer 1969). By the late eighteenth century it was still the case that Sultan bin Ahmad (r. 1796-1804) felt able to mount military campaigns in the Gulf independently of the British. It is significant that following the brief interlude of Badr bin Sayf (r. 1804-1806), Sa'id bin Sultan (r.1806-1856) felt it necessary to write to the British authorities in Bombay requesting recognition - a recognition that was not forthcoming for a year as the British were wary of committing themselves to different contenders for power in Omani politics (Bhacker 1992). However, thereafter the British, through a variety of measures, came to progressively dominate the rule of Sa'id bin Sultan who gradually found his room to manoeuvre progressively eliminated as he struggled to maintain his independence. At the same time that Britain benefited from its alliance with Sa'id bin Sultan it was taking actions that undercut his position and eventually made his successors completely dependent on Britain. This was achieved through two measures: firstly, the removal of Omani claims to tribute in the Gulf and, secondly, the curtailing of Arab commercial activities such as slaving and trading in guns. In Sa'id's father's lifetime Oman had lost its economic interests in India to the British. The 1820 General Treaty of Maritime Peace between Britain and the tribes of the lower Gulf removed any hopes of re-establishing Omani dominions in that area. With the British capture of Ile de France Britain lost interest in Oman or its overseas territories. Nevertheless, the only two actions of note in Omani-British rela-

tions in the 1820s had the effect of further undermining Sa'id bin Sultan (Bhacker 1992).

The slave trade from East Africa formed a substantial part of the economic base of the Omani empire. The Moresby Treaty of September 1822 was signed by Sultan Sa'id in Muscat and prohibited the sale of slaves to Christians in Zanzibar. The protection given to the Mazru'i of Mombassa by Captain Owen in February 1824 remained in force until 1826 although it was protested against by Sa'id and quickly repudiated by the British government. British interest in the activities of the Muscat ruler was rekindled in 1833 when Sa'id signed a treaty with the Americans. This was perceived by the British as a threat to their position in the area and motivated them to sign in 1839 a Commercial Treaty with Oman and Zanzibar. Cogan, who negotiated the treaty, saw its primary objective as to offset American commercial encroachment in the Indian Ocean area (Sheriff 1994:317). In 1845 Sa'id assented to a stronger treaty by which he agreed to prohibit any slave trade between his possessions in East Africa and Arabia and conferred on the East India Company the right to search and seize vessels. This trend was to culminate in the 1873 treaty which absolutely prohibited the importation of slaves into Oman and instigated the closure of public slave markets in Oman.

1857-1871: British arbitration in Omani affairs

The progressive severity of these treaties indicates the degree to which the British were increasingly dictating to the Al Bu Sa'id. This change in the nature of the Al Bu Sa'id-British relationship first became obvious with the arbitration of the succession dispute after Sa'id bin Sultan's death in 1856. Following the Coghlan Commission, the British-mediated Canning Award of 1861 presided over the division of the African domains from the Arabian lands which the Al Bu Sa'id ruled. It confirmed the existing separation and that the two rulers would now be officially addressed by the British as 'Sultans' like the Ottomans (Bhacker 1992: 191). The richer Zanzibar sultanate under Majid bin Sultan was to pay a subsidy of 40,000 Maria Theresa dollars (MT$)[3] a year to the Muscat sultanate ruled by Thuwaini bin Sa'id. When Majid 'defaulted' on this payment he was at first pressured into its payment with arrears and later the Government of India took over the payment of the actual money from its coffers. The Zanzibar subsidy, as it became to be known, was the first step towards the Muscat sultanate's financial dependence on the British. Furthermore, the withholding of the Zanzibar subsidy, as with the withholding of British recognition, became a powerful means of arbitration in Omani succession disputes without involving Britain in direct administration (Landen 1967: 201). The most notable demonstration of this was the collapse of the Imamate 1868-1871 after the British withheld the Zanzibar subsidy and demonstrated their decisive influence. In the late 19th century the British implicitly ordained succession by primogeniture and the designation of an heir apparent so that the family had to accept the choice of the Government of India as Sultan and so avoid succession disputes (Peterson 1978: 97).

1872 - 1920: Muscat - a de facto protectorate

In this period Muscat became a de facto British protectorate. This was the result of the 'forward policy' of the Government of India in the late nineteenth century and was expressed in a number of British-Muscat 'agreements'. In 1891 Sultan Faisal bin Turki pledged himself and his successors never to transfer Omani territory except to the British government; this was enforced in 1899 when, under threat of a British bombardment of his palace, Sultan Faisal withdrew his agreement to a French coaling station at Bandar Jissah. In 1895 the British undertook to protect the Muscat-Matrah area from future tribal attack. As a result Indian Army troops were dispatched to Muscat in 1913 and defended the town against besieging Imamate forces 1915-1920. On the accession of Taimur bin Faisal (r.1913 - 1931) in 1913 the British secured his commitment to seek British advice on all important matters (Peterson 1987: 8). The British official pretence that the Sultans were fully independent rulers crippled the Muscat regime.[4] The British held a view of the ideal Sultan: he would not be a financial liability, would maintain peace and order amongst his subjects and would of course take British 'advice' on matters involving British interest. However, as has been noted already, British actions inevitably made the Sultan dependent on the British both financially and militarily. The outcome was the notable tendency in Sultans from Faisal to Sa'id bin Taimur (r. 1932-1970) to want to abdicate or live away from Muscat.

France, the United States and Oman

Apart from occasioning greater British involvement the death of Sa'id bin Sultan had also stimulated interest from other Western powers in the fate of the Al Bu Sa'id dominions, particularly the French who were taking a renewed interest in Indian Ocean affairs. In 1862 Britain and France signed an agreement in which both pledged to respect the independence of the two, now separate, sultanates of Muscat and Zanzibar.[5] A commercial treaty arranged through the auspices of the British was signed with the Netherlands in 1877 (al-Musawi 1990: 93). The Americans, as has been noted, signed their first treaty with an Arab power when they concluded negotiations with Sa'id in 1833 (Halliday 1974: 269). The United States, conducting an active trade in dates, opened a consulate in 1880. However, these burgeoning contacts with a number of Western countries came to an end in the last decade of the nineteenth century, as the Arabian littoral became ever more firmly integrated into the British Indian imperial frontier. This integration meant that Britain became more involved in internal affairs as well as external affairs:

> In 1862 the official - and usually the actual policy of Britain in the Gulf was one of supervision of the foreign affairs, but one of non-interference in the internal affairs of the various local states. By 1900, however although the official policy remained unchanged, few Gulf rulers could escape without consulting British representatives when they considered important decisions concerning their internal administrations. (Landen 1968:163)

The position of a Sultan in Muscat became an onerous one, without freedom of manoeuvre in either external or internal affairs. The Sultans had no illusions about their independence and neither did Western powers other than the British. In 1915 the US consulate closed and the French consul was not replaced after the death of its occupant in 1918. Britain's strategic interest was only that other powers be excluded; the isolation of Muscat meant that her once busy port suffered depopulation and became stagnant. This was the making of Muscat's 'long sleep':[6] however, it was not a natural sleep born of exhaustion but one induced by the smothering effect of

British action in the Indian Ocean. The main focus of this section has been on British motives, policy and actions in Oman; we now turn to a more detailed look at the impact of British imperialism on Oman's economy, society and political organisation in the period up to 1920.

2.3: Impact of British Imperialism on Oman to 1920

British involvement had profound and fundamental consequences for Oman. British imperialism interrupted the historical pattern of Omani politics. This pattern reflected certain realities of life on the south-eastern corner of the Arabian peninsula which will be briefly examined in order to assess the consequences of British imperialism for Oman.

Geography and Ecology of Oman

The starting point is the physical geography of Oman.[7] Oman has been likened to an island on which two traditions developed: that of the mountainous interior (*dakhiliya*) - 'Oman' - and that of the coastal plain - 'Muscat'. The interior tradition is dominated by tribal politics and Ibadhism whilst the coastal tradition is that of sea faring and maritime trade. Research has often focused, depending on the individual researcher's preference, on either the interior or the coastal regions (Wilkinson 1987: ix). As a result, for a long time in the academic literature, the society of the interior and coast were seen as entirely separate. A consensus has now emerged that the two traditions are very much interconnected.[8] J.C. Wilkinson expresses it thus:

> So whilst we can conceive of 'Muscat' as the focal point of contact between outward and inward looking Oman, we should never think of Muscat and Oman as separate entities; rather as two sides of the same coin. (Wilkinson 1987:68)

He perceives the relationship between interior and coast as historically having a dynamic so regular as to be cyclical: its constitutes the 'Imamate cycle' (Peterson 1991: 1440). The constituent parts of this cycle and their relationship to the physical geography prior to the impact of the West will now be examined in more detail: the tribal system, Ibadhism and the Imamate, and maritime trade.

Tribes and confederations

Life in the interior was dictated by the imperatives of the level of agriculture permitted by the ancient irrigation system (Persian: *qanat*; Arabic: *aflaj*) - probably first constructed by the Persians during the Archaemenid occupation (Allen 1987: 23). The Arab tribal system of Oman had its origins in the migration of Arabs to the area starting in around the first century A.D. and which occurred in two successive waves. The two tribal confederations of the Hinawi and the Ghafiri are, according to custom, based on the original areas they came from: the first from the south, the second from the north. In addition, a correlation between Hinawi and adherence to Ibadhism and conversely a tribe's membership of the Ghafiri confederation with Sunnism, is often posited to amount to a fundamental dichotomy.[9] M. Reda Bhacker contends that such a view is seriously flawed. Rather, he argues, we should focus on the way that 'the tribal-cum-religious system of Oman, religious affiliations and dubious genealogies based on mythical ancestors have never played as significant role in this dichotomy as have the political ambitions of the major tamimas within each confederation' (1992:19). This became particularly significant for the election to the Imamate from the eighteenth century, a period to which we will return later in this section. It is first necessary to consider the distinctive version of Islam in Oman - Ibadhism - and its institution of the Imamate.

Ibadhism and the Imamate

The fundamental characteristic of life in the mountainous interior was its autonomy. This was reflected in the successful implantation of Ibadhism in the eighth century. This represented an 'anti- centralising ideology' well suited to the needs of a tribal society hostile to a distant imperial capital (Halliday 1974: 267). Ibadhism rejected both the prescriptions of Sunni and Shi'a Islam concerning the proper leadership of the Islamic community (Allen 1987: 9). It held that the original pure Islamic state had been corrupted by Uthman and sought to restore that community. In theory the leadership of this Islamic community was to be decided by an election in which any able bodied mature male of proper religious standing could stand. It was even possible in certain political conditions, such as an external tyrant (*jababira*), for the Imam to be concealed following the Ibadhi concept of secrecy (*kitman*) or even for there to be no Imam at all (Wilkinson 1987: 9; Bathurst 1972: 106). The Imamate had a minimalist form of government according to a strict interpretation of Islamic law. A standing army was forbidden and if an Imam departed from true Islamic principles then the community had a right even a duty to depose him.

In practice, however, the Imam was chosen from certain families and tribal groups and tended to 'degenerate' into dynastic power. These dynasties often lost interest in the tribal politics of the interior and concentrated on the other tradition 'Muscat'. This was the maritime tradition of Oman centring on the ports of the Batinah and concerned with the trading and commercial opportunities of the Indian Ocean littoral which periodically developed into overseas dominion. The tensions that this set up constitute the underlying dynamic of the 'Imamate cycle' to which we now turn.

Summary of the Imamate cycle
To start at one point of the cycle: at various times in history Ibadhi ideology has provided the basis for a unification of the tribal forces of the interior into a form of 'nation'. This allowed the Omanis to take control of their coast and benefit from the wealth accruing from the trading opportunities of the Indian Ocean and overseas territories. However, at this point the Imamate would degenerate into 'temporal' power and turn its back on the tribal politics of the interior. This would arouse the discontent of the interior forces who sought under Ibadhi ideology to depose the corrupt Imam. The ensuing conflict often resulted in an outside power occupying the coastal plain and even interior Oman, either at the behest of one of the parties or through an opportunistic appreciation of the situation. Faced with this external tyranny the interior tribes would again unite under Ibadhi ideology to elect a good and true Imam to free the country of the foreign power. This represents a full turn of the cycle. It was this cycle that was to be interrupted by the impact of British imperialism - that is the incorporation of the Arabian littoral into the Indian defence orbit and the resulting protection of the Al Bu Sa'id who, by the latter part of the nineteenth century, were to become client rulers. Let us now turn to a brief and selective overview of the history of this cycle prior to the election of the first Al Bu Sa'id Imam.

Imamate history to the first Al Bu Sa'id Imams

There have only been five dynasties of any lasting importance: the Julanda, the Yahmad-Kharus, the Nabahina, the Ya'aribah and the Al Bu Sa'id (Wilkinson 1987: 9). For our purposes the al-Ya'aribah dynasty is significant in that it led to the expulsion of the first Europeans to dominate the coast of Oman, the Portuguese, and furthermore they inaugurated what has been termed 'Oman's imperial age' of expansion and dominion in the Gulf, India and East Africa (Allen 1987: 35). It was this Omani empire that was to be dismembered by Britain.

The Portuguese in Oman

Portuguese control on the coast of Oman had been established in brutal fashion by Alfonso de Albuquerque who, in 1507, arrived off the Omani coast and explored from Ras al-Hadd to Sur, laying waste the town of Quriyat. Eventually the coast of Oman from Sur to Khor Fakkan was added to the Portuguese Indian Ocean empire and Muscat developed as the centre of their maritime and commercial operations. This required defending against the Arabs, Persians and Ottomans and it was during this time that the imposing forts of Jalani and Mirani, which still stand today, were built. The Portuguese were content to leave the Arabs and their Hormuzi overlords to their own devices as long as their annual tribute was paid. However, there were many Omani rebellions against the Portuguese control with varying degrees of success but it was not until the beginning of the Ya'aribah dynasty that the Omanis were able to unite sufficiently to expel the Portuguese from Oman for good (Allen 1987: 32-34).

The Ya'aribah Imams (1624 - 1749)

Nasir bin Murshid al-Ya'aribah (1624-1749) was one of the many contenders for control of Oman in the early seventeenth century.[10] With the backing of the ulema, he gained election to the office of Imam and thereafter imposed his authority in the face of opposition of rival warlords on Oman and the lower Gulf coast. Having established his position in interior Oman he proceeded to take on the Portuguese who were still in control of Muscat and the Batinah coast. The final expulsion of the Portuguese, however, was to fall to his son, Sultan bin Saif al-

Ya'aribah; the Portuguese were harried out and replaced by the Omanis from India to East Africa. The result was that Oman became the most formidable maritime power in the western Indian Ocean area and the period of the first three Ya'aribah Imams was a time of great prosperity for Oman.[11] Gradually their hereditary and outward-looking regime became increasingly suspect to the Ibadhi religious leaders, especially when there was no threat of foreign domination and on account of their great wealth. By the reign of Sultan bin Saif II (1711 - 1714) dissent had begun to become rife in the Omani polity. The issue came to a head with the election of a new Imam on the death of Sultan bin Saif, with rival candidates being backed by the religious leaders and the tribal chiefs. This became a civil war of the Omani tribes polarised around the Hinawi-Ghafiri divide, in which the Ghafiri-backed candidate invited in Persian support. Rather than an alliance, the Persians became a force of invasion and occupation. This occupation came to an end in 1744 when the Persians sought to withdraw and were slaughtered by the governor of Sohar, Ahmad bin Sa'id al Bu Sa'id, who had given them a guarantee of safe passage (Allen 1987: 35-38).

The Al Bu Sa'id dynasty

The Al Bu Sa'id dynasty was founded with the election of Ahmad bin Sa'id to the office of Imam in 1749 as a result of his role in resisting and expelling the Persian forces which had occupied the Batinah in the civil war which followed the decline of the Ya'aribah dynasty. Although Ahmad did not come from a traditional Imamate family he governed from the old Ya'aribah capital of Rustaq. Following his death a family power struggle ensued over the succession the outcome of which has been the subject of different interpretations. Calvin Allen contends that Ahmad's son, Sa'id bin Ahmad, held the title of Imam and resided in Muscat, whilst his son, Hamad bin Sa'id took control of Muscat and showed no interest in claiming the title of Imam or in establishing himself with the tribes of the interior (Allen 1978; 1982; 1987: 41). In contrast, he used the title of Sayyid which holds no connotations of religious authority and turned his attentions to the trading opportunities of the Indian Ocean. He characterises this as amounting to the establishment of an independent state. M. Reda Bhacker, in contrast, contends that this depiction is erroneous; he points out that the title of Sayyid was not an Al Bu Sa'id innovation but had been used by the Ya'aribah as a respectful form of address and does not possess the same religious significance in Ibadhism as it does in Shi'a Islam. Furthermore, he adduces evidence to show that Sa'id helped Hamad to take over Muscat and that they remained in close contact as 'they acted in concert in their effort to safeguard their own commercial interest faced as they were with persistent intrigues from other members of the Al Bu Sa'id.' Following Hamad's early death from smallpox Sa'id did not involve himself with Muscat affairs as his brother Sultan successfully challenged him for control of the city. There then followed an agreement between the three principal sons of Ahmad bin Sa'id which recognised Sultan as in control of Muscat, Qays in Sohar and Imam Sa'id to be pensioned off to Rustaq where his authority held sway, whilst the authority of other tribal leaders ran in their own tribal areas (Bhacker 1992: 25-26). Sultan continued the traditional attempts to exercise power in the Gulf, conducting campaigns to gain recognition of his right to tribute from the Utub of Bahrain and to counter the Sa'udi backed Qasimi foe. His death at their hands on the return from negotiations with the Ottoman *pasha* of Basra led to predictable upheaval in Oman (Allen 1987: 25-25). Sultan bin Sa'id came to power in 1806, having assassinated the Sa'udi sympathiser Badr bin Saif, and sought to develop his power base. Ultimately, he was forced, due to the growth of British power, to concentrate on the development and preservation of the Omani dominions in East Africa and to absent himself from Muscat.

Oman and East Africa
The turn of the eighteenth to the nineteenth century sees not only the development of the British into something more than a trading power but also the first manifestations of the expanding Saudi power and their doctrine of Wahhabism (Wilkinson 1987: 54; see also al-Rashid 1981, chapter 3). With the coastal areas of the lower Gulf coming under the British Trucial system in the 1820s and the expansion of Wahhabi power in the interior Sa'id had but one option: expansion in East Africa (Wilkinson 1987: 54-58). Ironically, it was the development of British protection in Oman that allowed Sayyid Sa'id to concentrate fully on this

and develop his 'African policy' beginning in the 1820s and culminating in the de facto transfer of his capital to Zanzibar. It would, however, be a mistake to see this in isolation to developments in the rest of the world. Thomas Bierschenk has characterised the expansion of Omani commerce in East Africa in the first part of the nineteenth century as a 'a secondary regional distribution centre in a world market increasingly dominated by Britain'(1989:20) and M. Reda Bhacker comes to a similar conclusion.[12] It was these same forces which had led to the development of Omani commerce in the first half of the nineteenth century - the spread of capitalism under its 'pioneer' of British imperialism - that dictated its decline thereafter.

Oman's economic decline
Following the Indian Mutiny British economic penetration of India gained pace and the British position in India became pivotal in Britain's world-wide empire (Bromley 1994: 67). The British sponsored separation from Zanzibar deprived the ruler of Muscat from this source of wealth and put into stark relief the economic consequences of other aspects of British action in the Indian Ocean area - in short, British paramountcy which had been designed to safeguard the economic wealth deriving from the Raj. These were the growing curtailment of slaving and gun trading, the opening of the Suez Canal and the introduction of steam ship technology which reduced Muscat's role as a stopover port. Furthermore, as the British domination of trade in the Indian Ocean area deepened commerce shifted from the silver to the gold standard; Oman's Maria Theresa dollar was based on silver and currency drained from Oman when silver prices fell in the late 19th century. Most significant was the elimination of the Omani cotton weaving handicraft industry at the hands of the European and British-sponsored Indian manufacturing - a force with which Oman could not compete. The result was that by the end of the century Oman, although still within the Indian Ocean trading area, had become relatively insignificant economically with a volume of trade that could only allow prosperity for a few merchants.[13] C.H. Allen advances the argument that the poverty of the ruling Al Bu Sa'id should not be correlated with a decline of trade in the 19th century; rather that trade passed into the hands of the Indian merchants, the Banians

(1978: 6). Whatever the case may be it is indisputable that the impecuniousness of the Al Bu Sa'id Sultans was to both increase the hostility of the interior tribes and the Sultans' dependence on the British either through the provision of military protection against the tribes or in the bailing out of their debts with the Indian merchants. Tribal resentment grew against the British-backed Sultans on the coast who neither allowed the development of traditional sources of revenue nor provided any largesse. We will examine the relations between the Sultanate and Imamate up to 1920 next.

Sultanate and Imamate

The term Sultan was first given to the rulers of Muscat by the British.[14] The term is an anathema to Ibadhis with its negative association with secular tyranny. In the normal course of the cycle the Al Bu Sa'id would have been swept away; it was only due to interventions by the British - militarily or through the intervention of subsidy - that the Al Bu Sa'id were restored after Imamate forces took control of Muscat 1868-1871. With the collapse of the Omani empire in the 1860s the tribes of the interior no longer saw the position of the Al Bu Sa'id Sultans on the coast as benefiting them. As in previous times they started to espouse a 'pure Islam' and elected an Imam, forming an anti-coastal alliance headed by the al-Harathi tribe. In 1868 this alliance led by Azzan bin Qais Al Bu Sa'id, representing a collateral branch of the Al Bu Sa'id, descended from the mountains, captured Muscat and drove out foreign merchants and all signs of alien corruption such as coffee houses (Halliday 1974: 270). This hostility to the outside world threatened British interests. In 1871 the British helped Turki bin Sa'id financially and militarily to expel the Imam from Muscat (Imam Azzan was killed in battle outside Mattrah) and re-installed this branch of the Al Bu Sa'id as Sultans - the switch from British alliance to British hegemony had occurred and Muscat became a de facto protectorate.[15] With this development also came the change in the relationship of the Sultans with the population from autocratic patrimon to foreign-supported puppet.[16] The beginning, as with the end of informal imperialism, is not as clearly defined as formal colonial annexations. The overthrow of the Imamate in 1871 and the restoration of the Sultan can be taken as the start of British informal imperialism in Muscat and Oman - a situation that was to last for the next hundred years. From 1871 - 1919 Muscat was a *de facto* protectorate with British control of its foreign relations. As we shall see in chapter three, with the greater involvement of the British in internal government from 1920, Muscat then became part of Britain's informal empire.

The British were also concerned that the Sultan might be overthrown from within; this problem highlighted one of the contradictions of imperial rule: while Britain benefited from the destruction of the Omani empire and brought it about, this end of empire weakened the Sultans internally who then required greater British intervention to support them - a 'crisis of collaboration' in Robinson's terms. The advent of imperialism both exacerbated the conflict between the Omani interior and the coast and did not allow of its resolution. The tribal uprising of 1868 and the occupation of Muscat by the tribes of the interior began a long series of British interventions in defence of their client sultans. After the restoration of the Sultan in 1871, and the intensification of British involvement there were further clashes in 1877 and 1883 when British warships bombarded and repelled tribesmen who were attacking Muscat (Halliday 1974: 271-272).

In 1895, after a tribal attack on Muscat, the British issued a warning to the tribes that they would not tolerate the eviction of Sultan Faisal from Muscat (Peterson 1976: 172; 1987: 8). In 1913 a new Imam, Salim bin Rushid al-Kharusi, was elected by disgruntled tribesman and an Indian Army force was dispatched to protect Muscat from besiegers 1915-1920. Flushed with success after some victorious skirmishes, Sultan Taimur bin Faisal was keen to try and extend his authority but Viceroy Harding preferred he seek some sort of settlement with the Imamate backed by British coercive power. Following the defeat of the Germany and the Ottoman Empire the British Political Agent in Muscat, Major L.B.H. Haworth, intimated this power in a letter to 'the Oman Chiefs' in 1919 advising Omani compliance with British plans: "...if we wished we could send aeroplanes which would destroy your towns and your forts and you surely do not think you could fight against us. We have 50,000 men in Iraq whom we no longer require there and a few thousand of these would be sufficient to take the whole of Oman if we wished to do so." (FO 371/3285 in El Solh 2000: 3). A British threat of a punitive tax on date exports from the interior brought Imamate forces to negotiation at Sib and a treaty was signed under British auspices in 1920 at Sib.[17] The Political Agent Muscat, Wingate was deliberately vague on the issue of sovereignty in order to get an agreement between the two parties (Bierschenk 1989: 211).

The Treaty of Sib

The Treaty of Sib defined relations between 'Oman' and 'Muscat' for the next thirty or so years. Effectively it left the interior to its own devices - both sides agreed not to interfere in each other's affairs and allow free trade and travel. So, at this stage the main consequence of Western involvement in Oman was the ossification of the Imamate cycle. The twentieth century Imamate was, in contrast to its predecessors, actually very isolated from the outside world due to the impact of British imperialism and the expansion of the capitalist system.[18] It was not to be until capitalistic forces developed an interest in the interior, that the cycle -which for the time being had merely been stopped - was to be dismantled, seemingly for ever.

Conclusion

By the end of 1920 and the settlement at Sib, Britain's position in Muscat was unchallenged by either other Western powers, Al Bu Sa'id aspirations of independence, interior tribal forces, or Saudi intrigues. Britain had no direct interest in Oman and was happy to ignore the interior as long as, as elsewhere in Arabia, its control of the littoral was secure and free from disturbance. The attainment of this position was the result of the incorporation of the Omani coastline into the imperial frontiers of British India - a connection first made at the turn of the eighteenth to the nineteenth century. This situation was not to change until the 1920s when economic and strategic interests intrinsic to Oman and the Arabian peninsula developed. The first prospecting for oil and the development of air routes and its effect on Britain's 'informal empire' in Oman are examined in the next chapter.

CHAPTER THREE:
Informal Empire in Oman 1921 - 1931

The collapse of the Ottoman empire and the creation of a new state system in the Middle East which followed World War One had a significant effect on British policy towards the Persian Gulf. The increased British involvement in the Middle East region as a whole led to increased military and civilian communications. In this context British strategic interests in Oman increased as a new air route was planned. American formal diplomatic representation was the responsibility of their Consul in Baghdad following the closure of its consulate in Muscat. However they showed great interest in information pertaining to explorations for oil and the relationship of the Sultan of Muscat to the British. British strategic interests were located in 'Muscat' territory; the Sultanate's administration was restructured to try and stop its reliance on the Government of India for defence against Imamate forces. However, it was the lure of oil that was to create new Western interests which would require control of Imamate territory itself: the first incursions into the interior of Oman in the search for oil took place in this period.

3.1: The international context 1921 - 1931
The introduction of air routes and the development of oil as a commodity meant the Arabian peninsula was perceived as an area of increasing geopolitical importance in its own right. The air age made its first impact on Arabia during World War One. Britain supplied Ibn Saud with four de Haviland biplanes and crew to use against the rebellious Ikhwan. This was mainly to pre-empt other European powers attempting to undermine the

British position. However, the introduction of air technology to the peninsula came about mainly through the uses of air power Britain found for its imperial interests. In the 1920s one of the main uses was for 'policing' operations to subdue troublesome tribesmen. The nascent RAF and its new strategy of air power faced considerable hostility from the other services fearful of an erosion of their role. However, the ease with which an aerial display or bombardment could assert British authority won the inter-service argument. The other application of air technology in this period was the development by the British of air routes around the fringes of the peninsula.

Air routes and empire

Whilst the discovery and exploitation of oil was to prove the more lasting and important Western concern with the Arabian peninsula, the need to develop air routes and the application of air power was the focus of British concerns with the security of the Peninsula in the 1920s (Peterson 1986: 18). New air routes, civil and military, were seen as buckling the British Empire together. These routes required the creation of airstrips at regular intervals along the route where supplies could be left. This in turn required making arrangements with the relevant sheikhs and rulers.

Theoretically, there were four possible routes for a passenger and mail service by air from Cairo to India. One was via the Red Sea to Aden and thence up the coast to Salalah and Muscat; however this was the longest route, lacked facilities and could be disrupted by the seasonal monsoon. Another was across the desert to Baghdad and then across central Persia to Quetta but this had operational as well as political problems. Remaining were two routes: along the Persian coast and onto Karachi or taking the Arab side of the Gulf to Oman and then over to the Makran coast. In terms of distance, climate and amenity to supply by sea the two routes were similar. However, the Persian Gulf route had the advantage that the Indo-European Telegraph's line was already in place there. Furthermore, there were perceived to be additional problems with the Arabian route: a political one of dealing with the various sheikhdoms on the Arab side, and a technical one - aircraft capable of safely making the hop across the sea from the Trucial to the Makran coast were only to come into existence in 1932. Accordingly, the Persian route was the one that was initially developed. However, it always suffered from serious problems relating to wider tensions in the Anglo-Persian relationship, German and Russian influence in Persia and the Persian preference for the central route (Peterson 1986: 21). The last leg of the Imperial Airways Cairo-Karachi flight was inaugurated along the Persian coast in April 1929 and continued on a regular basis until October 1932 when it was transferred to the Arabian littoral.

Work on the Arabian coast alternative started in 1929 but surprisingly, given the difficulties with the Persian route, the Air Ministry and Imperial airways only began to give it consideration in 1931(Peterson 1986: 64). Developing the air route involved surveying which was carried out by the RAF's No. 203 (Flying Boat) Squadron and negotiating with the rulers along the route which was conducted by the Political Resident Persian Gulf. Kuwait, Bahrain and Gwadur (under the jurisdiction of the Sultanate of Muscat and Oman) on the Makran coast posed few political problems as the rulers had long co-operated with the British. More difficult was Qatar and the Trucial Coast. Eventually, agreement was reached for a landing strip at Sharjah which could be utilised by landplanes although the passengers would be accommodated at the resthouse at Dubai. Although there still remained the issue of emergency landing grounds (especially on the other side of the Ru'us al-Jibal from Sharjah) the civil air route from Cairo to India switched to the Arabian side of the Gulf in late 1932.

In addition to this civil air route the RAF sought to institute a Basra-Aden route. Parts of this route were in place before the creation of the civil route but it was not finished until the completion of the civil route. This apparently anomalous situation is explained in that the RAF had long been active in Mesopotamia and around Aden and had laid down fuel supplies where ever a Political Agent was located. With the transfer of responsibility for the defence of Aden colony and the protectorate from the Indian Government to the RAF in 1928 the need for a permanent air linkage between Basra and Aden became even more pressing. In 1929, as the civil air route on the Arabian side of the Gulf was being developed, the Air Ministry instructed the Air Officer Commanding (AOC) Aden to extend the chain of landing strips eastward. Doing this in the protectorate was relatively easy as British authority was firmly established. Likewise, the Batinah coast of Oman was secure for such development. More problematic was the stretch of coast between Salalah and Muscat where the Sultan of Muscat and Oman's authority was purely nominal. The creation of this route in Oman was finished by 1936 and will be examined in section 3.2.

Air Power and Policing in the Arabian Peninsula
The advent of the air age to Arabia was not confined to the creation of civil and military routes (see Peterson 1986: 28-40). The applications developed from the use of aircraft in the First World War were applied to peacetime conditions in the expanded empire in the Middle East. This included their use in 'small wars' and imperial defence, and in colonial policing operations against tribal forces in which the low cost of air power was of particular appeal and used by the Air Command in the inter-service competition for defence responsibility. The use of air power on Sur in Oman was one such instance and was used by the Air Ministry to show the benefits of air power and this will also be examined in section 3.2.

Oil and empire: Britain and the Middle East after World War One
By the beginning of the First World War it had become abundantly clear to the British military that control of reserves of petroleum would be a key strategic component in any future military conflict; this was brought home to the British government by the oil shortages of 1917 and 1918. These reserves were to be found in the Middle East, notably Persia and what was then known as Mesopotamia. Sir Maurice Hankey, the secretary of the War Cabinet, wrote to the Foreign Secretary, Arthur Balfour that 'oil in the next war will occupy the place of coal or at least a parallel place to coal. The only big potential supply that we can get under British control is the Persian and Mesopotamian supply.' Therefore, Hankey said 'control over these oil supplies becomes a first-class British war aim'. In substance Foreign Secretary Balfour agreed with Hankey; Balfour sought to achieve the same objective but without using formulations that would appear to the Americans as unduly imperialistic and conflict with Woodrow Wilson's doctrine of national self-determination (Yergin 1991: 185-188).

The United States and the Open Door Policy

The American perception that the British were attempting to create a zone of supremacy in the Middle East and the consequences this would have for Americans motivated American policy in this period. As in Britain, the experience of petrol shortages during the war had had a similar galvanising affect on American policy makers to ensure that American oil companies were not shut out of Middle East oil (Yergin 1991: 194). The mechanism by which the exclusion of the US companies might have been achieved was the concessionary arrangement of the Turkish Petroleum Company (later the Iraqi Petroleum Company). Set up in 1912 this company, had been comprised of the Anglo-Persian Oil Company (later Anglo-Iranian), Royal Dutch Shell and the Deutsche Bank and had negotiated a concession with the Ottoman government to develop the potential oil-fields around Mosul. The companies in TPC had agreed not to prospect for oil in the area covered by the concession except under the aegis and conditions of the TPC; the boundaries of the concession were known as the 'self denying clause' of the 'Foreign Office Agreement' signed March 14 1914 (Yergin 1991: 187-188). During World War One this area was allocated to the French sphere of influence under the Sykes-Picot agreements. With British occupation at the end of the war the British had persuaded the French to hand over the Mosul area in return for Syria and a French involvement in the exploitation of the oil resources.

Although the Americans retreated into political isolationism at the end of World War One the other part of American foreign policy at this time was a determination to break open important markets and access to natural resources for American companies, foremost of which was oil. Hence, the Mineral Leasing Act of 1920 which denied drilling rights to foreign companies to oil resources on American public land in retaliation for the restrictions of the Dutch in the East Indies and the British in Mesopotamia. The Americans were determined to resist the 'old- fashioned imperialism' embodied by the San Remo Conference and press for their 'Open Door' policy. Initially the British were sceptical of American concerns of oil shortage noting that four fifths of world oil production was located in Texas; acrimonious diplomatic exchanges ensued between the Foreign

Office and the State Department (Yergin 1991: 195). Following American pressure the British decided that it would be better to have the Americans within the concession of IPC rather than outside attacking it. Furthermore the involvement of American finance would reduce the costs to the British tax payer of setting up the new Iraqi state (Bromley 1994: 79). After hard negotiations forced by the discovery of oil near Kirkuk in 1927, the concessionary area of the IPC became known, after Calouste Gulbenkians's pencil, as the 1928 'Red Line Agreement' comprising the interests of British, French and American oil companies and the Armenian financier's five per cent. It was to cover all of the major oil fields subsequently discovered in the Middle East with the exception of Kuwait and Iran and required that no member could take up a concession within the ex-Ottoman empire unless it was offered to the group as a whole (Yergin 1991: 205).

The Arabian Peninsula and the 'Red Line Agreement'
The oil fields of Saudi Arabia and the Gulf were to prove the greatest of these oil fields; however, in the 1920s this was not apparent. The Anglo-Persian Oil Company had little interest in the area on the other side of the Gulf as the geological formations did not match up with the known oil-bearing strata of the time, but this did not mean that they were keen to allow other companies to explore the area. Before the First World War the British had inserted 'nationality clauses' whereby only 'British interests' could be given oil concessions by the Gulf Shaikhs. Initially Gulf Oil acquired a concession to Bahrain; however when Gulf successfully gained entrance to the Turkish Petroleum Company in 1928 it became bound by the Red Line Agreement and could not prospect for oil in Bahrain. It therefore gave up its option to Standard Oil of California (SOCAL) which was not part of the TPC and so not bound by this agreement; however it ran into the barrier of the 'nationality clause'. There followed intense lobbying by the US government. The British reflection that by allowing American resources into oil development it would speed the development of resources for the Navy and reduce the demands of the shaikhs for subsidy meant that in 1929 Socal was allowed to enter into a concession with the Sheikh of Bahrain. This was on condition that all correspon-

dence between the company and the Sheikh went via the offices of the British representative. The concession was awarded to a Canadian subsidiary set up by SOCAL to maintain the facade that the concession was to a British company; drilling started in 1930. The discovery of oil in Bahrain and its consequences will be further examined in chapter four.

The increasing strategic importance of the Gulf
The development of strategic and civil air routes around the Peninsula reflected a growing shift in British involvement predicated on air power rather than for maritime reasons as had been the case earlier. Furthermore, with the discovery of oil in Persia and Iraq British involvement progressively intensified, and increasingly the Arab Gulf sheikhdoms were seen of intrinsic strategic importance rather than merely in terms of the security considerations of protecting the route to India (Peterson 1986: 40). The first major review of British policy in the Gulf in twenty years began in 1928 with the creation of the Persian Gulf Sub-Committee (PGSC) by the Committee of Imperial Defence (CID). The Sub-Committee agreed with the Chiefs of Staff that the 'maintenance of the British supremacy in the Persian Gulf is even more essential to the security of India and Imperial interests at the present time than it was in the past' and its related conclusion that 'it should be a cardinal feature of our policy to maintain our supremacy in the region'.[1]

The Arabian Peninsula and the world market
In conclusion, whilst the Arabian littoral still continued to be placed in its 'traditional' strategic context of one hundred and fifty years - that of its strategic importance on the approaches to India and a policy of minimal interference in the internal affairs of the Gulf sheikhdoms[2] - the development of oil as a commodity of crucial importance in the capitalist world economy and the changes this led to in the world market were to have increasing effects on the area. The region's incorporation into the capitalist world economy through the agency of British imperialism meant that the Arabian Peninsula was vulnerable to the vagaries of the world economy such as the Great Depression. Furthermore the oil companies had a need that had not existed in the traditional strategic context: the need for sovereign rulers,

that is, rulers who held authority and property rights in a territory defined by precise borders. They would thus be able to negotiate and sign concession agreements with the oil companies which would give the companies the right to prospect for oil in that area without hindrance.[3] This issue of authority in a given territory also impinged on the creation of landing strips on the South Arabian route. We now turn to consider how this international context affected Western involvement in Oman in the period 1921- 1932.

3.2: Western strategic interests in Oman 1921 - 1931

The developments surveyed in 3.1 led to a growing British involvement in Oman in two respects both of which reflected the consequences of the Treaty of Sib: the British-organised de facto division of Muscat and Oman. Firstly, the increase in the strategic importance of the Gulf required the maintenance of authority and British prestige in the coastal areas under the Sultan's jurisdiction; ultimately British air power was to win the day. Secondly, an initial expedition to prospect for oil took place in this period and encountered the problematic nature of Sultanate authority in the interior.

British support for the Sultanate

After the Treaty of Sib the authority of the Sultanate in effect was limited to the Batinah coastal plain, Muscat and Dhofar. Also deemed as part of Muscat territory but more problematic was the Musandam Peninsula and the port of Sur. Consequently, British military support for their client in the 1920s was required to put down a number of tribal rebellions in these areas against the payment of Sultanate taxes or jurisdiction; of paramount importance was the maintenance of British prestige at as low a cost as possible which was achieved through gunboat diplomacy and sometimes naval bombardment or the use of air power.

In late 1920 the Yal-Sa'd, the principal tribe of the Batinah staged an uprising against efforts to establish a customs post; it was not until 1922 that the Muscat Levy Corps supported by a British gunboat enforced compliance with the new taxation system. Another instance was the imprisonment in 1930 of Taimur's *wali* in Khasab in the Ru'us al-Jibal and the rejection of the Sultan's authority. Again, British gunboats bombarded

Khasab and the rebellious shaikh fled, returning to accept Muscati authority when he was unable to gain tribal support (Allen 1987: 62).

However, the most serious rebellion took place at the fishing village of Sur on the south-eastern tip of Oman by the Bani Bu Ali who had long bridled against the authority of the Sultan of Muscat over them; as mentioned in chapter two Sa'id bin Sultan had enlisted British support against them in the early nineteenth century. In 1923 the tribe refused to pay customs duty to the Sultan and in 1928 they built their own customs house in the suburb of al-Aqya hoisting a Saudi flag in an attempt to gain Saudi support. Unless the Sultan took action the Imam of Oman threatened to send his men into the area (Joyce 1995: 15). To lose control of Sur would halve the Sultan's revenues. However, the Sultan's limited armed forces were inadequate to oust the renegades and he requested British assistance (Peterson 1986: 38-39).

The British were determined to show that rebellion did not pay. The Political Agent Muscat recommended the posting of an Indian infantry battalion with the costs to be recouped through the customs revenue; Whitehall considered this but the Government of India thought such a dispatch of troops unnecessary (Joyce 1995: 29). Instead the vice admiral, Commander in Chief B. Thesiger, sailed to Sur and discussed the situation with Sayyid Sa'id, the Sultan's son. A number of shots were fired on the isolated fort from the sloop HMS Cyclamen which destroyed their target - thereafter the Saudi flag came down over Sur. The RAF levelled the fort in 1930 to demonstrate its capabilities in the rivalry between the services (Peterson 1986: 39).

Prospecting for oil in Oman in the 1920s

Although the exploration for oil in Oman was not to gather pace fully until the discovery of oil in Bahrain in 1932, the 1920s saw a number of expeditions made in Oman and also Dhofar. It was the beginning of what J.C. Wilkinson has termed the 'oil game': the struggle in Oman for the control of its oil resources. The different parties in this conflict were on one side the British oil company, the British government and their 'client' the Sultan of Muscat and on the other, the American oil company, the US government, the Saudis and the Imamate. The 'end game' in this dispute was to take place in the 1950s. The exploration process initially encompassed a number of features: the signing of agreements with imperial powers and oil companies, the delimitation of boundaries and actual expeditions.

In 1923 Sultan Taimur gave an assurance to '...not exploit any petroleum which may be found anywhere within our territory and will not grant permission for its exploration without consulting the Political Agent at Muscat and without the approval of the High Government of India' (Wilkinson 1987: 274). This was similar to undertakings procured earlier by Britain from the rulers of Kuwait, Qatar, Bahrain and the Trucial States. The first exploration party in the Sultanate of Muscat and Oman took place in 1925 when the d'Arcy Exploration company - effectively a subsidiary of Anglo-Iranian - obtained a two year exploration license. This document stated that 'the company recognises that certain parts of the Sultan's territory are not at present safe for its operations' and that 'the final decision on any attempt to enter an area lay with the Political Agent Muscat.' A geological party based on H.M.S. Triad, and accompanied by the British financial adviser Bertram Thomas and Captain Eccles of the Muscat Levies, made a number of excursions inland from the Batinah coast to look at likely oil-bearing strata in the Western Hajar. They were unable to do much work partly because of the disturbed situation resulting from the dispatch of an Imamate force to investigate the appearance of Saudi tax collectors in Buraimi for the first time in fifty years. The concession was allowed to lapse and there was no significant exploration for oil until the 1930s. The actual determining of boundaries would take place in the years after the discovery of oil in Bahrain but the essence of the process had been defined: it would be the extension by the British of the 'authority' of the Sultan of Muscat.

The American presence: missionaries and doctors
With the closure of the American consulate in Muscat in 1915 American involvement in Oman at this time was limited to medical missionaries. It was the responsibility of the American consul in Baghdad, John Randolph, to monitor news from Oman. To take up his post in Baghdad Randolph travelled on the British India Steam Navigation ship which stopped at Muscat for several hours; Randolph took the opportunity to meet the American

missionary Dr Sarah Hosman and discussed with her the difficulties she experienced with buying land and travelling outside of Muscat. Randolph later wrote to the Secretary of State that 'This reported attitude of the British as regards the purchase of land in Oman may be evidence that there is some truth in the report that, in return for the handsome subsidy paid the Sultan of Oman, the British hold treaty rights to the effect that no foreigners are to be permitted to purchase land in Oman.' The British consul, Major Hinde, and the Sultan were not keen for her to visit areas even where she had a guaranteed safe conduct and escorts from the shaikh. The reasons given by the consul were that should anything happen to her it would necessitate a punitive expedition 'in order prevent a loss of prestige by the white man' (quoted in Joyce 1995: 26). After Randolph made representations to the British Consul and the Resident at Bushire Hosman received permission from Hinde to briefly visit 'Suwaik and Hazam' where she preached the gospel and gave out medicine. In her report which she sent to Randolph she wrote 'I never saw so many sick bad eyes in all my life.' As she had to hurry back she only was able to perform one operation (Porter 1982: 25). Similar restrictions applied to other American missionaries that worked in Oman. In 1932 an American doctor slipped off to Dhofar without permission. The British Consul wrote to the Sultan, 'I trust that the American missionaries will realise the folly of their ways and repent their very bad manners' (quoted in Joyce 1995: 26).

Most significantly Randolph reported in March 1931 to his Secretary of State on the following topic: 'English Interest in Possible Oil Deposits in the Arabian Peninsula' (Porter 1982: 28-35). In this dispatch Randolph detailed his conversation with an English financier Sir John Cadnam who, Randolph implies, had been seeking to obscure the possibility of oil seepage in Bahrain. Furthermore, he reports on the reaction in the English and American colony in Bahrain of the arrival in February of Bertram Thomas on the island. Thomas evoked a mixed reaction in one conversation in which Randolph was involved. The officer commanding the Bahrain police was critical of Thomas for leaving his office in Muscat in bad order. Mr Walker the agent for the Mesopotamia Persia Corporation defended Thomas:

stating that British officials stationed in the Persian Gulf were well aware of the fact that Mr Thomas had not been sent to act as financial adviser to the Sultan of Oman solely, but that his main duties there were to explore the interior and to try to locate for the Anglo-Persian Oil Company oil seepage reported to have been discovered by Arab caravans in that section of Arabia. He added that British official were also aware of the fact that an Anglo-Persian Oil tanker had picked up Mr Thomas at Muscat and had landed him at Dhafur and that his journey while ostensibly undertaken as an exploratory trip over an unknown portion of Arabia was also taken to obtain all information possible for the Anglo-Persian Oil Company. To these statements Captain Parke made no answer but immediately changed the conversation. (see Porter 1982: 28).

The Americans were aware of the limitations on the Sultan's independence and that the Sultanate was part of Britain's 'informal empire'. The development of 'informal empire' in Oman will be examined in more detail in the next section.

3.3: Impact of British interests on Oman 1921 - 1931
In this section we examine the impact of British strategic interests on Muscat and Oman. Principally this was the re-organisation of government in Muscat. The Imamate was confined to the interior under the Treaty of Sib.

Institutions of Government in 'Muscat'
Following the Treaty of Sib the British instituted a series of reforms to government in the Sultanate. Their motivation was the concern of the Government of India that if something was not done then the Sultan would be removed by Imamate forces. The aim was to institute reforms which would strengthen the ability of the Sultanate to be self-reliant and thus reduce its dependence on the Government of India (Peterson 1978: 91). These reforms took place in the ordering of the Sultanate's finances, institutions of government and military all of which became British-run. Until the 1920s the British had been content to exert their influence of the Consul but now they became more and more involved in the daily affairs of the Sultanate. The out-

come was that in 1922 the British Resident in the Persian Gulf wrote to the government of British India: 'We have gradually but imperceptibly usurped the functions and authority of the State.' (Bierschenk 1989:209)

Finance was the immediate concern. We have seen how British actions in the nineteenth century - the separation of Zanzibar and the curtailing of slaving and gun running - had impoverished both the royal family and Omanis. Therefore, the remaining sources of finance were various customs revenues,[4] the religious tax (*zakat*) and various subsidies from the British. The problem was that due to the costs of maintaining the royal family expenses always exceeded income so that the Sultans were permanently in debt to various merchants. The solution as the British saw it was to clear the Sultan's debts to these merchants and to institute a financial adviser (*wazir*) to ensure the repayment of their debt.

The first finance minister was D.V. McCullum, previously a political agent in Kuwait. His briefing from PAM Wingate was:

> The very skeleton of reform of the administration is necessary. We only want to make the state pay its way and our loan and if possible make it stand on its own legs without continual propping from us. Make the customs pay and remove the more glaring faults and let the rest rip. Go very slow, be very tactful and try and remove any feeling the people may get that your coming is only the prelude to British occupation. In addition to the fact that this is not true such a rumour cannot but have a bad effect on our policy and our prestige elsewhere. Pay the greatest respect to local prejudices and above all to religion. It is not a difficult matter nowadays to raise anti-Christian sentiment, and the Omani fanatics are next door with whom we want to get some kind of agreement. (Peterson 1978: 76)

Wingate also created a Council of Ministers, ostensibly to assist Taimur but really to govern during Taimur's long absences from Muscat. It was composed of the Sultan's elder brother, Nadir bin Faisal as acting Sultan in Taimur's absence; the wali of Matrah, Muhammed bin Ahmad al-Ghashsham, as head of financial affairs, Zubayr bin Ali al-Huti, a Baluchi immigrant, as head of justice, and Rashid bin Uzayyiz al-Khubsaybi as head of religious affairs. In practice the Council was ineffective and largely for show and any major decisions were made by McCullum during the six months he stayed in his post and thereafter by successive PAMs and financial advisers.[5]

By 1924 the Sultan was in arrears with his loan repayments and the Sultanate's financial position was continuing to decline (Townsend 1977: 50). An appointment was made to reorganise the Customs Department. Initially an Imperial Customs expert name Bower undertook this on a temporary basis; however, it was recognised that a permanent appointment was required to overhaul the system. Accordingly, Bertram Thomas was appointed as Financial Adviser arriving in February 1925; he stayed in post for six years during which he devoted more time to his explorations. Despite this he acquired more and more power in the politics of Muscat and received permission from the Government of India to use the title of *wazir* and to serve on the Council of Ministers. Eventually the Government of India balked at Thomas's crossing of the Rub al-Khali and he was removed from post. His replacement, S.E. Hedgecock, was not sufficiently capable up and after a couple of months his duties were taken up by the military adviser, and often acting PAM, R.G.E.W. Alban. When Alban was invalided back to Britain shortly after, the new Sultan, Sa'id bin Taimur refused to accept a replacement. J.E. Peterson comments 'The period of direct British supervision over the Sultanate's administration had come to an inconsequential close' (Peterson 1978: 78). Whilst Muscat remained part of Britain's informal empire with a British interest and involvement in both the internal and external policy of the Sultanate, the particular character and approach of Sa'id bin Taimur did have an effect on the relationship with the British which will be examined in the next chapter.

Creation of the Muscat Levy Corps
The third area where the Government of India perceived reform was needed was the military (Peterson 1978: 90-92). The creation of the Muscat Levy Corps (MLC) in 1921 was part of the restructuring of the Muscati regime following the defence of Muscat against Imamate attack in 1913 and the eventual settlement at Sib. Prior to the MLC the Sultans had had resort to two types of military

capability of their own (of course, the forces of the British Empire had also been deployed for the defence of the Sultans 'rule'). These two forces were the garrisons of armed retainers ('*askari*), frequently Baluchi mercenaries, and then for specific campaigns, the Sultans could call upon tribes traditionally loyal to the sultans. It was apparent that these were inadequate to the task of maintaining the Sultanate against the interior. An initial proposal by PAM L.B.H. Haworth in 1917 was for a force of a thousand men from the Baluch with British officers in command, which would be able to take the attack to the interior. This aggressive policy went against the Government of India's desire to 'extricate' itself from the Sultanate's affairs and so was turned down.

Instead, following the Treaty of Sib, the MLC was created when Captain E.R McCarthy and the redundant Seistan Levy Corps, disembarked in Matrah, made their way to Bayt al-Falaj and relieved the Indian Army troops there. The MLC was essentially a garrison force of 200 - 300 men whose main tasks were the providing of arms for the Sultan's palace, the British Political Agency and the Sultanate's treasury. They also built the Muscat - Matrah road. It remained the Sultanate's only military force until the early 1950s.

The Muscat Levy Corps started the British organised development of Oman's armed forces and possessed a number of characteristics which were to be retained or repeated in the rest of the century. Firstly, it was a force composed of foreign mercenaries with British officers. Secondly there was an attempt to 'Arabize' the force which actually resulted in the replacement of Seistan Baluchis with Gwadur or Batinah Baluchis.[6] In 1917 the Government of India saw no need for a force capable of taking offensive action into the interior. The development of the oil reserves of the Peninsula, which shot to prominence with the Bahrain oil strike of 1932 was to change all this and ultimately led to the creation of more capable military force then the Muscat Levy Corps. The impact of the oil strike in Bahrain is the starting point for the next chapter.

Government in 'Oman'
The principal effect of British involvement and the development of informal empire in Muscat and Oman was the saving of the Sultan and the confinement of the Imamate to the interior. After the de

facto division of the coast and the mountainous interior following the Treaty of Sib different forms of government developed in these two areas. In the area controlled by the Sultan, which in effect was always dependent on British power, the British set about restructuring the administration. In these areas in the interior the institutions of the Imamate continued to function.

Functions of Imamate government

Under Ibadhi doctrine, government in all of the Imamates constituted a number of functions not all of which were the sole responsibility of the Imam.[7] For example his duty was to administer concepts of justice emerging by consensus from the *ulema*, of which he was one; but he was not, however, the mufti al-Islam and so could not overrule the views of the *ulema*. J.C. Wilkinson defines the Imam's role as '...the application and administration of justice, to rule by the laws of the community and to prohibit the disallowed, as he swears in his oath'(1987:177). Encapsulating this role there were four broad aspects of Imamate government: administration and consultation, finance, military, and relations with outsiders.

The Imam is the custodian of the Muslim commonwealth and its treasury and is fully empowered with its administration providing his acts are not injurious. He has a duty to consult informally and governed with the aid of a judge (*qadi*) and governor (*wali*). Sources of finance were booty (*ghanima*), residual estates, gifts and permitted taxes. As it was the duty of every true Muslim to take up arms against the community's enemies there was no need for a standing army – only for a small force for internal security at forts - the '*askaris*. Relations with the outside world were divided into relations with other Muslims (*ahl al-qibla*) and all non-Imamate rulers (*jababira*). The latter, J.C. Wilkinson notes

> ...has a subtle sense of gradation. In general it means *tyrannos*, an unconstitutional ruler, and is the collective term used for all non-Imamate rulers. Its predecessor in the earliest Ibadhi sources are the *ahl al-ahdath*, those who ruled by other than what God had revealed. At one end of this grade are *muluk*, usually local dynasts ruling like *amirs* outside Imamate control, at the other is *al-Sultan* (with the

implication of *Sultan al-jawr*) who is almost inevitably a foreign ruler or occupier; it is not surprising that the Al Bu Sa'id originally did not like the application of this title to them by the British! In the Ibadi literature *jubbar* tends to be local bad men but the genuine *jababira* often has the overtones of local rulers operating under foreign influence: the Al Bu Sa'id in the nineteenth century, for example. (1987: 190)

In contrast to its predecessors the twentieth century Imamate, started in 1913, was actually quite isolated from the rest of the world (Wilkinson 1987: 15-16). J.E. Peterson comments 'It is debatable whether the Imamate of the twentieth century should be considered a proper government in the same sense as the Sultanate' (1978:101). However, the Imamate's contention that it was the legitimate government of its territory which reached the climax in the 1950s started in this period. The Imam's capital was wherever the Imam happened to be since central administration consisted of no more than the Imam and his scribe and *qadi*. Under Muhammed bin Adullah al-Khalili the position of *qadi* was held by Amir bin Khamis al-Maliki who died in 1928 and then by Mansur bin Nasir al-Farisi. In the mid 1920s a counterpart to the Sultan's Council of Ministers was set up, composed of Sulayman al-Baruni as head, Sa'id bin Nasir al-Kindi, Amir bin Khamis al-Maliki, *wali* of Nizwa, and Majid bin Khamis al-Ibri. Al-Baruni acted as financial director with the assistance of Muhammed bin Isa al-Harithi until 1928 when opposition to his keen execution of his duties caused him to leave for Muscat (Peterson 1978: 102-103).

Conclusion: state formation in Oman 1921-1931

This period represents a distinct phase in the historical process of state formation in Oman. Developments in the broader international context - the application of aircraft technology and the development of the oil resources of the Middle East and the accompanying intra-Western rivalry - had their impact on Oman. Following the perception of British (Government of India) strategic interest in 1920, the Treaty of Sib brought about the de facto division of 'Muscat' from 'Oman'. In the interior, life continued under the institutions of the Imamate. In the Sultan's territory the authority of the restructured administration rested on British military power. This represented a 'crisis of collaboration' to use Ronald Robinson's phrase: the constant British undermining of the Sultans' wealth and authority meant the Sultans could not and would not govern necessitating greater British involvement to protect their interests. J.E. Peterson notes that the institutions that the British created in this time - financial, administrative and military - were to be the forerunners of the major building blocks of post 1970 society (Peterson 1978: 103). Thus the developments of the 1920s represent the British imperial origins of the modern Omani state.

CHAPTER FOUR:
The Expansion of the Sultanate 1932 – 1955

This chapter examines the next chronological phase of state formation in Oman which can be termed the expansion of the Sultanate. This phase is defined by the impact of oil leases following the discovery of oil in Bahrain in 1932 and the development of air routes around the Arabian peninsula. Sultan Sa'id bin Taimur (r.1932 – 1970) sought to take an active part in the government of Oman; his interest in obtaining any revenues from oil coincided with the interest of the British government and oil companies who wanted to gain access to that resource rather than allow American companies the opportunity. An important distinction must be made between the interests of oil company Petroleum Development Oman and those of the British government. Essentially the oil company was ambivalent as to with which ruler it signed oil concessions – all they required was a politically centralised state which would enable them to exploit the oil resources which they hoped to find in the interior (Biershenk 1984, chapter 3; 1989) However, the British government's perception of British strategic and economic interests in the Gulf as a whole required that Britain back the rulers with which it had formed relationships had been formed during the nineteenth century – in Oman this meant backing the Al Bu Sa'id ruler Sultan Sa'id bin Taimur. The outcome was the overturning of the de facto division of the coast and interior. This was achieved by the development of British financed and staffed armed forces which occupied Nizwa and ousted the Imamate in 1955; the Sultanate of Muscat and Oman became a reality. Thus, it was British strategic and economic interests which mediated the political impact on the Omani state of the search for a precious material resource to the international political system, that of oil. This chapter is divided into two chronological parts 1932 – 1945 and 1946 – 1955.

4.1: Oman and the West 1932 -1945

In the first part of this chapter we will examine the effect of the discovery of oil in Bahrain, on British policy in the Gulf; the development of British and American strategic interests in Oman during World War Two; and the way in which Sa'id bin Taimur sought to extricate himself from British domination.

4.1.1: The international context 1932 -1945

The discovery of oil in Bahrain in 1932 and the resulting change in the Western perception of the importance of the peninsula coincided with the declaration of the Saudi state in its modern form. The issue of the definition of boundaries and oil concessions became inextricably linked. It also involved the application of 'international law' - the legal structure of the capitalist state system - to lands which were ordered according to the precepts of tribal law and custom. With the development of the air routes and the realisation of the oil potential of the Peninsula British government policy towards the Persian Gulf began to change. There was the realisation that Britain could no longer sustain its policy of non-interference given its new strategic interests in aviation and oil. The debate over policy in the late 1930s was put to one side as the exigencies of wartime planning took priority. The impact of the war served to breakdown the peninsula's insulation further: the US military gained its first foothold on the peninsula.

Discovery of oil in Bahrain

The defining development of this period was the discovery of oil in Bahrain in 1932. Although this was not necessarily apparent at the time it had immense significance for the strategic significance of the Arabian peninsula; for the first time since the creation of the British Raj the focus of Western interest in the peninsula began to shift from the coast to the interior (Bierschenk 1989: 205). Oil had been discovered first in the Middle East in Iran in 1909 and subsequently Iraq. With the conversion of the British Navy to oil and the growing importance of oil to the capitalist industrial economies the acquiring of secure sources of cheap oil became a matter of immense importance.

However, at this time few of the 'experts' believed that the Arabian peninsula was a likely source. The conventional wisdom of the day was that as the geological character of existing known oil bearing rock formations was completely at variance with that of the Peninsula the likelihood of the discovery of oil there was remote.[1] An exception to this view was Frank Holmes who the Gulf Arabs came to know as Abu Naft - "the father of oil" (Yergin 1991:281). He was convinced that oil was to be found on the Arab side of the Gulf and eventually, despite many setbacks, his efforts proved him right. Holmes had secured an oil concession from the ruler of Bahrain in return for his discovery and drilling of water wells which at the time seemed of far greater importance to the Shaikh. Ridiculed in London he travelled to New York and linked up with first Gulf Oil and then SOCAL. After the First World War the British had inserted 'nationality clauses' whereby only 'British interests' could be given oil concessions by the Gulf Shaikhs. Gulf Oil, as part of its success in gaining entrance to the Turkish Petroleum Company was bound by the Red Line Agreement and could not prospect for oil in Bahrain. SOCAL, however was not bound by this agreement; however it ran into the barrier of the 'nationality clause'. The US government lobbied intensely to circumvent this clause. The British reflected that by allowing American resources into oil development the development of these resources for the Royal Navy would be enhanced and the demands of the Shaikhs for British subsidy would be reduced. In 1929 SOCAL was allowed to enter into a concession with the Sheikh of Bahrain with the proviso that all correspondence between the company and the Sheikh went via the offices of the British representative. Drilling started in 1930 and oil was discovered in small quantities in 1932. This news was a considerable shock. If oil was to be discovered in the off-shore island Bahrain, what were the prospects in the main land mass of the Peninsula only 30 miles distant and by all accounts with very similar anticlines? Thomas Bierschenk summarises the scramble to acquire oil concessions on the Arabian peninsula following the strike in Bahrain thus:

> With the exception of Iraq, IPC held its concessions mainly on the Arabian Peninsula. When American outsiders, Standard Oil of California and the Texas Oil Company, who

had managed to attain concessions for Eastern Saudi Arabia and Bahrain between 1928 and 1933, struck oil in Bahrain in 1932, between 1935 and 1939 IPC rushed to obtain the concessions for Qatar, Western Saudi Arabia, Aden, the Trucial States and Muscat and Oman through its subsidiary Petroleum Concessions. Already many years before, the British Government had made the rulers of these areas sign agreements that oil concessions would only be given with the agreement of the British Government. (1989: 210)

This was essentially a pre-emptive move that was to remain in place until after the World War Two[2] but the context in which the Arabian peninsula was to be placed for the rest of the century had begun to be framed. It represented a new stage of the incorporation of the Arabian peninsula into the capitalist world market and its state system. One of the first issues it impacted on was the need for property rights which required the creation of sovereign states with clearly defined boundaries.

Arabian boundaries and the Bahraini oil strike

With the discovery of oil in Bahrain in 1932, followed by that in the Hasa, the Western world began to impinge more deeply on the life of the peninsula: in contrast with the nineteenth century the British now had an interest in the interior of Arabia rather than merely the coast. This brought them into conflict with the emerging Saudi state declared in its newest form in 1932. The ideology of the Saudi state had expansionist tendencies which threatened the British clients on the coast:

> Only the universal claim to act as an Islamic ruler could override the political units of the shaikh and amir (shaikhdoms, emirates). The Wahhabi/al-Saud state was the most aggressive manifestation of the Islamic tribal state and recognised no compromise with others, Muslim or otherwise. (Wilkinson 1994: 98)

Thus, the scramble for oil concessions that followed the Bahraini oil strike coincided with a period of Saudi-British negotiations which attempted to settle the boundaries round the periphery of the Empty Quarter in the north and Aden in the south (see, especially, Wilkinson 1991; Schofield 1994b; al-Shamlan 1987). These negotiations, while they succeeded in laying down general parameters for future frontiers between the Fuad Hamza and Riyadh lines, ceased before any agreement was achieved, partly because of the outbreak of World War Two.[3] The Hamza line, offered to the British government by Deputy Foreign Minister Fuad Bey Hamza during April 1935, remained Saudi Arabia's claim to territory in southern and south-eastern Arabia until the extension of October 1949, when the Buraimi Oasis was claimed.[4] The failure of the negotiations in the 1930s led to the conflict of the 1950s which Britain resolved by force and will be examined in the next part of this chapter (4.2). The immediate effect of this new context of oil on British policy in the 1930s is examined next.

Changing British policy after 1932

It has been noted in chapter three (section 3.1) how despite the Political Resident's (PRPG) awareness of the changes that the development of the oil industry was initiating the optimal British policy in 1931 could still be stated in strictly 'minimal terms'. As the 1930s developed there was a change in the perception of both the new Political Residents and the Air Ministry (Peterson 1986: 45-48). In 1934 PRPG, T.C. Fowle, noted the growing British intrusion into the internal affairs of the Trucial Coast Sheikhdoms. Whilst traditional British concerns over the British Indian subjects, prevention of maritime hostilities were nothing new he noted that the exertion of British pressure over the air route had led the Sheikhs to fear future British interference. Whilst believing this fear to be unfounded Fowle did point out that for the first time Britain had, with the discovery of oil, a compelling interest in the internal affairs of the Sheikhdoms.[5]

Such a perception was shared by the Air Ministry who held that the creation of the air routes required a greater intervention to the extent of intervening in disputes between rulers on land. In this they were opposed by the Admiralty. To discuss this policy dispute a meeting of the Committee for Imperial Defence Official Sub-Committee on the Middle East was convened. G.W. Rendell, a counsellor at the Foreign Office observed

> Today the Persian Gulf is one of the world's highways, bordered by strongly nationalist States, whose interest in the Gulf was real and active, and the discovery of oil had led other foreign powers to take an increasing interest in Gulf affairs. In his view, the time had come, or at least was rapidly approaching, when His Majesty's Government would no longer be able to maintain their previous policy of merely keeping others out, and living, as it were, from hand to mouth, but would be faced with the necessity of going either forwards or backwards. (Peterson 1986:47)

He also noted that the ambiguous international status of the states would eventually need to be addressed as other countries apart from Britain became interested in oil, aviation and trade in the Gulf. The formal adoption of a new policy was thwarted by interdepartmental intransigence and thereafter the debates about the pros and cons of a forward policy was replaced by the exigencies of planning for the approaching world war. This was to raise the strategic importance of the air routes.

The importance of the Arabian peninsula during World War Two

World War Two was the first conflict that touched every part of the globe. The Middle East as a whole became an area of great geostrategic importance as a land-bridge between Europe and Asia. Although fighting was rare on the Arabian peninsula - in fact fewer military engagements occurred there than in World War One - it held considerable importance through its command of the air and sea passages to the areas east of Suez: the Indian Ocean, Asia and the Pacific. The peninsula and its air routes were utilised for a number of functions including Far Eastern arena reinforcements, anti-submarine operations, convoy escort, the East Africa campaign and the supply route to the Soviet Union. For these reasons the British Secretary of State for Foreign Affairs noted in 1943 that:

> It is of great importance that no international or inter-Arab rivalries should disturb the existing peaceful conditions (in the Arab Gulf states) and thus impede the development of the resources of the area or existing air communications. (quoted in J.E. Peterson 1986:51)

The American military and the peninsula in World War Two

By the beginning of the war American oil interests had gained representation in Kuwait, Saudi Arabia, Iraq and Bahrain; significantly, the war also forced the British to allow the US military onto the Peninsula including Oman. One way in which American participation took place was through the Persian Gulf Command whose task it was to channel military assistance to the Soviet Union via the Gulf and Iran. Towards the war's end and with the shift in focus from Europe to the Pacific, US forces made greater use of the Persian Gulf and South Arabian routes. While London recognised the necessity of USAAF use of these routes and airfields, permission was granted only grudgingly for PanAm's use of these routes as the British feared the establishment of claims to civilian traffic rights after the war (Peterson 1986: 112). The use of the South Arabian route meant that American aviators made use of the airstrips in the Sultanate of Muscat and Oman; this first foothold of the American military in Oman is examined in the next section.

4.1.2: Western involvement in Oman 1932 - 1945

Western strategic interest in Oman in this period was situated both on the coast and also in the interior. On the littoral the construction of the South Arabian Air Route and its subsequent use in World War Two meant both British interest in areas previously untouched by Sultanate authority and also an American military presence for the first time. In wartime the British were keen to avoid allowing the creation of a precedent for the granting of peacetime aviation rights to non-British concerns. These strategic interests relating to air power on the coast did not intrude on the Imamate in the interior. However the interest in oil did. The attempts to gain access to these territories in 1938 were the forerunner of the occupation of 1955.

Construction of the air route in Oman

The construction of the South Arabian air route required a greater degree of British involvement than the policing operations in Sur to enforce Sultanate authority in the 1920s. Planning for this route had begun in 1929 and in 1932 the work of actually constructing the facilities began with a meeting of AOCs (Air Officer Commanding) of Aden and Iraq at a mid point in the

Sultanate. In 1934 the Sultan and Britain signed a Civil Air Aviation Agreement.[6] Although this route would provide an alternative civilian flight route from Cairo to India if needed, it was always conceived primarily as a military, strategic route; it consisted primarily of refuelling and landing strips which meant dealing with the local population. To achieve this was relatively easy eastwards of Aden to the edge of the protectorate and from Muscat along the Batinah coast where British control was relatively secure. The difficult stretch was between Salalah in Dhofar to Muscat; the authority the Sultanate extended to these parts was purely nominal and the British had had no reason before to enforce it. The sheikhs of the Bedouin tribes had to be located and agreements negotiated in order to prevent disruptions to the landing stations. This was achieved either through the offering of incentives such as guard subsidies or threats of retribution if agreement was not forthcoming. Sometimes it took a number of visits by the Political Agent Muscat to determine in whose territory a prospective landing strip lay. For these reasons it took until 1936 to finally complete the route and carry out the first scheduled flight. In the Sultanate it consisted of landing strips and petrol stores at Salalah, Mirbat, Shuwaimiya, Sawqara, Masirah Island, Ras al Hadd, Sur, Muscat, Sohar and Shinas (Peterson 1978: 139; 1986: 24-29). The construction of the air route required an extension of Muscati authority to areas previously untouched by Western involvement. Because the air route followed the littoral it gave no impetus for an extension of British authority into the other remote area of the Sultanate - the mountainous interior. However the search for oil gave the outside world a reason to intrude into the Imamate. The initial probes took place in the 1920s; these efforts were intensified in the greater efforts which followed the discovery of oil in Bahrain in 1932. In Oman a new expedition took place in 1938.

The 1938 exploration for oil expedition

In contrast to the new oil company involved, Petroleum Development Oman (PDO),[7] Sa'id was in far less of a hurry to start exploring for oil in the interior. Thus, following the 1937 concession an expedition set out for the Dhahirah on the periphery of Imamate territory in the winter season 1938-39. The Sultan distributed some largesse to the tribes on the periphery of Imamate territory in order that they allowed passage for the geologists. However, there was no chance of entry into the Imamate proper. The Imam was of the opinion that the concession agreement signed with Sa'id only applied to Muscat territory and the expedition was forbidden to enter Imamate territory either on foot or for aerial surveying to take place (Wilkinson 1987: 276; Biershenk 1989: 212). The expedition was not a success; there was renewed optimism for the 1938/39 geological season with the emphatic statement from Sa'id that Buraimi did belong to him. However, the outbreak of World War Two curtailed any further exploration; the resumption of activities after the war is examined in the second part (4.2) of this chapter.

Use of military bases during the war by the United States and Britain

The establishment of the air route in the Sultanate took on further strategic significance with the approach of World War Two. J.E.Peterson identifies the air facilities in Sultanate territory as below (1986: 49).

Air facilities in Muscat territory on eve of World War Two

Location	Facilities
Shinas	Emergency landing ground with fuel
Sohar	Emergency landing ground
Muscat	RAF depot with wireless station; near by RAF aerodrome at Bayt al-Falaj and seaplane anchorage at Bandar Jissa
Ra's al-Hadd	RAF landing ground
Khawr Jarama	Seaplane anchorage; fuel and oil depot
Gwadur	Aerodrome 12 miles inland, used by RAF/ Imperial Airways
Masirah Island	Seaplane Anchorage; fuel and oil depot
Umm al-Rasaa	RAF landing ground; fuel and oil depot
Khawr Gharim	RAF landing ground
Shuwaymiya	RAF landing ground
Mirbat	RAF landing ground; seaplane anchor age; fuel and oil depot
Salalah	RAF landing ground

These facilities were required by the US during the course of its supply operations.

Before the creation of a department of the air force the US army was responsible for running the Air Transport Command (ATC). In 1942 the US Army sought intermediate landing rights for the ATC between Khartoum and Karachi. With the British Government of India managing the external affairs of the Sultanate of Muscat and Oman the Department of State, through the American Officer in charge in New Delhi, asked for permission to station the necessary military and civilian ground crews at Salalah and Ra's al-Hadd. This was granted by the joint secretary of the government of India after he had issued a reprimand for the unauthorised landing of four civilian Pan American Airways personnel at Salalah. These personnel had stated that they had 'come to establish a staging post for a Pan American Airways service between Khartoum and Karachi, that more of their men are expected within a few days with wireless equipment, that they expect to carry private passengers if bookings of government priority passages permit this, and that they wish to negotiate with the Sultan of Muscat for a camping site, local labour and supply of provisions.' The British rebuke 'on behalf of the Sultan' was backed up with the advice that Pan American would have to 'come under complete military ownership and control and that its operations [would have to be] determined absolutely by the War Department, and that nothing now done will have or is intended to have any effect in establishing commercial rights' (Hurewitz 1979: 606-608). The strategic Anglo-American rivalry in Southeast Arabia had begun. It was a rivalry which was to determine the fate of the local rulers who were competing to be defined as 'sovereign rulers' and thus benefit from the concession payments from the oil company. Although he sought to develop his independence from the British, Sultan Sa'id's lot was thrown in with the old imperial power; it was to be a mixed blessing, as we will see next.

4.1.3: the impact of the West on Oman 1932 - 1945
The main focus of this section is on the beginning of the reign of Sultan Sa'id bin Taimur: his strategy for independence and how he sought to implement it.

Sultan Sa'id bin Taimur and his strategy for independence
With the British acceptance of Taimur's abdication Sultan Sa'id bin Taimur became Sultan in 1932 although he had been acting

as President of the Council of Ministers since 1929. He had been educated first in Baghdad and then at a school for princes in India and was literate, speaking excellent English and some Urdu and Hindi as well as his native Arabic. For the first twenty four years of his reign he was, in effect, to be only the Sultan of Muscat: his authority extended only along the Batinah from Muscat to Sohar and Shinas, the Musandam peninsula, the port of Sur and Dhofar.[8]

The reign of Sultan Sa'id bin Taimur (r. 1932-1970) can be conveniently divided into two parts (Peterson 1987: 11). The first consists of the period up to the occupation of the interior in 1955 when he pursued a relatively 'activist' policy. The second is from 1955 to his deposition when he retreated to Salalah in Dhofar and sought to stall the intrusion of most aspects of the modern world. Initially, he was regarded as a good prospect by the British who hoped to be able to relinquish the day-to-day running of the Sultanate's administration: Sa'id they thought might be a 'capable' sultan. In 1932 PRPG Biscoe wrote to the Government of India:

> ...we now have in Muscat a young Sultan who, if tactfully handled, should, I think, turn out to be a good ruler. He should, I think, be given every chance to administer his State on Arab lines, and every effort should be made to free him from those relics of the past which are galling to him, while we should try, at the same time, to build up a facade of independence in the eyes of the world. (quoted in Peterson 1978: 52)

The contradiction within the British view of a capable Sultan has already been noted. Sa'id was forced to sign the same humiliating letter as his father and grandfather on his accession which obliged him to accept British advice on all important matters. However, he sought to assert his own independence wherever he could.

Sa'id resented the British domination of the Sultanate and had dreams of real independence for his regime. To cultivate this image of independence he embarked on a world tour (arranged of course by the British) in 1937 taking in Japan, the United States, England Italy and India. The US State Department summarised the issue of the Sultan's independence in the following manner:

> Although independent in the sense that he may enter into relations with foreign states the Sultan is in special treaty relations with the British of a protective nature, one of the stipulations of which is that territory may not be ceded to any foreign power other than the British. The British Political Agent at Muscat exercised a very considerable degree of influence in the Government of the Sultanate, both as regards internal and external affairs. It is understood, however, that the present Sultan is somewhat sensitive in the matter of British control and is inclined to become increasingly assertive on that point.[9]

He perceived that the cause of the Sultans' dependence was financial; with the decline of the Omani economy (see 2.3) the Sultanate became dependent on Government of India subsidies to pay off debts to the Indian merchants who resided in Muscat. His strategy was to free himself from the financial dependence on Britain, to omanize his administration and to work towards regaining control of the interior (Bierschenk 1989: 212). By bringing the administration under his control (he abolished the Council of Ministers in 1932) and through stringent economising Sa'id erased both public and private debt by the 1940s; he even started to invest in Newfoundland stock and Government of India war bonds (Peterson 1978: 87).

A further source of revenue would be oil concessions from oil companies wanting to search for oil in the interior. In the early 1930s the Sultan urged the British government to negotiate a concession for him and eventually forced the issue by starting negotiations with an American oil company, Standard Oil of California.[10] He was subsequently sharply reminded by the British of his obligation, under the 1923 agreement signed by his father which he had also been required to sign on his accession, to seek British advice on all important matters.[11] The outcome was a concession with a subsidiary of IPC, Petroleum Concessions Ltd, rather than Standard Oil, the forerunner of ARAMCO. The oil company were aware that as Sa'id was entitled the Sultan of Muscat and Oman he had some claim to the territory beyond the mountains but it was believed at the time by the oil company that Sa'id would not include the territory of the Imamate in any concessions he signed. However, Sa'id would make no such exclusion and he refused to let the oil company see the Treaty of Sib lest it diminish his authority in their eyes. The problem of the Sultan's authority in certain areas of the option agreement signed in June 1937 was skirted round by using a clause of the 1925 D'Arcy agreement which stated:

> The company recognises that certain parts of the Sultan's territory are not at present safe for its operations. The Sultan undertakes on his part to use his good offices with a view to making it possible for representatives of the company to enter such parts and will inform the company as soon as such parts become safe. (Wilkinson 1987: 276)

It was thus decided that oil company personnel should only enter an area once the Sultan had given his explicit agreement.

Sa'id's use of concession revenue

Having secured a new source of income he now tried to start building his authority in the interior through the settling of tribal disputes and by improving relations with tribal leaders through the giving of presents. Bierschenk comments:

> This policy to outbuy the Imam, who was unable to compete with it financially, was remarkably, successful. Between 1937 and 1939, the Sultan of Muscat was visited by the two leading sheikhs of the Eastern Province (al-sharqiqa), Ali Abdullah al-Hamuda of the Bani Bu Ali and Isa Salih al-Harthi, leader of the Hinawi faction of the Omani tribes, Sheikh Ahmad Muhammad, the son-in-law of the Imam, as well as by the leading men of the Dhahirah tribes. They all left Muscat showered with gifts and arms. (1989: 213)

Furthermore, the income from the oil concession meant that Sa'id could pay higher salaries than the Imam, allowing him, to attract a number of the Imam's officials to appointments in the Sultanate's administration. Ali Abdullah, the brother of the

Imam, was made governor (*wali*) of Boshar, whilst Nasir Rashid al-Kharusi, the brother of the predecessor of the Imam and judge (*qadi*) of the Imam in Rustaq was appointed as judge of Suwaiq on the Batinah coast (Bierschenk 1989: 213). Thus, the late 1930s, Bierschenk argues, can be seen as the start of the Sultan's campaign to integrate the interior into the Sultanate.

The administration of Said bin Taimur
Sultan Sa'id's examples were the independent princes of British India although he did not attempt to compete with them in displays of extravagance; rather he lived a frugal life. He had been educated away from Oman and throughout his reign sought to keep a distance from the Omani people. This helped him to avoid expenditure: by refusing to see the many supplicants for aid at his palace in Muscat and by spending ever more of his time in Salalah he reduced the need to pay out subsidies unless it suited him. His closest acquaintance was an Indian merchant in Muscat with whom he conducted a lot of business to their mutual profit; otherwise he mixed socially with the British officers and advisers (Townsend 1976: 57).

Sultan Sa'id achieved one of his first objectives quite quickly: that of removing the Sultanate from a position of debt. Townsend comments 'Sultan Sa'id's own achievement in balancing the budget and keeping out of debt within a short period of his coming to power should not be underestimated' (Townsend 1976: 57). Through draconian measures the budget deficit which had been running at an annual average of two *lakhs* from 1925 until after Said took control in 1929 was reduced to put the budget into the black by half a *lakh* in 1931.[12] This modest surplus continued until the substantial inflows from British military subsidies during World War Two and afterward when the sultanate piled up reserves of twelve *lakhs* in 1943, nearly nineteen *lakhs* in 1944 and over twenty one lakhs in 1945. Even by 1947 there was a surplus of nearly thirteen lakhs. As a result the financial position of the state was favourable until the events of the 1950s (Peterson 1978: 90). We examine the events of the post war years and their impact on the Sultanate in the next part of this chapter.

4.2: Oman and the West 1946 - 1955

In this second part of chapter two we examine the changing international context in which British and America interests in south-east Arabia were situated. Notably the tensions of British-American rivalry and co-operation in a Cold War context which played themselves out in the Buraimi Crisis. Local rulers such as the Saudis, the Imam in Oman and the Sultan of Muscat sought to pursue their goals in this framework and establish themselves as sovereign rulers by proclaiming property rights over territories whose borders were disputed by their neighbours.

4.2.1: The international context 1946-1955

In this section we consider the effects of World War Two on world politics, the development of the Cold War on the Middle East and Anglo-American rivalry in the region.

The effects of World War Two on the international system

World War Two accelerated and compressed major changes in the international system which had been underway since the early decades of the twentieth century. The start of the global competition between the ascendant Western power, the United States, and the Soviet Union developed as the central feature of world politics at the end of the war. Notably, the war contributed towards the weakening of the end of the West European empires and the encouragement of nationalist movements (Bromley 1994: 108). For Britain the most significant change in its colonial empire was the attainment by India of independence in 1947. We have seen in chapter two how it had been the need to safeguard the sea routes to India which had been the basis for British policy towards the Persian Gulf and the Middle East as a whole. Also of great significance was the growth of Arab nationalism and particularly the Free Officers coup in 1952 in Egypt; from then on Britain would be caught between a powerful combination of forces in the Middle East: Nasserism and US antipathy to European colonialism in the region.

The start of the Cold War and the Middle East

Despite the imminent independence of India, near the end of the war the strategic importance of the Middle East to Britain was already being re-affirmed by the Middle Eastern Defence

Committee of the Cabinet:

> The Middle East is a region of life and death consequences for the Britain and the British Empire in four ways, (a) as an indispensable channel of communications between the Empire's Western, Eastern and Southern territories; (b) as a strategic centre, control of which would enable an enemy to disrupt and destroy a considerable part of the British imperial system and influence as a major power; (c) as the empires main reservoir of mineral oil; (d) as a region in which British political method must make good, if the British way of life is to survive. The vital importance of these considerations has been established by hard experience in both World Wars. (quoted in Peterson 1986:60)

With the start of the Cold War a major review of British defence planning in 1946 addressed itself to a scenario of conflict with the Soviet Union. Such wartime requirements to defend the northern Gulf from a Soviet advance were seen to include operational naval bases at Aden with forward bases at Tobruk, Haifa, Port Sudan, Bahrain and Masirah Island. It was also going to be necessary to involve the United States:

> Even allowing for the timely arrival of the Americans, it might still not be possible to hold the oil fields at the head of the Persian Gulf... We consider, therefore, that it should be a definite part of our policy to associate the United States in the defence of the Middle East oil-fields. (quoted in Peterson 1986:62)

Anglo-American Rivalry in the Middle East
This need to involve the Americans in the British planning for the imperial security of the Middle East was especially galling for the British. This period witnessed the development of bitter Anglo-American rivalry in the Middle East as Britain's ineluctable imperial withdrawal began. On the Arabian peninsula, the US government, at the behest of the American 'majors' (the largest American oil companies) was determined to break down the exclusive access agreements which had been formulated by the

IPC. The main objective of US oil policy formulated in Washington between 1944 and 1947 was expressed in a memorandum as 'to remove or modify existing barriers (legal, contractual or otherwise) to the expansion of American foreign oil operations and facilitate the entry or re-entry of private foreign capital into countries where the absence of such capital inhibits oil development.' Furthermore 'Washington... should promote, by advice and assistance...the entry of additional firms into all phases of foreign oil operations.' The immediate outcome of this policy was the renegotiation of the Red Line Agreement and the resulting increased access to the oil reserves of the Middle East for US interests (Bierschenk 1989: 210).

In 1948 the Arabian-American Oil Company (ARAMCO) was formed by SOCAL, Mobil and Texaco to develop concessions in Saudi Arabia.

In 1952 Britain was still the dominant power in the Middle East and determined to maintain this position. The British controlled enormous oil reserves which helped their economy and believed that the Middle East was vital to their strength as a great power. As well as a massive base in Egypt with 80,000 troops the British possessed naval facilities in Jordan, air bases of significance in Iraq, reserves in Malta and Cyprus and protectorates along the Persian Gulf. The British perception was that in return for British support for US NATO policies and burgeoning American commitments throughout the world, the United States would support the British position in the Middle East. Prime Minister Churchill sought a meeting with President-elect Eisenhower hoping to re-establish their wartime alliance and Anglo-American unity. A briefing paper prepared for Churchill stated 'each power must support the other fully and be seen by all to do so. Lack of positive support and an affectation of impartiality by either power will be interpreted as disagreement with the other and exploited to the detriment of both.' The Americans, however did not share this view. Eisenhower recorded in his diary that Churchill was old and feeble and surely due for retirement; Anglo-American unity was only a move by the British to maintain their position in the Middle East. The State Department agreed; Anglo-American friction in the Middle East was happening because frank discussions had yet to take place over their change of roles. As the British were failing to maintain security or come to terms with Arab nationalism it fell to the United States to expand its role lest an expansion of Soviet influence come about (Petersen 1992: 73-74). From this political involvement the US government also saw an opportunity for US oil companies to supplant British ones. With the Anglo-American overthrow of Mosadegh in Iran in 1953 the US replaced Britain as the pre-eminent Western power in Iran as well as Saudi Arabia. This was due to the diminishing ability of Britain to influence wider events, the activities of the CIA and aggressive lobbying by the United States. With regards to the effect of this changing international context on Oman Bierschenk argues:

> It is solely against this background of the shift in British Near Eastern policy from protection of the sea route to India to exploitation of the region's oil potential, and the replacement of British imperial hegemony by British-American rivalry that the Omani-Saudi Arabian border conflicts as well as the dispute in the 1950s between the Sultan of Muscat and the Imam of Oman over control of the interior, can adequately be interpreted. (1989: 211)

We now turn to see how these changes in the wider strategic and international political context affected British and American involvement in south-east Arabia 1946 -1955.

4.2.2: Western strategic involvement in Oman 1946 - 1955
The focus here is on the attempts by PDO to prospect for oil in the interior in the area of the concession it had signed with Sa'id bin Taimur and the way in which this intersected with the British government's strategic interest.

The resumption of oil prospecting in Oman
The start of World War Two had suited the Sultan as it stopped any further prospecting by Petroleum Concessions and the subsidies he received from the RAF increased the resources at his disposal to gain favour with the tribes of the interior (Bierschenk 1989: 213). By these means he hoped to accumulate so much political credit that when the elderly Imam died the tribes would renounce the election of a new Imam and accept Sa'id's reintegration of the

interior more easily. In 1946 the Imam was reported to be fatally ill and his death expected. Sa'id received friendly letters from influential shaikhs in the interior, one of whom vouchsafed that he 'intended to take no part in the future of the Imamate' (Timpe 1992: 166). On the Imam's death Sa'id bin Taimur planned to immediately occupy the interior with a force of tribesman loyal to him. The Sultan made a request to the Political Agent Muscat for some light arms, one British officer and some Indian officers and RAF support. The British initially supported his plan; the Political Agent wrote to his superiors 'Now that the Petroleum Concessions Ltd are in a position to open up their operations it is obviously in our interest that the state [i.e. Muscat] should be in a position to support them in their journeys and ensure their safe conduct wherever they wish to go.' From the oil company's point of view such a development would be advantageous because it would give them access to promising areas such as Jebel Fahud. In London the Labour Government 'recognise[d] reasons in favour of proposal as a means of hastening the time when PC Ltd will be able to survey the possible oil bearing areas of interior inaccessible on the ground'. It also considered that oil development should take place as soon as possible and therefore agreed to the supply of arms and officers. However, fearful of public opinion they declined to offer RAF support and instead suggested using financial inducements in the Sultan's name to gain support of tribal chiefs in the interior. Sa'id was so incensed with this that he rejected the offer of arms and officers and also refused to take any responsibility for the negotiations between the oil company and the interior tribes. In the event the Imam recovered and the Sultan remained on good terms with him until al-Khalili died in 1954: Sultan Sa'id's plans had to be postponed (Bierschenk 1989: 214).

The political significance of oil concessions
From the perspective of the oil company Petroleum Concessions (PC) the refusal of the British government to provide the Sultan with the military force he wanted meant they were compelled to consider alternatives such as gaining their co-operation through financial means. In 1948 the PC Representative assessed the situation thus:

I doubt if we shall get permission for the geologist to go beyond Dhank until either an understanding can be brought about between the Sultan and Suleiman or the latter is paid handsomely by us/given a separate agreement...It is time that His Majesty's Government faced facts and, if upholding the Sultan's sovereignty over Oman implies refusing to allow the de facto rulers of the Interior to negotiate concessions with the Company, there is no prospect whatsoever of developing Oman's probably very considerable resources. (quoted in Bierschenk 1989: 214)

Negotiations were started with the semi-bedu Al Bu Shamis of the Dhahirah, the Na'imi Shaikh of Hafit and the Bani Ka'b Shaikh (Wilkinson 1992: 251); these threatened to exclude the Sultan and take on the status of negotiations with independent rulers. From PDO's point of view this was the only option given the Sultan's lack of military strength without the British government's backing. Both the Sultan and the tribal sheikhs of the interior were aware of the political significance of these concessions: that of attaining the status of supreme political authority in an area and thus able to grant the property rights required by the oil company and benefit accordingly from the concession fee. Bird of PC wrote to the Political Agent Muscat noting that 'the Sultan was extremely perturbed by the Company's direct approach to the tribes...He feared that the Al Bu Shamis negotiations would tend to encourage every tribe in the Dhahirah to assert its independence by dealing direct with us.' In 1950 Suleiman bin Himyar of the Jebel Akhdar asked for recognition by the British government as an independent ruler and an agreement with the PC. This situation demanded that the British define their policy in south-east Arabia. The PRPG, Sir Rupert Hay, wrote to London that the alternative was either to 'adopt a more realistic attitude towards the Sultan and treat him as Ruler only of the places under his effective control, viz. the eastern coast of the Gulf and Oman from the Batinah to Sur inclusive and Dhofar...[or] to allow the existing situation to continue for the present in spite of its fictitious character.' The reasons the PRPG gave for favouring the latter option were that

firstly, if we adopt the attitude that [inner Oman including the Dhahirah and up to Buraimi] are not included in the

Sultan's dominions we have no *locus standi* to negotiate regarding their boundaries with Ibn Saud and we shall find it difficult to object if he should endeavour to bring them under his influence. Secondly, the Iraq Petroleum Company hold concessions from the Sultan covering all his dominions except Gwadur. Our action would automatically cancel their rights in all these areas and open them up to all comers. Thirdly, we should bitterly offend the Sultan...which might well affect our position in the Gulf Sheikhdoms generally. (quoted in Bierschenk 1989: 215)

Bierschenk argues that

It was hence the importance of the British interests in the region - in contrast to the *local* interest of the PC in Oman - which caused the British Foreign Office to continue supporting the Sultan...To safeguard its strategic interests in the region, which at this stage largely consisted in the exploitation by British concerns of the regions oil reserves, the British Government decided to continue basing its Arabian policy on the assumption that the Sultan was sovereign over the whole of Oman. Direct negotiations by the PC with the tribes of the interior were now clearly excluded. (Bierschenk 1989: 215)

With this clarification of British policy in 1950 the stage was set for the different actors to take their parts in the dispute that put south-east Arabia in the world headlines.

The Buraimi Oasis Dispute and Anglo-American Rivalry
This development of this dispute eventually came to involve two sides. Firstly, the Imamate forces of the interior, the Saudis, and behind them the American oil company in Saudi Arabia, ARAMCO, backed by the tacit agreement of the US government.[13] On the other side were the Sultan of Muscat, the British government and the British oil company - Petroleum Development Oman. Essentially it was a dispute over who would benefit from the development of any oil reserves in the interior of Oman. The Americans supported the Saudis because they would receive any oil concessions resulting from an extension of Saudi territo-

ry. Significantly, Saudi and Sultanate papers prepared for an arbitration committee were written by American and British officials respectively.

As we have seen, the treaty of Sib of 1920 arranged by the British, had secured peace in the Sultanate by recognising the de facto autonomy of the interior under the Imamate; the interior remained calm for the next three decades under Imam al-Khalili and the *tamimah* of the important Hirth tribe Isa bin Salih. Isa bin Salih died in 1946 and was succeeded by his weak son Muhammed. A power struggle ensued within the Hirth tribe between Salih bin Isa supported by his brother Ibrahim, and Muhammed's son Ahmad. Salih triumphed and Ahmad began communicating with Sa'id bin Taimur. Through the Hirth power struggle Sulaiman bin Himyar of the Jebel Akhdar became the leading secular force in the Imamate and he began making overtures to the Saudis (Allen 1987: 64).

The Saudi occupation of Buraimi and the British response

In October 1952 Saudis (encouraged by the Arabian-American Oil Company -ARAMCO) occupied the Buraimi oasis on the western edge of Imamate territory and appointed a governor (Petersen 1992: 71). From 1954 onwards the Imamate was to be allied to the Saudis but in 1952 this was not the case with al-Khalili; he wrote in protest to the Saudi governor of Buraimi: 'Your statement that in view of repeated requests from your subjects in Oman to appoint a representative on your behalf among them, you have appointed Turki bin Abdullah bin 'Uteishan, has astonished us, because we do not know that you have subjects in Oman' (quoted in Bierschenk 1989: 216). In association with the Imam Sa'id assembled a force of tribesmen at Sohar to march to Buraimi to expel the Saudis; however, due to American pressure, the British instructed him not to march - they were too aware of American involvement to allow anything precipitate to happen.[14] Sa'id bin Taimur had the sense to make sure that the instruction not to march to Buraimi was read to him in full public view by the British Counsul General Chauncy who had rushed at top speed along the Batinah coast to deliver the message as instructed by London. The tribesmen dispersed and returned to their homes. In May 1954 Imam al Khalili died after a long period of poor health and tribal leaders assembled in

Nizwa to elect a successor from a number of proposed candidates. Sultan Sa'id was rejected on religious grounds, others on tribal affinities. The eventual choice was Ghalib bin Ali al-Hinawi who was favoured by Sulaiman bin Himyar and his Saudi allies (Allen 1987: 64).

The oil company and the Muscat and Oman Field Force
With the change of Imam in the interior PDO saw an opportunity to explore Jebal Fahud in its concession in the interior given by Sa'id. The British government, having prevented the oil company from signing a concession with parties other than Sa'id and refused RAF support, was happy for the oil company to finance the creation of the Muscat and Oman Field Force (MOFF) under the command of a British officer, the first significant expansion of the Sultanate's military forces since the creation of the Muscat Levy Corps in the 1920s (Bierschenk 1989:215). The PC saw this as in its interest:

> It would be a wise investment on our part, it is the only solution to these backward areas, and it might lead to the opening up of an extremely favourably placed oil field with a terminal on the Arabian Ocean as opposed to the Persia Gulf or the Gulf of Oman... and it would very likely pay handsome dividends. (quoted in Bierschenk 1989:216)

It was agreed that the company would pay £143,000 (£55,000 direct and £88,0000 through the Sultan) and £100,000 in any consecutive year (Bierschenk 1989: 216). In December 1954 the four hundred strong MOFF accompanied a PDO surveying team from al-Duqm on the coast to Fahud. A detachment marched on and occupied Ibri against explicit instructions from Sa'id not to do so. Sulaiman bin Himyar persuaded Ghalib to attempt to retake Ibri. At this point the Sultan approved offensive action to occupy the whole of the interior. The Batinah Force marched into the Ghadaf where it defeated Imamate forces under Talib bin Ali the brother of the Imam. The Trucial Oman Scouts expelled the Saudis from Buraimi in October 1955 thereby denying the Imamate of military supplies and money. Finally, the MOFF occupied Nizwa unopposed in December 1955. Ghalib resigned as Imam, Sulaiman bin Himyar retired to

Tanuf and Talib bin Ali and Salih bin Isa fled to Saudi Arabia. Sa'id made a cross desert journey from Salalah and embarked on a tour of the interior appointing Ahmad bin Muhammed as *tamimah* of the Hirth and governor of Nizwa.[15]

Anglo-American diplomatic relations and south-east Arabia
As has been already indicated, behind these events in South East Arabia lay the whole dynamic of change in the British and American positions in the Middle East; Anglo-American diplomatic relations reflected this as the following diplomatic exchange on the Sultanate's occupation of Nizwa in 1955 illustrates. On 24 November 1955 the Cabinet gave consideration as to whether to give the Americans advance warning of the Sultan's move into Nizwa and it was decided not to do so. On 12 December the Foreign Office informed Secretary of State Dulles that the Sultan of Muscat had initiated an offensive against the Imam. Dulles replied that had he known earlier he would have urged restraint as the Saudis might now consider asking the Security Council to place Buraimi on its agenda. Foreign Office officials were livid with this American response. Permanent Under-Secretary, Kirkpatrick, was observed 'breathing fire' and summoned Walworth Barbour, the Minister-Counsellor at the American Embassy in London. Against the news that the Sultan had occupied Nizwa without opposition and that the Imam had fled to Saudi Arabia, Kirkpatrick professed bewilderment at American policy. The Americans were supporting the Saudis who seemed at best to be pursuing a neutralist policy and at worst taking delivery of Soviet arms, opposing the Northern Tier arrangements and generally taking an anti-Western stance. The Americans he contended were supporting the Saudis in their bid to absorb the pro-Western states of south-east Arabia. Kirkpatrick asserted that if Washington did not believe that the Sultan of Muscat should take action he deemed appropriate to restore his authority in what he believed to be his territory then the Americans were 'inevitably supporting the establishment of Oman as a Saudi puppet preparatory to its inclusion in Saudi Arabia' (quoted in Ovendale 1996: 128). On Buraimi Barbour admitted that the Saudis had broken the arbitration agreement but protested that the Americans regarded the Saudis as staunchly anti-Soviet.

These diplomatic exchanges illustrate the intensity of the Anglo-American friction in this period leading up to Suez. The events of 1956 in Egypt and their relation to events in Oman will be assessed in the next chapter. With the occupation of Nizwa in 1955 the authority of the Sultanate had finally been exerted over the interior. However, as the above narrative indicates, the decisive factor was the interest of the British oil company in controlling the development of any oil reserves there. Petroleum Concessions sought to achieve this interest in a situation where the British government had forbidden the oil company from signing a concession with the interior tribes due to the consideration of the British government's strategic position in the region as a whole. Sultan Sa'id's strategy for unification was successful because it coincided with the interests of the British government and oil company for whom he was a useful 'collaborator'. Furthermore it was not long before Sa'id's authority was to be rejected again in the interior and then in what he regarded as his personal estate - Dhofar - the subject of chapter five. So far in this chapter the focus has been on the strategic interests and involvement of Britain and America in Oman - it remains to reflect on the impact this had on a number of aspects of politics in south-east Arabia, most notably the development of the state system of the area up to this point.

4.2.3: The impact of the West on Oman 1946 - 1955

We can at this point survey the progressively interventionist role of Britain in the processes of Omani society as the British pursued their strategic interests in the area. Britain had first perpetuated the Al Bu Sa'id Sultans (late 19th century), then isolated the Imamate in the interior (1920) and now had occupied the interior and overturned the Imamate. This was part of the wider process of British involvement in the development of the state system of the Gulf region. As George Joffé puts it:

> The modern sovereign political structures of the Arab states of the Gulf region are, in virtually every respect, a testimony to British imperial policy, spurred on by a desire for oil and for commercial control. This is particularly true of the small states along the Gulf littoral of the Arabian peninsula, but it is also true, to a greater or lesser extent, of the three major states of the region: Iran, Iraq and Saudi Arabia.

Although at least two of them had a sovereign existence before the British-dominated colonial period in the Gulf region began, nonetheless the actual form of sovereignty manifested by all of them today clearly shows the consequences of British interest. This, in turn, derived from concern over access to India and over commerce during the nineteenth century and over control of oil production during the first half of the twentieth century. (Joffé 1994: 78)

The British drawing of borders in south-east Arabia
One of the main consequences of this aspect of the intrusion of the West was the imposition or adoption of Western concepts, most notably of sovereignty and state.[16] With the realisation that vast oil deposits lay under the Arabian peninsula the British realised that there was an urgent need to define the territories of the quasi-states they had created; previously they had not been particularly interested as long as calm prevailed. This meant the application of international law to lands previously organised in terms of tribal concepts of territory (*dar*).[17] This tribal law often centred around usufructory rights which allowed the mobility on which the peninsula with its sparse natural resources (until the oil age) depended. In contrast international, that is, Western law had developed in feudal Europe and then been applied to colonial division in Africa and linked sovereignty to territory:

> ...the corpus of international law relevant to deciding sovereignty over sparsely populated territory was singularly ill suited to the needs of the region. All territorial boundaries are in some measure artificial, but the imposition onto Arabia of sovereignty concepts that basically started with feudal rule over areas of sedentary subsistence agriculture and ended up with European rules designed to partition Africa, inevitably cut across the very flows of migration, trade and political loyalty that permitted the local population to exist in its traditional way of life. (Wilkinson 1994: 97)

Associated with territorial sovereignty was the Western concept of state which in international law has a particular meaning: 'states are entities with populations living in territories effectively controlled by governments, which are also capable of conducting international relations with other states' (Joffé 1994: 78). Until the oil age and the events of the 1950s this had been problematic in Oman as it was completely at variance with the traditional practices of power and political organisation there:

> Political power could also certainly translate itself into terms of regional sovereignty. Resource-rich areas in the traditional geographic cores of Greater Bahrain, Greater Yemen and Greater Oman offered opportunities for a degree of social stratification and the development of a quasi permanent central government system. The fact that in such areas 'circulation' patterns were relatively highly internalised also helped reinforce a sense of regional identity. But the tribal ideology that prevailed in all areas of Arabia was geared to minimizing such centralisation of power and wealth. So even when rulers developed a hold over commercial or tribal empires, they were never able to transform their society into the hierarchically organised social, urban and administrative structure that characterises full, permanent statehood. Arabia remained at the two-tiered "chiefdom" level in state and class formation. (Wilkinson 1994: 98)

In the dominant ideology of the area only the universal claims of an Islamic ruler could take precedence over the political units of the shaikhs and emirs. The Zaydi Imam in Yemen, the al Wahhab-Saudi state and the Ibadhi Imam of Oman were all therefore opposed to what they regarded as the illegitimate forms of government of the British-protected rulers on the coast. Thus Wilkinson comments : 'The Islamic state order was therefore fundamentally in conflict with British rule in Arabia, and although in Oman and Yemen, unlike the case of the Wahhabi state, the Imamates could constitutionally accept some constraints on their sovereignty, these concessions never extended to permanently limiting their territories' (Wilkinson 1994: 99).

These concepts of sovereignty and political order were, in Oman, overturned by the imposition of the sovereignty of the capitalist state system which required authority and property rights to enable the development of the oil reserves by the international oil companies.

Conclusion: the expansion of the Sultanate 1932 – 1955

In 1932 the area of effective control of the Sultanate was in Muscat and Matrah, the Batinah and Dhofar. The Sultanate's expansion into the interior was primarily due to the desire of the oil company (PDO) to develop its concession and the British government's policy of supporting Sa'id bin Taimur in the context of its strategic interests in the Gulf as a whole. This contract of collaboration was necessary but after 1955 the shifts in the international expectations of a ruler began to progressively undermine the contract between the British and Sa'id bin Taimur. It became clear in this time that the new developments that have been outlined in this chapter were changing the Arabia that had existed within the cocoon Britain had spun around it. The cocoon was crumbling and Arabia exposed to the air of the outside world. Hence, the title of David Holden's account of this time, *Farewell to Arabia*, (1966). Two of the winds that were to blow into the Sultanate, Arab nationalism and revolutionary Marxism, are examined in the next chapter.

CHAPTER FIVE:
The consolidation of the Omani state
1956 – 1977

The period 1956 – 1977 forms a distinct period in the process of state formation in Oman. It is defined by the impact of Arab nationalism and Arab radicalism on the British position in the Middle East. Up to this point the British protected shaikhdoms of the Persian Gulf had seemed isolated from developments in other parts of the Arab world. However, the effects of the rise of Arab nationalism and radicalism gradually percolated through to the British-protected rulers on the Arabian peninsula including the Sultan of Muscat and Oman. In the international arena the Suez War demonstrated that the European powers could no longer act in the Middle East if they did not have the acquiescence, if not active support, of the United States. Timpe concludes that the 'events of Suez had no apparent effect on Britain's relationship with Oman. The record clearly indicates that Suez was not responsible for any change in the substance or style of the patron-client relationship that had developed between Great Britain and Oman' (1991: 321). While this may have been true on the level of relations between British officials and the Sultan perhaps this is not where we should look to find an effect. The effect of Suez was far more at the level of British policy to the whole East-of-Suez arena: the failure to assert British hegemony in Egypt meant that Britain's position in the Gulf and Oman was now set increasingly in the context of attempts to secure British interests after British imperial withdrawal from the area. A key objective of the political movements of Arab nationalism after 1956 and later the left-wing radicalism of the 1960s and 1970s in South Yemen and Dhofar was to remove the British from their position of overbearing influence on the Arabian peninsula from Aden to Kuwait. The pressure of these political movements forced the British to initiate schemes for economic and political development on occasionally reluctant rulers.

In Oman ultimately the culmination of these pressures meant that Sa'id bin Taimur was deposed in 1970 and his son Qabus installed as Sultan. British strategic and military involvement was essential for the attempts to consolidate the Omani state in the face of renewed rebellions. Firstly, in the interior, the integration of 'Oman' in to the Sultanate of Muscat and Oman was contested, and then in Dhofar where a new challenge was posed to the regime of Sa'id bin Taimur. The need to defeat these rebels required a number of reviews of the British relationship with Sa'id bin Taimur which, as already noted, eventually led to his removal and to Qabus becoming Sultan. Lying behind all these developments was the bid to develop the oil resources of the Sultanate and to institute some form of development before the rebels could oust the Al Bu Sa'id and the British with them. The development of a centralised *rentier* state, made possible by the occupation of the interior in 1955, was brought to fruition in this period.

5.1.1: The international context 1956 -1967
In this section we examine the aftermath of Suez and Anglo-American relations as they sought to develop an overall strategy for the protection of Middle East oil in a Cold War context. We also look at how in this context the British government's policy towards Oman underwent reviews in 1958 and 1960.

Suez and its aftermath
The wider strategic developments affecting Oman and the Arabian peninsula in this decade were the aftermath of the Suez War of 1956 and continuing adjustments in the East-of-Suez role which had followed Indian independence (Peterson 1986: 77). Indian independence in 1947 had removed the original justification for a British military apparatus in the Indian Ocean; logically it should have led to a run-down in the British presence east of Suez for a number of reasons. Firstly, on economic grounds: Britain no longer derived so much revenue from India and had been seriously weakened by World War Two. Furthermore, in the postwar years the advent of nuclear weapons necessitated a complete re-think in strategic thinking. However, what in fact

happened was that the East-of-Suez presence was justified on new grounds and indeed it remained one of the last areas in which Britain maintained a military capability outside the North Atlantic/European theatre.

The main reason for this was inertia - a habit of mind of thinking as a global power. Additionally, three specific factors can be noted. Firstly, the difficulty of considering withdrawal when British forces were continually involved in East-of-Suez contingencies. Secondly, the commitment of the three services to a world role partly through tradition and also the inter-service politics of a declining defence budget. Thirdly, the inability of successive British governments to take long term decisions. The result was that:

> The defence system originally designed to safeguard the Indian Empire was maintained through the fifties to secure what were thought to be Britain's interests and responsibilities in the Middle East, the Far East and Africa. And in the early sixties, when Britain's colonial empire had gone the way of the Indian Empire it was refashioned, and in some ways strengthened to meet the requirements of the post imperial order. (Darby 1973: 327)

British defence policy and the Sandys White Paper

British participation in the 1956 invasion of the Suez Canal was unquestionably a tremendous debacle, particularly as it affected Britain's relations with the Arab world and thus its military presence in many Arab states. Its effect on strategic thinking was somewhat paradoxical. On the one hand, there was an instinctive feeling that all Britain's spending on conventional forces had gone for nought - they might as well be got rid of and the money spent more wisely on nuclear defence. This seemed to be the message of the 1957 Sandys White Paper, which stressed a nuclear priority, smaller but more mobile conventional forces, an eventual end to conscription and cuts in defence expenditure (Peterson 1986: 83).

At the same time it was held by others that the poor showing in military terms at Suez was due to the starving of conventional forces. By this view, the lesson of Suez was that Britain needed to upgrade its forces and mobile capability, since its overseas commitments would require British assistance for some time to come. This view was backed by service lobbying: even the navy began to show an interest in the concept of limited war. The government sought to balance opposing views by emphasising the nuclear umbrella and at the same time relying heavily on the potential of an airlifted strategic reserve. Thus, the key effect of Suez and the emerging air and sea barrier was to stimulate consideration of the East-of-Suez arena as a theatre in its own right and to open up British strategic debate from sole concentration on a potential total war to fighting limited wars. J.E. Peterson comments: 'As a consequence, strategic mobility became an integral part of British defence policy from the late 1950s through the economic collapse of 1967, and the concept was put to the test in the Arabian Peninsula during the Oman and Kuwait crises'(1986: 84). Kuwait and its oil and sterling balances were the cornerstones of the British position in the entire Gulf area.

Anglo-American relations, the Gulf and Oman
The British position in Kuwait was discussed as part of Anglo-American planning to ensure continued access to the petroleum reserves of the Middle East. Although one strand of opinion in America held that Britain should encourage reform in the Gulf states, Loy Henderson, the deputy Under Secretary of State, was opposed to such a stance (Ovendale 1996: 186). The British ambassador at Ankara observed that the Americans needed to be convinced that the British position in the Gulf was important for the West in general and was not just an 'out-dated relic' of British imperialism. Preservation of the rule of the al-Sabah family depended 'in large measure on the relationship between the ruling family and the United Kingdom', and this was an important part of the wider system of the relationship between Britain and the Gulf rulers. Britain insisted that it could do nothing more to ease the situation over Buraimi (Ovendale 1996: 187). London informed Washington of its intervention to support the Sultan of Oman, when, in the middle of July 1957 tribesmen took over the mountains near Nizwa in Oman. Britain considered once again that the establishment of a separate state under the Imam of Oman in central Oman would be used by Egypt, Syria and Saudi Arabia as a centre for intrigue against British interests in the area. Primeminister Macmillan told President

Eisenhower that Nasser was encouraging the trouble and that the Saudis were involved. Foreign Secretary Selwyn Lloyd told the Americans it was a minor matter on the military side: 'sending 50 men or so and shooting up a fort or two.' Eisenhower assumed it was the latest incident in the old Buraimi affair, and refuted the rumours current in London that the troubles had been brought about by the efforts of American oil companies to damage British oil possessions in the region.

In a statement to the Commons on 28 July 1957 Selwyn Lloyd justified the government's decision to help the Sultan of Muscat and Oman. There were implicit obligations to a friendly ruler and because direct British interests were involved in connection with the importance of the Persian Gulf to Britain. Selwyn Lloyd then proceeded to make an important statement about the government's view of its commitments in the Persian Gulf, noting that although Britain's obligation to the Gulf Sheikhdoms were of two kinds

> the difference between a formal obligation and the obligations of a long standing relationship of friendship is not readily apparent to the local rulers and people. If we were to fail in one area it would begin to be assumed elsewhere that perhaps the anti-British propaganda of our enemies had some basis to it, and that the Government were no longer willing or able to help their friends. (Darby 1973:131)

American intelligence found no evidence of official Saudi support for the Imam of Oman. Secretary of States Dulles feared a small Suez. He warned Eisenhower on 3 August that the Arab world could be drawn into opposition to Britain, Nasser would have a new chance to assert Arab leadership, and Washington would be caught between its desire to maintain an influence with some of the Arab countries, particularly Saudi Arabia, and the desire to maintain good ties with Britain (Ovendale 1996: 189). Washington decided to abstain over the inscription of the Oman problem on the agenda of the Security Council. The ambassador at Washington, Sir Harold Caccia, warned the Americans over the danger of such a move for public opinion in Britain, and for Anglo-American relations. In the end Washington did abstain, but the vote in the Security Council was five to four against, and the 'Oman question' was not placed on the agenda.

The Oman situation turned out to be more serious than had been supposed, and the question of air action was raised in October. The Cabinet Defence Committee, however thought that bombing was unacceptable on political grounds. MacMillan used his son-in-law, Julian Amery, who sent in the Special Air Service in actions in Oman over the following two years to pacify the rebels. As part of the settlement in September 1958 the Sultan of Muscat ceded Gwadur, his small possession off the coast of Baluchistan, to the government of Pakistan (Ovendale 1996: 188).

Kuwait Oil and the Domino theory
By November 1957 the joint planning with the Americans had brought forward proposals from Washington for the protection of Middle Eastern oil. On 14 November Sir William Stratton, the Vice Chief of the Imperial General Staff warned the Chiefs of Staff that the size of the force which Britain could muster constituted a major limitation, and that it might be worth considering planning to use joint Anglo-American forces in these circumstances. But R.W.J Hooper, who headed the Permanent Under Secretary's Department at the Foreign Office, advised that there would be political difficulties if Americans were part of any forces destined for protection measures in the Gulf Shaikhdoms. At this time the Foreign Office, in response to the disturbed situation in Muscat and Oman, outlined a British policy in which the British position in the Gulf and Southern Arabia was viewed as a 'single whole whose parts were mutually self supporting'. This amounted to a domino theory: 'Our withdrawal from any one of these territories for whose protection we were now responsible would thus fundamentally weaken the whole of the present system and if it did not destroy it would at least hasten its final collapse' (quoted in Ovendale 1996: 189). It was in this context that the request of Sultan Said for British help against the renewed Imamate rebellion of May 1957 (this will be examined in more detail in section 5.1.2) led to the formulation of a new British policy towards Muscat and Oman whereby the British provided aid for an expansion of the military forces of the Sultanate and a civil development programme. The diplomatic protocol for this new policy was an Exchange of Letters.

The 1958 Agreement

The 1958 Exchange of Letters indicates the different aspects of British support: military aid in the form of subsidy and secondment of personnel and civil development.

> "In pursuance of the common interest of Your Highness and Her Majesty's Government in furthering the progress of the Sultanate of Muscat and Oman, Her Majesty's Government in the United Kingdom have agreed to extend assistance towards the strengthening of Your Highness's Army. Her Majesty's Government will also, at Your Highness's request, make available regular officers on secondment from the British Army, who will, while serving in the Sultanate, form an integral part of your Highness's armed forces. The terms and conditions of service of these seconded British officers have been agreed with Your Highness. Her Majesty's Government will also provide training facilities for members of Your Highness's armed forces and will make advice available on training and other matters as may be required by Your Highness."

> "Her Majesty's Government will also assist Your Highness in the establishment of an Air Force as an integral part of Your Highness's armed forces, and they will make available personnel to this Air Force."

> "Your Highness has approved the conclusion of an agreement for the extension of the present arrangements regarding civil aviation and the use by the Royal Air Force of the airfields at Salalah and Masirah."

> "We also discussed the economic and development problems of the Sultanate and Her Majesty's Government agreed to assist Your Highness in carrying out a civil development programme which will include the improvement of roads, medical and educational facilities and an agricultural research programme."
> (British and Foreign State Papers 1957-58, H.M.S.O., 1966)

Under the 1958 agreement the RAF maintained a base at Masirah Island which became a dispersal point for nuclear armed Vulcan bombers from Cyprus, the only British aircraft with nuclear capability; regular training missions took place involving deployments to Masirah (Winn 1994: 546; Kechichian 1995: 145).

Given the political and strategic significance of the Sultanate it is not surprising that the disturbances in Oman caused considerable debate as to the best British policy towards the Sultan. In July 1959 M.C.G. Man the Acting Political Resident in Bahrain proposed:

> If the Sultan will not do what we think is necessary to crush a rebellion, or to prevent a recurrence, or as is more likely he prevaricates, we shall have to be prepared to compel him, or to overthrow him in favour of someone who will do as we want. If we decide...to proceed at once to installing a new Sultan who will do better than the one we have, we must likewise be prepared to back our man to the full during this inevitable rebellion, and when it is crushed, hope that he will be able to prevent another. (quoted in Timpe 1991: 292)

This was one view from the Gulf of the best policy towards the Sultan of Muscat and Oman. Of course, eventually this was the option chosen by the British. Sa'id bin Taimur, like Shakhbut of Abu Dhabi earlier, was removed in 1970. But for the time being the British continued their policy of supporting their existing client, Sa'id bin Taimur; however alternatives were considered.

Britain and the Sultanate of Muscat and Oman: the Cabinet Paper, July 1960

Options for change were being considered at all levels of the British government. In July 1960 the Secretary of State for Foreign Affairs Selwyn Lloyd presented a paper to the Cabinet which outlined policy alternatives for the Sultanate of Muscat and Oman in the context of British strategic interests in the Gulf as a whole.

He first affirmed that 'it is important that the Sultanate of Muscat and Oman should remain effectively controlled in friendly hands'. The necessity of this was based on the wider context of British interests in the Gulf which he identified as:

(a) *Economic* - To retain access on favourable terms to oil produced in the States bordering on the Persian Gulf, and to maintain acceptable arrangements for Kuwait's sterling balances.

(b) *Strategic* - To maintain rights over Masirah Airfield. This is likely to grow in importance, both as an air staging post providing flexibility on air routes to the Far East, and also possibly in the long term as an alternative to air bases which we possess at present elsewhere in the area.

(c) *Political* - To defend the area against the spread of Communism or pseudo-Communism. (CAB 129/102 Part 1 p.82)

To be able to achieve these three interests he argued that 'certain political and military requirements in the area must be met. We have to retain the confidence of the Rulers in our will and our ability to protect them, and we must maintain the military facilities needed for successful intervention. These requirements have developed substantially in recent years.'

He argued for an increase in the amount of subsidy to the Sultan of Muscat and Oman in order to implement the 1958 policy properly. He also outlined a number of alternative policies such as strategic disengagement from the Sultanate as a whole, and support for a British-protected state in inner Oman. These were all argued against on the grounds that they would erode the British position in the Gulf. A far greater erosive force was Britain's economic problems which led to the official British withdrawal at the beginning of the next decade (see 5.2.1). The developments in the international context we have examined in this period were reflected in British military involvement in Oman to defend its client the Sultan.

5.1.2: British military involvement in Oman 1956-1967
In the period 1957-67 two 'quasi nationalist' armed rebellions - on the Jebel Akhdar and in Dhofar - were to indicate the difficulties Britain would have in securing a pro-Western state in Oman.

The Imamate rebellion in the interior and British reoccupation
The extension of Sultanate authority into the interior in 1955 was initially short lived - only with a further introduction of British

forces was the interior finally pacified. With the fall of Nizwa Talib bin Ali the erstwhile Imam's brother had made his way to Saudi Arabia where he started recruiting Omani labourers to the Oman Revolutionary Movement (ORM). He started planning a revolt in Oman with his brother Ghalib, Sulaiman bin Himyar and Sulaiman bin Isa al-Hirthi. In May 1957 Ghalib reasserted his claim to the Imamate at Bilad Sait and was immediately besieged by the MOFF. Talib's ORM, armed with US made arms and mines supplied by the Saudis made their way into Oman via the Batinah and broke the siege; the Sultan's forces withdrew to Firq and subsequently to Fahud. Ghalib's army once again raised the white Imamate flag over Nizwa (Allen 1987: 67). Sa'id sought the help of his British supporters. After a parliamentary debate (Britain was still coming to terms with the Suez fiasco) the British government agreed to provide assistance. A company of Cameronians under General J.A.R. Robertson was sent to Oman and air cover from Sharjah was promised (Allen 1987: 68). Together with the Trucial Oman Scouts this force easily reoccupied Firq, Nizwa (where Venom fighters strafed the fort) and Bahla; the Cameronians were withdrawn in August 1957 as Britain sought to cover itself against attack at the United Nations. Ghalib, Talib and Sulaiman bin Himyar withdrew with their supporters to the plateau at the top of the mountain Jebel al-Akhdar. Here they were well entrenched - the many caves providing hiding for supplies provided by friendly villages and arms from Saudi Arabia. They continued to lay mines and ambush government convoys and pursue their case in international fora from an office in Cairo.

The Jebal Akhdar campaign and Anglo-American relations
The British remained concerned with rebel activity against the Sultan. London decided to increases the British military presence in the Sultan's territory and to utilise the Special Air Services Regiment. The Foreign Office informed Secretary Dulles of its decision: 'in the event of this news leaking later, we should have more chance to defend ourselves against any charge of having kept the Americans in the dark'. According to London, the American Secretary of State 'attempts to relate the Oman Trouble to the general unresolved issues of sovereignty and boundaries in this area.' The Foreign Office admitted that settlement of out-

standing differences with Saudi Arabia might contribute to a peaceful solution in Oman but also that 'a settlement on terms acceptable to Saudi Arabia would in the long run serve only to disrupt our position in South East Arabia generally. The Foreign Office sent Secretary of State Dulles a message noting his concern that 'further British military action in Oman might prejudice a peace settlement, however in dealing with people like the Omani rebels pressure of this kind is probably the best means available of creating the frame of mind in which a satisfactory settlement will be possible.' Then on 23 December the Foreign Office informed its Washington embassy that additional soldiers would be sent to Oman, another seventy to one hundred men because of the difficult terrain. The embassy was instructed to pass on the information to the State Department, but did not communicate directly to prevent the possibility that the United States might 'attach undue importance' to the dispatch of additional troops (Joyce 1995: 150). The British perception of the American attitude was that it should move forward with plans to increase its force in Oman because the 'Americans have no sympathy for anyone who having decided to use force does not use it in more than adequate or absurdly overwhelming strength in order to finish the job quickly' (quoted in Joyce 1995: 150). This was to be achieved by the introduction of the SAS.

The SAS and the conquest of the Jebel Akhdar

Colonel David Smiley, who had been seconded to organise the Sultan's Armed Forces, managed to isolate the mountain in Autumn 1958 and found a route up to the plateau from Wadi Bani Kharu, which due to its sheerness of its incline was undefended. For the storming of the mountain a contingent of the SAS were diverted to Oman on return from counter-insurgency operations in Borneo. On the evening 27th January 1959 they occupied the mountain in a surprise operation.[1] Ghalib, Talib and Sulaiman managed to escape to Saudi Arabia and the Imamate cause was promoted until interest gradually petered out by the 1970s.

British building of the Omani military in the 1960s

The 1958 agreement with the British allowed a steady expansion of the military, and their commitment was reaffirmed as a result of a report submitted in March 1960 by War Office

Representative, Brigadier M.R.J. Hope-Thompson who spent six weeks in Oman. His terms of reference were 'to recommend the long-term measures which must be taken in order to ensure the security of the Sultanate. To this end to examine and advise on the way the SAF should be organised, trained and equipped.' The terms of reference were qualified with the proviso that 'no significant increase in the number of seconded British officers could be considered'.[2] The first product of this military expansion was the Oman Gendarmerie, established in mid-1959 with headquarters first at Sohar, then at Azaiba and finally at Sib. Originally it was conceived as a sort of rural police with the responsibility of patrolling the northern borders of the Sultanate but was later reconstituted as a regular regiment. Soon afterwards the Sultan of Oman's Air Force (SOAF) was created with a nucleus of three Provost T52 and two pioneer aircraft (Peterson 1978: 95). This military force was to be required in the Sultanate but not in 'Oman' - increasingly the military threat was to come in the area separated from Muscat and Oman by 500 miles of gravel desert and always geographically and culturally distinct: Dhofar.

Geography and Ecology of Dhofar

Although territorially contiguous to Oman, Dhofar is separated by a five hundred mile expanse of desert. Like Oman, it is in many respects an island: it is bordered by the Rub al-Khali, and the Indian Ocean; while the Mahra and Hadramhawt are natural extensions to the west the rugged nature of the terrain in effect forms a natural barrier (Peterson 1978: 187). Geographically it consists of three distinct areas: the Salalah Plain, thirty miles long and ten miles wide, so named after the main town of Dhofar which is situated there on the coast facing the Arabian sea; a line of mountains consisting of Jabal Samhan in the east, the Jabal Qara in the centre and the Jabal Qamar in the west; and behind these mountains, the Najd, a stony plateau. A further distinctive aspect of Oman's ecology is that it is the only part of Arabia which is touched by the monsoon system. Hence for three months of the year the *kharif* brings low mists which cover the hills transforming them into verdant rolling downs. The Arab population is mainly of the Kathir tribe; the inhabitants of the mountains, the *jebalis*, are thought to be descended from ethnic groups particular to South Arabia: the Qara, the Mahra and the Shera (Peterson 1978: 187). They possess a separate culture and language.[3]

Establishment of Omani control in Dhofar
Dhofar had not had links to Oman until the nineteenth century when Omani domination began. Dhofar was first occupied by Sayyid Sa'id bin Sultan in 1829 following the death of the chieftain Sayyid Muhammed bin Aqil. Political control remained loose and it was not until an occupation following the Omani expedition of 1879 that Omani control was more effectively imposed (Janzen 1982). Faisal was the first sultan to spend more time in the province and this trend was continued by Taimur culminating in Sa'id who initially extended sultanate authority throughout Salalah plain and into the mountains. As early as 1935 Sa'id improved the palace at al-Husn and developed agricultural estates. Sa'id spent much of World War Two there and resided there fully after 1958. He treated Dhofar as his personal estate and imposed many petty restrictions on the inhabitants causing many Dhofaris to leave secretly to work in the Gulf (Peterson 1978: 187). Said had a particular distaste for the *jebalis* whom he called 'cattle thieves' (Pimlott 1985: 27).

Rebellion in Dhofar: The Dhofar Liberation Front
In 1960 British Foreign Office officials wrote of Dhofar:

> There is no serious threat to the Sultan's authority here. The Sultan likes to keep this province as separate as possible from the remainder of his country.[4]

This situation was soon to change; a rebellion in Dhofar became the most serious threat to Sa'id's regime and indeed British schemes for a new state system in the Gulf. This threat ultimately required Sa'id's ousting and a massive expenditure to integrate Dhofar into the Sultanate. In Dhofar rebellion against Sa'id started amongst disgruntled mountain tribesmen in 1962. They made their way to Saudi Arabia and then Ba'athist Iraq where they received training. In 1963 and 1964 sporadic raids were carried out. In 1964 the Dhofar Liberation Front (DLF) was formed from the merger of the Dhofar Benevolent Society, the

Dhofar Soldier's Organisation and the local branch of the Arab Nationalists' Movement. As early as December 1962 acts of sabotage were carried out at RAF Salalah and in April 1963 oil company vehicles were ambushed on the mid way road (Pimlott 1985: 27). The Muscat Annual Report for the Year 1964 summarised the anti government activity in Dhofar:

> The most serious incident was the explosion of a British Mark 7 mine in July beneath a RAF vehicle in Salalah. A British NCO was killed. Other incidents occurred in Dhofar, including the blowing up of the Salalah Midway Road, a RAF five ton crane destroyed by a mine and a ferret scout blown up by a mine. All are believed to be the work of a band led by Musallan bin Mufl al-Kathiri. A small reconnaisance party of SAF, including an element from SOAF, moved to Dhofar early in December. The air route to Salalah via Masirah has been opened up for SOAF and the road route marked so that it can be covered in three days driving; all with the intention of the force being effective, if necessary in Dhofar.[5]

The DLF held its first conference in central Dhofar in 1965 electing an 18 man executive and issuing a manifesto calling for the overthrow of the sultan and an end to foreign influence (Pimlott 1985: 28). Subsequently a government patrol was attacked. In March 1966 the rebels activities had become such that William Luce, PRPG telegraphed the Foreign Office in London stating:

> In view of the danger of attack on the R.A.F. airfield and camp at Salalah by the considerable force of dissidents now being hunted by the R.A.F., I have today authorised the despatch of a platoon of the second parachute battalion from here to Salalah to assist in local defence of the R.A.F. establishment...I note from your telegram No.90 to me (not to all) that the Sultan has accepted the principle that we can take such steps so long as British troops do not go outside the airfield. I leave it to you whether to inform him direct of the present move or give the information to his military secretary and let him pass it on.[6]

Subsequently, the Sultan's military secretary, Waterfield, replied that either the Sultan or his wali in Dhofar should always be consulted on such a development. This is indicative of how the obfuscating 'protocol' of informal empire was beginning to break down under the pressure of the Dhofar rebels so that, increasingly, British power would be unmasked. In 1966 an assassination attempt on Sa'id narrowly failed;[7] after this Sa'id never left his palace and brought the predominantly Baluchi SAF to Salalah, excluding all Dhofaris. At this point the rebellion was supported by Dhofaris who saw it as a continuation of attempts to break away from Al Bu Sa'id rule. It suffered from a lack of resources; this was to change with the advent to power of the radical NLF to power in Aden in November 1967 and the subsequent creation of the Peoples Democratic Republic of Yemen. The radicalisation of the DLF and the course of the Dhofar rebellion after this are examined in section 5.2.2.

The military response to the DLF
The Sultan's military response was weak, chiefly because he lacked both information about the threat and the means to gain that information. His army comprised only two British-officered battalions - The Northern Frontier Regiment (NFR) and the Muscat Regiment (MR) neither of which was stationed in Dhofar nor contained Dhofaris, and when the Commander, Sultan's Armed Forces, Colonel Anthony Lewis, led an NFR company onto the Jebel in search of the DLF in October 1964, he faced enormous problems. Approaching the mountains from the north, Lewis had had:

> a cold start for getting to know the enemy, the inhabitants and the terrain. Fortunately the DLF was just as weak, lacking men, materiel and an organised infrastructure, and no contacts were made, but it was a poor start to a counter-insurgency campaign. Better results were achieved in May and June 1965, when two MR companies patrolled the *wadis* above Salalah in Operation Rainbow - on two separate occasions DLF groups were found and defeated - but once the monsoon began SAF troops were withdrawn and the mountains left to the rebels. (quoted in Pimlott 1985: 28)

The monsoon was one problem the SAF faced; another, which was to become more acute with British withdrawal from Aden in 1967, was the use by the Dhofari rebels of the port of Hauf in the East Aden Protectorate as a 'safe zone' where they could rest and recuperate. In autumn 1966 planning proceeded in British officialdom for a military operation to deny this port to the Dhofari rebels. On 25 October the Secretary of State of the Foreign Office authorised Operation Fate which was carried out three days later. Troops of the First Battalion, the Irish Guards, with helicopter support from HMS Fearless carried out a cordon and search operation; achieving complete surprise they encountered no opposition and sustained no casualties. Twenty two members of the Dhofar Liberation Front were arrested and deported to Dhofar.[8] British officials regarded it as a success – 'a considerable setback to the Dhofar rebels' – and a minute was sent to the Defence Secretary and copied to the Prime Minister conveying the congratulations of the Sultan of Muscat and Oman. Knowledge of the conflict in Dhofar and British military operations there went to the top of the British political system, in this case, the then Prime Minister, Harold Wilson.[9] This deployment of the resources of the British armed forces was to be crucial in the eventual suppression of the rebellion in Dhofar which will be examined in the next part of this chapter. It was a deployment that was obscured through a number of measures so that more than any counter insurgency campaign in the post war British imperial retreat it merits fully the title of one participant's account: the secret war.[10]

5.1.3: The impact of the West on Oman 1956 -1967

In this section we focus on the regime of Sa'id bin Taimur and its relationship with the outside world. The outside world was piercing the British cocoon which had isolated Oman: the United States showed interest in developing its relationship with the Sultanate whilst at the United Nations Sa'id's reliance on Britain was criticised as a type of imperialism. British support of Sa'id bin Taimur at this time meant that whilst it prevented his regime from being overthrown it now also put pressure on him to end the isolation of the Sultanate and allow the development of the country. His failure to do this adequately, which we will examine later in this section, both alienated the populace and undermined British commitment to him. This dynamic of imperial development meant there was an increasing shift to 'sell the Sultan down the river'.[11] Under the pressure of resistance to Sa'id's regime this is what was to happen when the British eventually dropped Sa'id bin Taimur to secure their wider interests. First we look at the context and significance of the 1959 Treaty of Amity, Economic Relations and Commercial Rights between the United States and the Sultan of Muscat and Oman.

Oman and the United States

In February 1949 the American Vice Consul in Dhahran had written to his Secretary of State:

> With the vast and dynamically expanding American interests in the Persian Gulf, I am sure that the Department is not unaware of the increasing strategic significance of the Sultanate of Muscat and Oman, lying as it does athwart the narrow entrance commanding the sea access to the Gulf. With the paucity of current information on this area, it is especially important that this consulate effectively discharge its responsibilities to report on this region, to protect and promote American interests there and to cultivate friendly and cordial relations with the Sultan and people of Muscat. (text from Porter 1982: 81)

An opportunity to develop 'friendly and cordial relations' was presented by the negotiations to replace the 1833 treaty between Oman and the United States - this was the last treaty granting the United States extraterritorial rights (see section 2.2). This treaty was replaced with a Treaty of Amity, Economic Relations and Commercial Rights in 1959 despite almost nonexistent trade relations (Joyce 1994: 145; Rigsbee 1990: 130).

The 1959 Treaty of Amity, Economic Relations and Commercial Rights

The State Department underlined the prospects of substantial further development of Muscat's oil resources by American business. To this end a treaty was required to facilitate the establishment of a consulate and thus make available to American citizens the services of consular officers having access to the ruler.

> For all practical purposes, there is now a vacuum in our relations with Muscat in that we have neither a satisfactory treaty nor even a more limited agreement of the type now in effect with Saudi Arabia and Yemen. This is a matter of more than ordinary concern where a country with an absolute ruler is involved. In such a case a treaty can serve to deter the ruler from capricious use of his power in an manner detrimental to US interests. (quoted in Joyce 1994: 149)

The treaty would allow right of entry to the Sultanate for American business and guarantee American protection of property. Agreement had been reached by the beginning of March on all points but one - Washington's proposal that disputes be referred to the International Court of Justice. The Sultan continued to say no; he suggested that if a dispute arose, the treaty be abrogated. Schwinn reported to Washington that there were three reasons for the Sultan's refusal to send unresolved disputes to the International court: his existing treaties with Britain and India did not contain such procedures; he was completely uninformed about the functions of the International Court; and he was reluctant to permit any third party to interfere in a treaty between the two nations. The Sultan explained: 'I, as ruler, am now free; once a paper is signed, I am restricted.' The Secretary of State was informed that while willing to listen to the points made by the American negotiator the Sultan 'proved tenacious and firm once he has made up his mind.' The Sultan contented that he did not need a new treaty and would be quite happy with abrogation of the defunct treaty of 1833 (Joyce 1994: 149). The choice appeared to be either to accept the Sultan's position or to forgo the treaty. The State Department emphasised the prospect of substantial further development of Muscat's oil resources by American business, which at this point consisted of the Cities Service oil concessions in Dhofar and the American share in the Iraq Petroleum Company concessions in Oman (Joyce 1994: 153). The US conceded defeat; a text for the treaty was agreed that did not contain the provision for recourse to the international court.

The Imamate and Saudi reaction to the US/Muscat Treaty
In the eyes of the Omani rebels the United States had, in concluding the treaty, aligned the US with the British in an unwarranted

interference in Oman through support for Sultan Sa'id bin Taimur, which amounted to a violation of the Charter of the United Nations. In Damascus a representative of a leader of the Imam of Oman, issued a statement deploring President Dwight D. Eisenhower's request to Congress to expedite ratify of the treaty and urged Congress to refuse ratification (Joyce 1994: 150).

The State Department sent a copy of the treaty to the Saudi Arabian ambassador in Washington emphasising that the treaty was a standard economic and consular agreement and held no political significance. However, strong objections were made by Acting Head of the Saudi Foreign Office Shaikh Omar Saggaf to the American embassy in Jedda. Saggaf protested that American recognition of rights for the Sultan outside Muscat demonstrated Washington's support for 'British aggression against Kingdom Saudi Arabia.' Jedda maintained the treaty contradicted the text of a joint communiqué signed on 8 February 1957 in Washington by Eisenhower and the Saudi monarch. That statement pledged the two governments to settle Middle East problems by peaceful means within the framework of the United Nations charter, with both leaders declaring their firm opposition to the use of force from any source. Jedda wanted Washington to revise the American position, which for the Saudis was 'subject astonishment and amazement'. Shaikh Saggaf felt that misunderstanding might have been avoided if prior to concluding the treaty Washington had consulted Jedda informally. Sweeny (*Charge d'Affaires ad Interim,* American embassy in Saudi Arabia) explained: 'Our understanding is that the Saudis are bothered by the term "dependencies" fear the British have taken us in'. The American *Charge d'Affaires* acknowledged that on the issue of boundaries Saudi opinion was often 'unrealistic', given that most Saudis believe their national destiny should include all of the Arabian peninsula except for the Yemen.

From Dhahran Schwinn indicated that when the Sultan insisted on using the phrase 'Kingdom Of Oman' in the treaty he did so in order to indirectly obtain, Washington's acknowledgement of his claims to Oman. Schwinn suggested that the American position should be that in using names and titles in current international usage the United States was not in any way taking a position on border disputes between the Sultan and his neighbours (Joyce 1994: 151).

The Question of Oman at the UN

Following the collapse of the rebels' military position in Oman their Arab supporters attempted to put the 'question of Oman' on the agenda of the United Nations (Peterson 1978: 151). The only substantive results of UN consideration were reports submitted in 1963 and 1965. Herbert de Ribbing, the Swedish Ambassador to Spain was appointed by the Secretary-General to investigate the situation. He visited Oman, Saudi Arabia and London in 1962 and submitted his report in the autumn of 1963. His conclusions were substantially in line with the Sultan's position, observing that the rebellion was long over, that the majority of the populace denied the existence of political repression, and that the British officers in SAF were apparently not involved in general policy-making. He also recommended that UN assistance be made available to help improve health and social conditions in Oman. Nevertheless, the Arab states continued to press for UN action favourable to their position. As a result, in December 1963, the General Assembly created an ad hoc Committee to engage not only in a fact-finding mission on Oman but also to give a judgement on the conflicting views of the parties to the dispute. This committee held discussions in London, Dammam, Kuwait and Cairo; Said bin Taimur did not allow members of the committee to enter Oman and Said requested that Britain represent him at the UN (Halliday 1974: 279). Partly as a result of this attitude, the committee declared Britain's presence was imperialistic and that all troops should be removed (Wilkinson 1987: 326). This was not the case due to the start of rebellion in the southern province of Dhofar.

Sa'id bin Taimur and development in Oman

It would seem that Sa'id believed that by isolating Oman from the outside world he might be able to perpetuate his form of rule. Many writers have contended that under Sa'id there was a range of official petty restrictions such as a ban on radios and spectacles, although this has been rejected as erroneous by a British official who was based in Oman at the time (Pridham 1986: 133). Furthermore Sa'id was not eager to start development projects such as hospitals or education. The reason he gave was absence of revenue in his treasury; however, in 1958 he received a windfall of three million pounds from the sale of the Omani enclave of

Gwadur on the Makran coast to the government of Pakistan. This money was deposited in a Swiss Bank account. In the late 1950s the Sultanate had an annual income of about two million pounds of which one and a half million was British subsidy. After the Jebal Akhdar rebellion the British sought to institute some form of development to ward off further discontent. A further reason was to cover up the damaging effects of the disproportionate response to the Jebel Akhdar rebels: the British civil development programme of 1960s was the necessary accompaniment of military pacification in the interior (Holden 1965: 234). Holden notes that when Lieutenant Wellsted had climbed the Jebel Akhdar in the 19th century that he was able to do this because with the proceeds of the slave trade Sultan's writ ran large. Wellsted found every sign of a flourishing agriculture on the plateau. As we have seen the decline of the slave trade meant the end of prosperity in the interior and led to migrations to Zanzibar and the coast. The irrigation channels fell into disuse and their destruction was completed in the air raids on the *jebel* in 1959 - the remaining villagers on the mountain prepared to abandon villages for good. The British government sent the Royal Engineers and an agricultural adviser, Jack Eyre, who restored the channels, distributed diesel pumps and opened an agricultural research station in Nizwa to host a vegetable show. Villages were being repopulated by the end of 1962 as migrants heard the news in Zanzibar and sought to return to their ancestral plots (Holden 1965: 235).

However, Sa'id stalled these development efforts with his extreme caution particularly in the areas of education and health; before 1970 only one hospital existed in Oman run by the Arabian Mission of America and much of the population was chronically sick and living in abject poverty (Allen 1987: 101). This had consequences for the security of all parts of the Sultanate as dissatisfied groups tried to obtain an improvement in their standard of living.

In 1966 the British Political Agent in Dubai, D.A. Roberts, warned off Sheikh Saqr of Ras al-Khaimah from an attempt to take over all of Muscat territory on the Musandam Peninsula. In his letter to Consul General Carden he concluded:

> It is gratifying to see that my warning to Sheikh Saqr had some effect but it is clear that so long as the people of the

Musandam Peninsula are dissatisfied they will continue to scheme with Shaikh Saqr or anyone else to improve their lot. The Sultan's refusal to do anything about this area will remain a constant source of trouble and embarrassment for us here. I hope that when his oil money starts to come in he may be pressed to spend some of it on his subjects here in the north.[12]

Carden replied:

I should be less than honest if, by remaining silent, I led you to think that the Sultan was likely to earmark much of his oil money in the initial phases for the Musandam Peninsula. From his standpoint Muscat and Matrah, Oman, the Batinah coast, and Dhofar are all of greater political importance. It would therefore be unrealistic to expect the Sultan to allocate to his part of the peninsular sums comparable to those available to Ras al Khaimah anyway before 1969.[13]

The official British pretence that Oman had an independent ruler meant that Britain could, to an extent, wash its hands of the state of the Omani populace. It was only when revolutionary forces threatened to overthrow Western influence in Oman that the British really concerned themselves with the nature of their client's regime. Ironically, in contrast to the days of the Indian Raj when they had sought to exclude any other Western presence in the Sultanate, the British now welcomed it as a buttress to their position:

According to one well placed witness a consortium of major German companies are interested in obtaining a sea-bed concession and held discussions on the subject with the Sultan in December. Dr Wendell Phillips had put them in touch with him. If this leads to the Germans getting the concession it will have the advantage that a further Western country will have a vested interest in the sovereignty of the Sultan and the territorial integrity of his country. Countries with such a stake now are limited to the U.K, the U.S.A. and the Netherlands.[14]

The emigration of Omanis to the oil states

One effect of the situation in Oman was the emigration of large number of Omanis to Gulf states experiencing oil-based development such as Kuwait, Bahrain and eastern Saudi Arabia. In July 1957, some tribes loyal to Sa'id bin Taimur were ordered to destroy the houses, date palms, and irrigation channels of communities which had rebelled (Eickelman 1985: 19). Following the Jebal Akhdar war and continuing throughout the 1960s there was an acceleration of working-age male emigration to the significant communities of Omani manual labourers and shopkeepers in Kuwait, Bahrain, and eastern Saudi Arabia (Eickelman 1985: 20). This was because after the submission of the Jebel Akhdar and the escape of the rebel leaders in 1959, punitive restrictions were placed on the region's inhabitants and a campaign of systematic reprisal began. They were denied regular access to the markets of neighbouring towns and forbidden to obtain passports to seek work outside Oman. They nonetheless usually found alternative means of leaving the country. The result was that by the late 1960s there were over 50,000 Omanis living in neighbouring Gulf states (Eickelman 1985: 20). For the same reasons many merchants moved to Dubai to escape the anti-commercial policies of the Sultan (Halliday 1974: 287).

Sultan Sa'id's regime in Oman

With the rebellion in the interior 1957-1959 Sultan Sa'id withdrew to Salalah, never to return to Muscat. He conducted government business by radio wire and the residents of Muscat were subject to the whims of some members of the royal family. For example Sayyid Shihab refused to issue passports for the Hajj without payment of a substantial deposit which in practice was very difficult to get back. Shihab claimed that his intention was to prevent dissatisfied subjects from using the *Hajj* as a cover to leave the country to work, which was illegal, or worse to join the rebellion (Joyce 1995: 96). The Sultan invited retired British Consul General to return to Muscat to work as his personal adviser; after consulting with the Foreign Office Chauncey took up the post (Joyce 1995: 96).

At this time British officialdom was concerned about possible adverse public relations which might stem from public executions in the Sultanate. One such execution had involved the fifteen year old son of the victim firing an eighteenth century rifle which had misfired three times. Eventually the boy handed the rifle to an older relative who having hit the prisoner's chest, fired a second shot five minutes later hitting the forehead. A later execution was filmed by a member of the royal family. Britain was concerned about the impact if knowledge of the public executions became public in Britain. However, it was the Sultan's aim 'not to expose himself to any accusations by the bigoted Ibadhis that he is departing from the strict letter of the Sharia law.' Political Resident William Luce pointed out that Britain was not in a position to pressure the Sultan, with the need for military facilities in connection with the defence of Kuwait (Joyce 1995: 92-93).

In 1965 Amnesty International groups in the UK began a letter writing campaign on behalf of what they regarded as 'non-violent prisoners of conscience' such as Saif bin Humaid al-Jabiri imprisoned in Jalali prison. In rebutting the allegations made in a letter from David Roberts of the Bristol Amnesty International group the Consul General, D.C. Carden wrote to M.S. Weir in the Arabian Department on the improvements that had been made in conditions in Jalali prison since 1960:

> Conditions in the fort have improved considerably over the past five years. I have no reason to think that they will not continued to improve. On virtually every point raised by Mr Roberts, there has been a marked improvement since Major Anderson gave us his 1960 report. Indeed taking into account the living conditions of the average Omani, the prisoners are quite well off, with free clothing, food and medical treatment. [15]

This is gives an indication of the privations that the rest of Sa'id bin Taimurs subjects had to endure. When Amnesty International members directed letters to their Member of Parliament the tactic of the Foreign Office officials was to issue two letters. One was for the constituent's consumption and stated that the Sultanate of Muscat and Oman was a fully independent state and that Britain had no basis to intervene. The other went to the MP stating, in confidence, that Britain was trying to influence the Sultan but that this was best done by gentle prompting rather than direct confrontation which would be counter-productive.[16]

Sa'id's system of rule

In the late 1950s and 1960s Sultan Sa'id often repeated to his British advisers his belief that 'if Oman's little rulers are all right then so is Oman.' He was referring to the country's tribal sheikhs upon whom he depended to maintain order. The scope of governmental activities remained what it was prior to 1955 except for a small military presence and a small network of individuals personally commissioned by the Sultan to write confidential reports on local events. Reliance upon tribal sheikhs provided an inexpensive means of government in the interior, but at the cost of maintaining an administrative system with neither the capacity nor the resources to initiate development projects of any sort or to assess local needs in any significant way (Eickelman 1985; 17).

Sa'id bin Taimur and Dhofar

Said treated Dhofar as his own personal domain where he might escape from the interference of the British and also the demands for financial largesse from tribal delegations.[17] Sa'id was a thoroughly obnoxious character - in the 1950s when he resided in Muscat one of his favourite past times was to make his slaves swim under his balcony and then shoot at the fish around them (Halliday 1974: 277). Sa'id's presence in Dhofar meant that his regime there was particularly oppressive. The UN Committee on Oman interviewed two persons from Dhofar and gave this summary of their interview

> The people of Dhofar, the Committee was told, were treated by the Sultan as slaves. He was cruel and imposed many arbitrary restrictions on the people. They could not travel outside; they were not permitted to build houses; food could only be bought in one walled market where the quantity that could be bought was fixed; and they were not allowed to import or export goods. Further, there was no work in Dhofar, no schools, no hospitals, no economic life, no equality and no right to participate in politics. For instance, in 1957 when the oil company came, people

from outside the country were given jobs, although local people had wished to work. However, the young people of Dhofar had held secret meetings about these matters and although they had had no education, some of them had travelled and they all knew their rights. (UN Report of the Ad Hoc Committee on Oman, 1965, p.164)

After the assassination attempt Sa'id ordered a blockade of the mountains and sealed off Salalah which prevented the *jebali* from gaining access to their traditional markets and alienated uncommitted *jebali* (Pimlott 1985: 28). Although until this point it had been the Imamate forces of the interior that had posed the most persistent threat to the British supported Sultans of Muscat, it was in Dhofar that a rebellion started that at one point seriously threatened the rule of the Al Bu Sa'id Sultans and Western influence in Oman. It was to precipitate a greater external military involvement than the Sultanate had seenbefore and the creation of a new post-colonial order in Oman.

Sa'id bin Taimur and the parameters of collaboration
In his discussion on the end of the British empire in the Persian Gulf, Glen Balfour-Paul comments on Halliday's assertion of the colonial status of Muscat and Oman:

'The only counter observation offered here is that, if Muscat and Oman was ever a colony in Halliday's *de facto* sense, it had certainly ceased to be so by the period we are concerned with. Any British representative (the author was one) who sought in that period to tender advice to Sultan Sa'id bin Taimur on the governing of his country soon found how constitutionally (in both senses of that word) impermeable he was.' (Balfour-Paul 1991: 199).

Sa'id was clearly a wily character and knew how to play the British officials at their own game - or 'obstinate' as some of the British in Oman liked to call it. He had the power to stall, and a limited power to manoeuvre and was certainly not a 'puppet'. However the parameters of collaboration meant that while Sa'id could ignore British advice his usefulness was becoming outlived. In January 1966 the Consul General in Muscat, Bill Carden wrote to William Luce, PRPG that

The next five years will be a contest with the rebels and their friends trying to oust the Sultan and us before he can consolidate his position by expenditure of oil revenues.[18]

Ultimately, it was to be the British who, towards the end of that five year period, ousted the Sultan so that they could retain their position in Oman and maintain the Al Bu Sa'id dynasty in power through the expenditure of oil revenues. The further development of the Dhofar conflict examined in the next part of this chapter meant that their erstwhile collaborator, Sa'id bin Taimur, had to be dispensed with.

5.2: Oman and the West 1968 - 1977

The second part of chapter five reviews the changes in Western security arrangements for the Gulf, the development of the conflict in Dhofar in this context and the resulting removal of Sa'id bin Taimur. The development of the Omani rentier state under the regime of Qabus is examined.

5.2.1: The international context 1968 - 1977

The British withdrawal from the Gulf and the Twin Pillars policy were the two key developments in Western security projects for the Gulf in this period. This change reflected the growth of regional powers of Iran and Saudi Arabia and their relationship with the dominant Western power the United States.

The British Withdrawal from Aden and the Gulf

The gathering pace of British withdrawal from the Persian Gulf which came to a head in this period is characterised by Sir Anthony Parsons, a British diplomat in Bahrain at the time, with a metaphor from cricket:

> Governments, Labour and Conservative, were like teams embarking on what they believed to be a timeless, at least, a five day Test Match. Suddenly, they discovered that the rules of the game had been changed: they were playing a limited-overs game and, at the beginning of each session, the umpire reduced the number of overs remaining. Long term strategy and planning, if any, gave way to hasty improvisation, the important lost priority of the urgent,

decisions were made for the wrong reasons, or were not made at all, advice from the region was ignored or rejected. (see his foreword in Balfour-Paul 1991: xvi)

As this indicates, British policy regarding military bases east of Suez continually changed as each successive revision to attempt to conduct a viable policy was undercut by events on the ground. The eviction from the Egypt Canal Zone and the debacle of Suez led to the building up of Aden as the RAF's major base in the Middle East only to see British rule there face sustained and eventually successful opposition.[19] It was clear that British imperialism was in terminal decline; efforts turned to securing post-colonial states on the Arabian peninsula conducive to Western and specifically British interests. However, developments in the Arab-Israeli conflict between 1967 and 1973 made this more difficult by catapulting the Arabian peninsula into world attention and breaking down its insulation from the destabilising force of the Arab-Israeli conflict (Halliday 1980: 212). Fred Halliday comments:

The context of those years needs little summary: globally, the final death throes of the European empires, the rise of the revolutionary movements in Indochina, the conflict between Russia and China for influence in the third world; regionally, the crisis of the Arab nationalist movement that followed the defeat in the 1967 war, the consolidation of a new pro-western bloc headed by Saudi Arabia and Iran, the rise of a revolutionary movement in South Arabia, beginning with the Yemeni revolution of 1962, leading onto the anti-British guerrilla movement in South Yemen between 1963 and 1967, and the outbreak of guerrilla warfare in Dhofar in 1965. (Halliday 1997)

In Aden and South Yemen British attempts to construct a pro-Western government failed: in 1967 the Marxist NLF came to power (see, especially, Kostiner 1984). In Oman, by contrast, the British were successful - eventually. On 16 January 1968 the Prime Minister, Harold Wilson, in a supplementary question on defence policy announced Britain's intention to withdraw all armed forces by the end of 1971 from the remaining British-protected states in the Gulf: Bahrain, Qatar and the shaikhdoms of the lower Gulf known as the Trucial States (Jones and Stone 1997: 2). This declaration was made in response to chronic economic problems and the need to make defence cuts following the devaluation of the pound in November 1967.[20] The United States, preoccupied as it was with Vietnam, opposed the British decision. Whilst the Conservative Party in opposition argued against it, it did not reverse the decision on coming to power in June 1970: Britain's imperial withdrawal was not to be halted. There was though a significant difference in the approach of the Conservatives; a supplementary statement on defence issued in July stated unambiguously that the UK should 'resume, within her resources, a proper share of responsibility for the preservation of peace and stability in the world.' In effect this meant the commitments of Britain's colonial past and the demands of the Cold War: whilst Britain was going to terminate its official protection agreements in the Gulf it would not be the end of Britain's strategic involvement in the area (Jones and Stone 1997: 2).

The US and the Twin Pillars Strategy

The US perceived that the British withdrawal would leave a power vacuum in the Gulf, an area whose oil reserves were becoming of increasing importance to the US; in accordance with the Nixon doctrine this vacuum was to be filled by strong regional pro-Western powers friendly to the West. In the Gulf this took the form of the 'Twin Pillars' policy which envisaged the building up of the military capabilities of Iran and Saudi Arabia. In reality, Iran was the military power of the Twin Pillars whilst Saudi Arabia used its financial muscle. The 1973 Arab-Israeli war and ensuing oil crisis further elevated the economic and strategic importance of the Gulf: it became an area of vital US interest (Cordesman 1984: 55-59). In particular the oil of the eastern Gulf had to pass through the Straits of Hormuz. Sovereignty over the Musandam Peninsula meant that the shipping lanes lay in Omani territorial waters: Oman's resulting strategic importance focused Western policy-makers on the necessity of defeating the Dhofar rebels who since 1968 had adopted a Marxist-Leninist orientation and become the Peoples Front for the Liberation of Oman (PFLO). With the coming to power of the NLF in South Yemen in 1967 the Dhofar rebels were to pose a more serious threat to Western interests than either the Oman Revolutionary Movement or the Dhofar Liberation Front. The efforts of Britain and pro-Western allies in the area to defeat the rebels is examined in the next section.

5.2.2: Western involvement in Oman 1968 - 1977

In this section we will review the change that took place in the political stance of the rebels in Dhofar. The success of the rebellion led to the ousting of Sa'id; a vigorous counter-insurgency campaign combined with international support for the Qabus regime defeated the PFLO and British withdrawal from the bases in Salalah and Masirah took place in 1977.

The Radicalisation of the Rebellion in Dhofar

Britain's treaty relations with the Trucial States were terminated in December 1971 in a peaceful transfer of power to local elites (Said Zahlan 1991: 90). British withdrawal from Oman was made more difficult by the conflict in Dhofar which became increasingly serious (Allen 1987: 101). At the second conference of the DLF at Hamrin in 1968 the existing nationalist leadership of the rebellion was replaced by committed Marxists; one of the most influential figures in the new leadership was Muhammed al-Sayl al-Ghassani (Peterson 1986: 100; Janzen 1986: 166). Reflecting this change in direction the DLF became the Popular Front for the Liberation of the Occupied Arab Gulf. Its declared aim was to overthrow the entire post-colonial structure Britain was trying to erect in the Gulf. This shift towards the left was largely due to the changes in South Yemen where the British had withdrawn in 1967 to be replaced by the People's Democratic Republic of Yemen. The rebels benefited from the advent to power of the radical government in Aden which gave them supplies and bases just inside the South Yemen border. Also the defeat of Egypt by Israel in the Six Day War removed Nasserist support; from then on the rebellion in Dhofar could only obtain material support from communist countries (Janzen 1986: 166). Since 1967 China had supplied arms, training and political literature to the Front (Halliday 1990: 143). The rebellion gathered momentum pushing back the ineffectual SAF until by early 1970 Sultanate authority in Dhofar was confined to three towns on the narrow coastal plain: Salalah, Taqa and Mirbat. Travelling between these enclaves of Sultanate authority was perilous for the SAF (Pimlott 1985: 20).

The 1970 coup

The British became increasingly concerned about the ability of Sa'id's regime to win the conflict. Brigadier John Watts, commanding officer of 22 SAS was horrified as he completed his preliminary reconnaissance of Dhofar in response to a belated request from Sultan Sa'id for help:

> The road was cut and the only resupply was by air or sometime by sea... There were no Dhofaris in SAF, which was virtually an army of occupation. Everybody on the jebel was with the enemy, some convinced, some out of boredom, some intimidated; SAF had only a few jebali guides. It was crazy - we were on a hiding to nothing. (quoted in Pimlott 1985:30)

Said had ignored one of the most basic rules of counter-insurgency: to understand your opponents' grievances.[21] As late as April 1970 he told the new CSAF, Brigadier John Graham, that the *jebalis* were 'evil and dangerous men - I want you to destroy them' (Pimlott 1985: 30). On 12 June 1970 there was an attempt to extend the conflict to northern Oman, not far from the PDO oilfields, with attacks in Ibri and Nizwa by the National Democratic Front for the Liberation of Oman and the Occupied Arab Gulf. Such an extension would threaten the whole of the post- colonial structure which was being planned for the Gulf. The Shell oil company pressed action on the British government. Following the general election of 20 June a Conservative government was elected and the risks of staging a coup prior to an election, which had perhaps weighed on the Labour government, could be ignored (Halliday 1974: 288). Whitehall saw the coup as a solution to the problem of Sa'id: a Foreign Official was purported to have commented in April 1970 'we need an Omani Zayid for Sa'id's Shakhbut'.[22] The Consul-General in Muscat, David G. Crawford and the PRPG, Geoffrey Arthur and the seconded SAF commander, therefore cooperated with the plans to remove Sa'id drawn up a group of British officers and Sa'id's son, Qabus (Peterson 1978: 202). The long term expatriate community in the Sultanate had been divided for some time into those loyal to Sa'id and those keen to see him replaced. Of the first group the Military Secretary Brigadier P.R.G. Waterfield was the most prominent; in January 1970 he retired and was replaced by Colonel Hugh Oldham, a former SAF Commander. This removed a potential obstacle to the smoothness of any operation to remove Sa'id. A key figure was Tim Landon, an SAF intelligence officer and Sandhurst classmate of Qabus. Other Omanis involved apart from Qabus were Burayk bin Hamud al-Ghafiri, the son of the *wali* of Dhofar and Hamud bin Hamud Al Bu Sa'id, the Secretary to Sultan Sa'id. Although Sa'id's brother Tariq had more experience internationally than Qabus, he was considered to hold 'nationalist attitudes' and was not, therefore, to the British liking as a potential Sultan (Bebehani 1981: 152). A meeting of the head of the Sultanate's intelligence service with Tariq in Dubai in April 1970 ensured his agreement to Qabus becoming Sultan. This group prevaricated until the rocket attack at Izki pushed them to implement their plans for the ousting of Sa'id (Peterson 1978: 202). On July 23rd 1970, the guards having been bribed to turn a blind eye, a small force entered Sa'id's palace in Salalah. After a brief exchange in which a slave was shot and in which Sa'id shot himself in the foot, Sa'id relented and was forced to sign a letter of abdication. He was immediately flown out of the country, first to Bahrain for medical treatment and then to London where he resided in the Dorchester hotel until his death in 1972 (Graz 1992: 283).

Development of the Counter-Insurgency Campaign
The priority for the new regime was to win the war in Dhofar. With Qabus installed it was now possible to pursue the classic elements of a counter insurgency campaign. John Pimlott identifies a number of the key features of such a campaign: the understanding of rebel grievances and countering with reforms; government propaganda to encourage defection from rebel ranks - the winning of 'hearts and minds'; military campaigns based on good intelligence within a clear political strategy; military operations conducted by a well-resourced army (Pimlott 1985: 30). The Front's Marxist-Leninist ideology with its commitment to women's emancipation was not popular with some of the jebali whose society was based on the Moslem religion and tribal traditions (Pimlott 1985: 34). Due to these changes a conflict ensued within the Dhofar rebels and one group led by Salim Mubarak handed themselves over to the Sultan's forces. Qabus announced a pardon for all surrendering rebels. These men were organised into military companies called *firqats* which formed an invaluable resource for the Sultanate's forces

with their knowledge of the local terrain and PFLOAG tactics. This was exploited by the 'information experts' of 22 SAS who were organising leaflet drops onto the *jebel* to encourage more members of the Front to change sides.[23]

Operation Storm: the SAS in Dhofar
With their expertise in counter-insurgency the SAS played a key role in the outcome of the Dhofar conflict.[24] The SAS had been returning to Oman regularly on training missions since the storming of the Jebel Akhdar in 1959. Confronted with the state of the beleaguered military situation in Dhofar three senior SAS officers discussed notes in Easter 1970 and identified the key aspects of a strategy to win the war (Geraghty 1980; Pimlott 1985: 32). These were a medical campaign to provide aid to the 50,000 *jebalis* in the mountain; a veterinary campaign to help the *jebali* with their livestock such as the digging of wells; improved intelligence on the enemy to break down their morale; a psychological operation to persuade the rebels to change sides; and a policy of directly involving the Dhofaris in the fight for their province. The SAS were inserted into Dhofar under the guise of British Army Training Team (BATT) allowing the government to deny they had been deployed there purely on a combat role (Jones and Stone 1997: 4). To a limited degree this was the case - as conceived in the strategy described their main job was to bring initial medical aid for the *jebalis* and to organise the *firqats* which were the first military units to start challenging the Front's control of the mountainous interior of Dhofar.[25] The SAS also attacked Hauf on a number of occasions to pressure the PDRY to end its support for the rebels (Cordesman 1997: 126). The most significant military battle in which the SAS was involved was at Mirbat in July 1972 when the BATT team there withheld a sustained attack from the PFLOAG in July 1972 in an engagement which was seen as a turning point in the war. The Front's attempt to demonstrate it still had the ability to mount a major offensive suffered an irreversible setback.[26]

The Dhofar Conflict: a British-run war
Whilst the role of the SAS units played an crucial part it was the massive combined international involvement which eventually decided the war's outcome in which different external powers

played different roles: the British, Americans, Iranians, Jordanians, Pakistanis, Saudis and Emirates all contributed as they all had a stake in the outcome:

> Although Britain was initially the sole outside party involved, the conflict in Dhofar became a highly internationalised one, in which at least nine foreign powers participated in the campaigns to crush the guerrillas. The participation of these powers is illustrative not only of the fact that the suppression of the Dhofar guerrillas was essential to the region's stability, but also of a new interstate system being built in the Gulf. (Halliday1977: 24)

Halliday's identification of the far-reaching implications of the outcome of this war is echoed by the British military commander, Major General Timothy Creasy who arrived in September 1972 to become the Commander, Sultan's Armed Forces. The stakes in Dhofar were high:

> He who controls Oman, and particularly the Musandam, controls the Gulf. He who controls the Gulf controls the Gulf oil supplies, and these are crucial to both the West and Russia. The fall of Dhofar would lead inevitably to the fall of Northern Oman and the Musandam, and thus of the Gulf - a classic example of the Domino theory. (quoted in Skeet 1992: 168)

As a result of the significance attached to the outcome of the war extra British officers were seconded to command the SAF which was expanded and reorganised; fifty per cent of the Sultanate's budget was allocated to the military. By the end of the rebellion in 1975 the British presence numbered over 1500 including 220 officers on private contract, sixty Special Air Service members, 75 men from the Royal Engineers and 147 RAF personnel at RAF Salalah (Halliday 1977: 103; Peterson 1986: 103). In contrast to Vietnam where the involvement of American servicemen was covered by the media, the British-directed war effort in Dhofar was concealed by a strict policy of news management (see Halliday 1987a); this secrecy was helped by the fact that the war was paid for out of the Sultanate's oil revenues which started in 1967 (Halliday 1977: 48). Although, in contrast to Vietnam, the war in Dhofar was kept secret, in other respects it was a similar campaign such as in some of its tactics in dealing with a guerrilla army in mountainous territory: the use of napalm to deprive them of cover.[27]

Weaponry supplied by Britain
Such bombing raids were made possible by the supply of military aircraft to Oman by Britain. Orders were placed in April 1968 for Jet Provost trainer aircraft, in September 1970 for five Skyvan transport planes with more ordered in September 1971, followed by an order for a dozen Strikemaster fighters and various naval patrol aircraft. The culmination of these purchases came in late 1974 when the sultanate contracted for 12 Anglo-French Jaguar fighters and 28 Rapier missiles, at a cost of between £71million and £83million (Peterson 1986: 104). These aircraft were used to support advances by infantry in the campaign to oust the rebels from the areas they controlled in the mountains.

The Military Campaign to establish Sultanate control in Dhofar
The repelling of the Front's assault on Mirbat in 1972 represented a turning point. From then on the Front was seeking to stem Sultanate advances; it still required a considerable effort to return all of the mountains to Sultanate control. A number of fortified lines were built progressively from east to west in Dhofar bisecting rebel held territory thus breaking supply lines. By early 1973 government troops had begun to capture key points on the western Jebal Qamar; 'Operation Thimble' recovered and permanently held the Thumrait road re-opening a ground link between Salalah and Muscat. Previously the rebels had been able to retake this road during the monsoon season and thus regain any ground denied to them by Sultanate forces. It was clear that the Sultanate forces were gaining the upper hand and were on their way to victory.

The Sultanate forces gained the upper hand in the Dhofar conflict in 1973 but it was to require two more years to finally crush the rebellion. In July 1974, in an indication of its reduced horizons PFLOAG divided into the Popular Front for the Liberation of Oman and a People's Front in Bahrain. The PFLO continued the guerrilla struggle in Oman whilst the latter continued underground political work in Bahrain (Halliday 1990: 144). In September government forces accelerated their offensive with action around Sarfait. An Omani-Iranian attack on Rakhyut which involved a heavy loss of Iranian lives led to the capture of the town on January 5th 1975. This allowed the construction of the Damavend line northward from Rakhyut. At the close of the 1975 monsoon season SAF and Iranian troops moved into areas north of Rakhyut while the PFLO base in Hauf, South Yemen was attacked by Sultanate aircraft. With other Iranian units moving south from Sarfait towards the sea Sultanate forces occupied the remaining towns in the west of Dhofar as the guerrillas slipped back into PDRY territory. On the 11th December Sultan Qabus declared the war officially over (Peterson 1986: 103). The British, from their perspective, had prevented another 'Aden' with their contribution to the massive external military intervention on behalf of the Sultanate. Conversely, they had avoided a British 'Vietnam'.

The American Concern
The American approach to the Dhofar conflict was shaped by two factors: the Cold War and Vietnam (Peterson 1978: 193). This meant that whilst the US was extremely concerned to avoid a communist take-over in Dhofar they were unable to get involved in any serious way themselves. Instead, under the Nixon Doctrine this responsibility was to be assigned to regional powers, supplied with the latest American weaponry - US proxy military forces. Thus, the Americans kept a close eye on events in Oman. On coming to power Sultan Qabus had quickly established links to the US to prevent a similar fate to his father. Initially this took the form of covert CIA funding for his personal security and intelligence force (Stork 1980b: 11). The objective was to get Oman 'out from under the dominance of the British'.[28] In 1973 Oman became eligible for American military assistance and the Americans also inquired about access to the RAF air strip at Masirah. In September 1973 US Army Colonel George Maloney made a three-week visit to Oman. His report concentrated mainly on the situation in Dhofar and stressed the potential usefulness of the airstrip on Masirah Island (Stork 1980b: 11). In 1974 Secretary of State Kissinger sent the following memorandum to President Gerald Ford:

Maintaining Oman's stability in the face of the war is a great concern to both the Saudis and Iranians. The Shah, King Faisal and other moderate Arab leaders are encouraging us to develop closer relations with Oman, particularly since its strategic location at the mouth of the Gulf means that two-thirds of the world's oil exports transit its territorial waters. (quoted in Joyce 1995: 106)

Oman received its first significant supplies of American arms in 1975 when anti-tank (TOW) missiles were transported to the Sultanate with a small training team (Halliday 1977: 36). In January 1975 Qabus visited Washington: the Americans raised the possibility of access to the RAF bases, especially Masirah Island, asking Britain and Oman simultaneously (Kechichian 1995: 146). Following the Sultan's meeting with the President, the State Department prepared a draft statement for the possible use of the White House press secretary. The statement said that Washington welcomed and strongly supported the efforts of all regional states, including Oman, to strengthen security. The only American programme in the Sultanate at the time was a thirty-member Peace Corps operation. The White House planned to declare that no new programmes were discussed. Nevertheless, the United States 'would be as responsive as possible' to any Omani request for aid. A Washington Post article reported that when the Sultan hosted a reception at Blair House 'some pretty big guns attended' including Secretary of Defense James Schlesinger and William Colby, director of the Central Intelligence Agency (Joyce 1995: 107). After the Sultan's visit to the United States, cooperation between Washington and Muscat increased: an informal agreement had been reached in which in exchange for access to Masirah Island the US airlifted 10 launchers, 180 anti-tank missiles and two advisers. These missiles were set up in the Dhofar region for use in any possible conflict with the PDRY (Halliday 1977: 66; Stork 1980:11; Kechichian 1995: 146). Joseph Kechichian comments:

Even after all these years, it remains to be determined whether this informal agreement involving the TOWs in exchange for access to Masirah Island was initiated by the administration, or by Secretary Henry Kissinger without the knowledge of the State Department, the Pentagon, or the National Security Council. (1995: 146)

One of the advantages of Oman to US strategic planners was Qabus's willingness to cooperate and unambiguous pro-Western stance. Although at this stage the Omani-American military arrangement was an informal one, a Congressional study in December 1977 noted that, 'the absence of FMS [Foreign Military Sales] prospects...does not accurately reflect the reality of an apparently intense desire among Omani officials for discreet assistance, especially in the area of training' (quoted in Stork 1980b: 11). A formal US-Omani agreement was to come about after the Iranian revolution and the Soviet invasion of Afghanistan. These events and the agreement are examined in more detail in the next chapter. American support for the Sultanate in the conflict in Dhofar was facilitated through the policy of the time - reliance on the Twin Pillars of Pahlavi Iran and Saudi Arabia. In military terms this meant the contribution of thousands of Iranian troops and their US-supplied equipment (Stork 1980b: 11).

The Iranian intervention

In November and December 1973 several thousand Iranian troops were deployed by the Shah in support of Sultan Qabus (Halliday 1990: 145). Dhofar presented the Shah with a rare opportunity to provide combat training for his troops, and the rapid rotation of Iranians fighting in Dhofar was alleged to have resulted in nearly 200 deaths. Iranian helicopters and paratroopers were sent to Dhofar in early 1973. Iranian paratroopers were key elements in 'Operation Thimble' of December 1973 when the Thamarit Road was recovered and permanently held open, providing the first ground link between Muscat and Salalah in several years (Peterson 1986: 102). By the end of 1974 Iranian troops totalled over 2000 growing to over 5000 in 1975. A local headquarters was established at the sprawling air base at Thamarit and Iranian F-5 Phantoms patrolled the PDRY border, while Iranian destroyers shelled the rebel-held Dhofari coast. The Iranians were at the centre of Rakhyut's capture in January 1975 and they played a prominent role in the 'big push' in December.

The support of Arab monarchies for the Sultanate
Iranian involvement in Dhofar was viewed with suspicion by most other Arab states, including Oman's neighbours in the Gulf. Nevertheless, Saudi Arabia and the UAE provided the Sultanate with welcome financial assistance while Jordan contributed staff officers and NCOs, intelligence officers, engineer units and a combat battalion in 1975 (Peterson 1986: 104). This gave an extra dimension to the Sultanate effort. Whereas from 1970-72 many of the propaganda leaflets failed as they were written in the Arabic of British intelligence officers, they had more effect when Jordanian intelligence officers were brought in to help with this aspect of the campaign (Halliday 1977: 56).

The British withdrawal from RAF Masira and Salalah
As we have seen the outcome of this massive support for the Sultanate was the effective military defeat of the Popular Front in Dhofar. In December 1975 Commander SOAF Watts informed the Sultan that Dhofar was ready for civil development - development in the Sultanate is examined in the next section (5.2.3). Having successfully defeated the rebels in Dhofar and secured a pro-Western Omani government Britain announced in July 1976 that it would hand over its air bases at Salalah and Masira; this took place in March 1977 (Peterson 1978: 155; Halliday 1977:32). This was not, however, the end of Britain's military links with the Sultanate; the nature of British military involvement with Oman in the 1980s and 1990s is examined in chapter six.

5.2.3: The impact of the West on Oman 1968-1977
In this section we examine the modernising regime of Qabus and the composition of the state elite. The end of Oman's isolation and the establishment of foreign relations is also reviewed. We also consider the debate on the extent to which the Qabus regime differed in this time from that of his father.

The 'modernising' regime of Qabus: the Omani rentier state
The post-colonial state that was to develop after the British staged coup that brought Qabus to power was a *rentier* state. A key feature of such a state is that the rent derived from a single product allows the ruling elite to act independently of other elite groups with which it previously had to negotiate.[29] Thus, in the

era of revenue from oil exports which started shortly before Qabus came to power, Oman has experienced an ever increasing concentration of power in the hands of the Sultan and the diminution of previously influential groups, most significantly the tribal leaders. M.E. Yapp writes:

> As elsewhere in the Gulf one may see the new political elite in terms of concentric circles composed of ruler, household, notables and citizens, narrowly defined. One may also observe the same process of the elevation of the ruler and his household above other groups. In particular the role of tribal leaders declined after 1970, for example Ahmad ibn Muhammed al-Harithi, whose support had been vital to the success of the Sultan in his struggle with the tribal rebels in 1957 and who had played a major role in Omani politics thereafter was arrested in 1970. (Yapp 1996:375)

On becoming Sultan, Qabus quickly established complete domination over the government on an official level; initially his uncle, Tariq, was brought back as prime minister but at the end of 1971 Qabus took direct control of the government and of the ministries of foreign affairs, defence and finance (Yapp 1996: 375). Tariq spoke of Oman gradually becoming a constitutional monarchy.[30] Qabus, however, never seriously considered involving his subjects in government at this stage. In 1972 Qabus told a Lebanese journalist: 'It was not possible to follow the Western tradition of democratic systems. We are not yet ready to embark on this stage. We have no constitution. We have no chamber of deputies' (Townsend 1976: 93). What did happen in the governmental system was that members of the Al Bu Sa'id staffed the departments of government which were greatly increased to accommodate them and others. A key trend in the years after 1970 was the monopoly of government posts by Omani Arabs at the expense of those of Zanzibari, Baluchi and Indian origin who had previously staffed the administration (Yapp 1996: 375).

Qabus renamed the state the Sultanate of Oman to signify the intention to unify and modernise the Sultanate; the failure of Sa'id to do this was perceived as one of the causes of the rebellion. In his accession speech Qabus explained why he had deposed his father:

I have taken this action against my father in an effort to place the country along the path of reconstruction and development. (quoted in Kechichian 1995: 37)

Modernisation programmes were initiated in all areas: military, education, health and economic infrastructure. In this the new regime was considerably helped by growing oil revenues. A commercially viable well had been developed at Fahud in 1964 and oil exports started in 1967. Oman developed as a *rentier* state; the *rentier* state controls the rent from oil which is the most important material resource of Omani society.[31] Although Oman is an oil producer its reserves are nowhere in the league of Saudi Arabia or Abu Dhabi.

With the effective ending of the war in 1975 the non-military modernisation programmes gathered apace. An ambitious five year plan was drawn up in which with the growing oil revenues sought to create a basis economic infrastructure and health and educational system. The government emphasised private sector participation in the achievement of these plans. Business growth was phenomenal with Western companies profiting greatly from the boom conditions in Oman. The awarding of these contracts was in the hands of a small group of Al-Sa'id family members and long-time associates who accordingly prospered greatly.

Bierschenk (1984) identifies four groups in the *rentier* state that initially emerged after the 1970 coup and which together formed a 'stateclass': the 'Palace' (*diwan*) and 'Courtiers', merchant class, the Ibadhis and the Zanzibaris. The merchant class, the Ibadhis and the Zanzibaris are termed coopted groups; this means they have no direct share in power through access to the key decision making process. They have been 'bought off' with material opportunities and exclude themselves from making inputs to the decision-making process. In the merchant class an important distinction is that between the Hindu merchants which chose to retain their Indian citizenship and who lost out in the Omanisation process to the Khojas - Indians of Sunni Muslim extraction. The 'Ibadhis' are representatives of the traditional notables of the tribal society of inner Oman. The Zanzibaris had technical skills and were strongly represented in the oil company, Petroleum Development Oman.

The most important social group is the *diwan* consisting of the Sultan and a small group of 'courtiers'. Bierschenk questions whether it is the Sultan that rules or the courtiers through the Sultan (Bierschenk 1984: 219). The courtiers have high official positions such as minister, governor of a province for key areas such as the capital or Dhofar, or as officers in the military apparatus, police or secret service. Independently of the official description of their political position, they are sponsors for foreign construction firms or old established Hindu merchant families which, with the 'Omanisation' policy of the government, required a partner of Omani nationality in order to win business. They are partners in banks and furthermore they have their own business and financial enterprises with international connections in Europe and the USA. They used their connections to the Sultan, who ultimately could control all oil rents, to gain his agreement to make funds available for particular projects in which they had an interest e.g. the construction of a road.

An example of these courtiers at this time were the brothers Qais and Omar Zawawi. Their grandfather Yusuf al-Zawawi, originated from Taif in Saudi Arabia and was a merchant who became an adviser to the Sultan in Muscat at the end of the 19th century. His son Abdul Muneim apparently lived in Pakistan for a time which is where his son Qais and Omar received their school education. Omar trained as a dentist and Qais managed a Pepsi Cola distribution centre in Kuwait in the 1960s. They returned to Oman in 1970 in the expectation of an upturn in the economy and to build up their family business again. Their first enterprise was the Muscat Pharmacy in the Matrah *suq* (Bierschenk 1984: 222).

The political climb of the Zawawi brothers began in 1973 as Qais became Minister for Foreign Relations - the Sultan is Foreign Minister himself. His appointment was part of the Omanisation of the government, whereas in the first years after the coup of 1970 all the top positions were held by foreigners. He was also the deputy chairman of the Development Council which had responsibility for the control of the five year plans and therefore determined the development policy of the Sultanate, as well as of the Finance Council which had the last word on all state expenses. The chairman of these two councils was the Sultan but he appeared to have little interest in economic policy and therefore allowed himself to be represented by Zawawi. Zawawi was, therefore in all three political functions the direct representative of the Sultan. His brother Omar was also on the Finance Council so the Zawawis had two of the ten votes there (Bierschenk 1984: 222).

Bierschenk (1984: 223) lists the extensive business interests of the Zawawi brothers by the early 1980s which reflected the developments of the 1970s. They had business interests in nearly all sectors of the economy. Companies they controlled or had shares in included Zawawi Trading which was one of the ten largest trading firms in Oman and amongst others, the agent for Mercedes and IBM, two important suppliers to the Omani ministries. Other Zawawi interests were Oman Mechanical Services which represented General Electric and gained the order for the delivery of the gas turbines for the copper project at Sohar. Wimpey Alawi was a joint venture with the British construction company Wimpey and one of the largest road building firms in Oman. A further construction company, Qurm Contractors, was partly owned by the Zawawis. The Lebanese construction company, Consolidated Contractors Company hired the Zawawis as unofficial sponsors and gained the largest road project at the time, the main road from the north to Dhofar. The Zawawis also had shares in the Bank of Oman, Bahrain and Kuwait which is the second largest local bank in which leading Omani, Bahraini and Kuwaiti business people have shares and which also has a management contract with the American Chemical Bank. Finally, Omar Zawawi Enterprises employed former US military officers and was responsible for procuring the majority of Oman's weapon imports (Bierschenk 1984: 223).

It was this mixing of private and public interest, of which the Zawawi brothers were a prime example, that led to the comment in the Financial Times in 1979 that: 'It has been pointed out by foreign observers, sympathetic and unsympathetic Arab states and even some officials inside Oman that a small number of corrupt advisers are deciding the allocation of key civil and military projects' (quoted in Bierschenk 1984: 221). Furthermore, these corrupt officials had available to them a wide-reaching security apparatus consisting of the army, police and secret service.

Establishment of foreign relations and international recognition

The Qabus regime sought to institute foreign relations, perhaps most importantly with his fellow monarchies in the Gulf. He created an Oman Friendship Committee to tour the Gulf states to assess the attitude of his Gulf neighbours. Under the chairmanship of the Minister for Education, Shaikh Sa'ud al-Khalili (from a well known Imamate family), the Oman Friendship Committee visited Riyadh in January 1971 (Kechichian 1995: 71). This paved the way for Qabus's state visit to Saudi Arabia in December 1971 where he met with King Faisal; both heads of state shared an antipathy towards the regime in South Yemen and its foreign policy. Saudi support for the Imam Ghalib and the Oman Revolutionary Army was toned down and traditional suspicions lessened: boundary issues were discussed and the Buraimi oasis territorial issue was dealt with on an interim basis in 1974 (Joffé 1994: 91). Oman started to receive considerable financial aid from Saudi Arabia - between 1972 and 1975 Oman received $150 million from the Saudis (Kechichian 1995: 73). Also significant in this regard was the connection with Shaikh Zaid of Abu Dhabi. Zaid was the first foreign head of state to visit Oman after Qabus became Sultan and he pledged his support. A further visit by Zaid took place in 1972 with Qabus going to Abu Dhabi in 1973; in this year Abu Dhabi granted Muscat a total of $200 million.

The beginning of such contacts with his Gulf neighbours helped to clear the way for Oman's membership of international organisations. In the UN the 'Question of Oman' which had been debated annually by the 4th Committee since the 1960s was shelved in autumn 1970 in a resolution which recommended reconsideration of the question of Oman's independence after a year (Skeet 1992: 57). The Arab delegations did not want to commit themselves before the matter was considered by the Arab League; in September 1971 the League accepted Oman as its seventeenth member - the PDRY was opposed but Saudi Arabia's change of position due to meetings between the Sultan and the Imam carried the day. On 4 October 1971 the Security Council unanimously recommended that Oman be admitted to UN membership and Oman was officially admitted on 7 October. Voting was 117 in favour, one against (PDRY) and two abstentions (Cuba and Saudi Arabia) (Skeet 1992: 58). The question of Oman at the UN had finally been resolved.

The changes in Oman after the 1970 coup: an Omani renaissance?

The sudden rush for modernisation that occurred in the decade after the 1970 coup produced change that was extensive and dramatic. B.R. Pridham (1986) has noted that these changes led to a number of published accounts heralding the 'rebirth' of Oman and identifying the accession of Qabus as a distinct break with the past.[32] These accounts he comments, formed a new 'conventional wisdom'. Pridham emphasises the similarities between the two regimes in giving a partial justification of Sa'id's rule. The key to understanding the changes in Oman in the decade after the coup is an appreciation of the political context of the Qabus regime. Qabus came to power with the help of outside forces - specifically Sandhurst classmates - and remained an absolute monarch surrounded by British and US advisers. At this point there were none of the consultative councils which were to appear later.[33] He was reluctant to widen participation in the decision making process (in 1985 he was to abrogate experimental elected rural councils) and seemed fearful of 'his' populace - generally the first government building constructed in a town in the interior was a police station. For the time being the Qabus regime was accepted; this domestic stability was largely dependent on economic conditions. However, if these had deteriorated, for example, with a severe collapse of the oil market, there seemed potential for considerable unrest. The many ethnic divisions and long term acceptability of the Al-Sa'id regime to Ibadhi and tribal leaders could then come to the fore. Furthermore, there did not exist a clear successor to Qabus. If he had been killed or suddenly incapacitated it could have precipitated power struggles both within the ruling family and the country as a whole. Many of these points became increasingly less than hypothetical in the 1980s and 1990s and are discussed in chapter six.

The end of British informal empire in Oman

In the chapters so far we have examined the involvement of the West, principally Britain, and the impact on Omani society from 1920 to 1977. This involvement was predicated on the strategic interests that accrued as a result of wider strategic developments affecting the Arabian peninsula. The Western interest in Oman changed from the British concern for the security frontier of the Raj in India through the gradual withdrawal of the British to an increasing American interest in the country. The British imperial withdrawal from the Gulf officially took place in 1971 but as we have seen Britain's informal empire remained in the Gulf area: the British maintained RAF bases in Oman until 1977. The end of British informal empire in Oman started with the ousting of Said and the withdrawal from RAF Salalah and Masirah represents its final termination (Halliday 1988: 97). Unlike formal empire whose beginning and end can be easily identified with proclamations of annexation and imperial withdrawal, the onset of informal empire and its passing is, by definition, more gradual, indirect and unacknowledged. It can, perhaps, be likened to the process of ageing: at the time it is difficult to see it but you know it's happened looking back.[34] If we want to find a ceremony and a point in time to take as the end of British informal empire in Oman the lowering of the Union Jack at RAF Salalah and Masirah is as good as any. From this point on relations between Oman and Britain and the United States were the politics of influence in a system of international inequality between states. The development of Western and particularly American strategic interests in the contemporary Omani state is the subject of the next chapter.

CHAPTER SIX:
Western strategic interests in the contemporary Omani state

This chapter is concerned with the development of Western strategic interests in Oman since 1978 and the integration of the Omani *rentier* state in the international capitalist state system. In contrast to the nature of Western influence in the British 'informal empire' in Muscat and Oman which has been examined in the previous chapters, Western relations with the Sultanate in this period can best be characterised as being conducted in an in international system of inequality between states.

6.1.1: The international context 1978 -1989
The developments in the wider context of international relations and policy that were to be the most significant for the development of Western strategic interests in Oman in this period were the Iranian revolution and the events in the 'arc of crisis': the resulting Carter Doctrine, the Reagan Doctrine, the unfolding of the Iran-Iraq War, and the end of the Cold War.

The Iranian Revolution, the 'Arc of Crisis' and the Carter Doctrine
By the middle of 1978 it became clear that the regime of Muhammed Reza Shah was in deep trouble. When the Shah left, never to return, the stage was set for the return of Ayatollah Khomeini and the eventual creation of the Islamic Republic of Iran. The Iranian revolution meant the crumbling of the "Twin Pillar" policy and coupled with the Soviet intervention in Afghanistan it was perceived as a major setback for US policy in the region. The Persian Gulf, with the Straits of Hormuz as its 'chokepoint,' came to be seen as being in the centre of an "Arc of Crisis" extending from Afghanistan through the Gulf and

South Yemen into the Horn of Africa in which US interests were threatened by a Soviet willingness to exploit opportunities to increase their influence.[1] On 23 January 1980 President Carter, as part of his State of the Union Address enunciated, much to the surprise of the Gulf States who had not been informed of it, the Carter Doctrine:

> An attempt by any outside force to gain control of the Persian Gulf region will be regarded as a an assault on the vital interests of the USA, and such an assault will be repelled by any means necessary, including military force. (quoted in Skeet 1992: 83)

Pentagon military planners had been developing the concept of a Rapid Deployment Force on paper since the late 1970s - the Carter Doctrine gave further impetus to turn it from a paper-pushing exercise into a practical proposition (see Acharya 1989 and Stork 1980: 3-4). Funds for the RDF were budgeted, facilities at Diego Garcia further improved and negotiations for access facilities stepped up. The US naval presence in the Indian Ocean rose to around 25 ships, including two aircraft carriers and 150 planes. The situation in the Gulf in 1980 was assessed by the US analyst, Gary Sick, thus:

> Not only was the US military presence [in the Gulf] at its highest level in history but there was also an underlying conviction that this region represented a major strategic zone of vital interests, demanding both sustained attention at the highest levels of US policy-making and direct US engagement in support of specifically US interests. That was without precedent. (quoted in Skeet 1992: 84)

The Department of Defense, quoted in the New York Times, made this clear to anyone who had doubts: 'Our principal objectives are to assure continued access to Persian Gulf oil and to prevent the Soviets from acquiring political of military control directly or through proxies' (quoted in Skeet 1992: 84).

The Reagan Doctrine

Ronald Reagan, who took over the Presidency of the United States from Jimmy Carter in January 1981 doubled expenditure on the RDJTF and, on 1 January 1983 reconstituted it as the US Central

Command. He assumed, and spoke of but did not define, a 'strategic consensus' in the area. It was undefinable since the Gulf Co-operation Council's defence policy was formally based on non-alignment. However, the military assumption behind 'strategic consensus' was that access ought to mean access for land as well as naval forces In the words of Deputy Secretary of Defense, Frank Carlucci:

> The fact is that for the most effective deterrent we need both sea based and land based forces and once our determination becomes clear to our friends and allies in the Middle East, they will become more forthcoming on the kinds of access we need. (quoted in Skeet 1992: 84)

This expansion of base infrastructure in sensitive parts of the world such as the Persian Gulf was one of the essential components of what became known as the Reagan Doctrine; a further significant aspect was the regular exercises by US armed forces in pro-Western Third World states situated close to states deemed hostile to the West (Halliday 1987b: 30).

The Iran-Iraq War

In September 1980 Iraq invaded Iran leading to the start of the longest war since World War Two (Chubin and Tripp 1988: 1). The war galvanised the Gulf monarchical states of Saudi Arabia, Kuwait, Bahrain Qatar, UAE and Oman into the creation of the Gulf Cooperation Council (GCC) in February 1981 (Peterson 1986: 213-218). Initial Iraqi advances had turned by 1982 into an Iranian offensive that threatened to break through the stalemate and overwhelm Iraq (and it was feared Kuwait, Saudi Arabia, indeed the whole Middle East) with larger reserves of manpower (Peterson 1986: 131). In this situation Iraqi strategy was to raise the cost of the war to Iran, elicit support from Arab states and to draw in superpower involvement, a strategy in which it was largely successful (Yapp 1996: 427). Iraqi attacks on Iranian oil installations led to Iranian retaliation against Iraq and those Arab states supporting Iraq financially and militarily and an Iranian threat to close the Straits of Hormuz . US military officials were concerned about the implications of an Iranian breakthrough in this war (Halliday 1987: 31). In addition to helping to arm Iraq the US, to be specific the CIA, established a secret intelligence link with Baghdad through which it shared information gathered from spy satellites and US-manned AWACs flying out of Riyadh (Timmerman 1986: 314). The US sought to publicly persuade Saudi Arabia and the UAE to allow it to station USAF fighters in GCC airfields (Peterson 1986: 132). The 'tanker war' which started in Spring 1984 eventually led in May 1987 to the US agreement to escort Kuwaiti tankers under the American flag in order to counter the Soviet Union's initial offer to Kuwait. This was an operation in which US warships were brought into action against Iranian craft. In 1988, with Iraq utilizing its superior airforce and stock of chemical weapons, the impetus of the war turned once again against Iran and in July Ayatollah Khomeini accepted UN resolution 598 and the resulting 'draw'.

The Second Cold War and its End
Developments in the Persian Gulf region contributed to and were placed in the context of the deterioration in US-USSR relations which marked the 'Second Cold War' (see Halliday 1986). The Americans received the strongest backing for their policies from the Conservative government of Margaret Thatcher elected in May 1979. However with the advent of the Gorbachov era in the mid-1980s condemnation of the 'evil empire' gave way to fireside chats with the 'man we can do business with.' The final collapse of communism in Eastern Europe in 1989 and the end of the USSR's rivalry and confrontation with the West marked the end of the Cold War.[2] Soviet troops withdrew from Afghanistan in 1989.

6.1.2: Western strategic interests in Oman 1978- 1989
How did these developments in the wider international picture affect British and American strategic interests in Oman? Broadly, it greatly increased the strategic importance of Oman to the West. With the fall of the Shah and the establishment of the Islamic Republic of Iran hostile to Western influence in the area, the fact that the shipping lanes through the Straits of Hormuz ran through Omani territorial waters suddenly obtained immense significance. Furthermore Oman was willing to allow the US access to its military facilities and openly took a pro-Western policy stance in a number of areas.[3] Britain retained considerable influence in the Sultanate.

The Straits of Hormuz

The fall of the Shah was a bitter blow to American plans for Gulf security - it denoted the crumbling of the 'Twin Pillars policy' which in military terms had in effect always relied solely on the Shah of Iran as witnessed by his contribution to the crushing of the Dhofar rebellion. An important aspect to this role was the 'policing' of the Straits of Hormuz. The Straits of Hormuz are 24 miles wide at their narrowest point and Oman and Iran both claim 12 mile territorial waters overlapping at this point. Most significantly the shipping lanes through the Straits of Hormuz ran in Omani territorial waters due to its sovereignty over the enclave of the Musandam Peninsula. At the time over 60% of Western Europe and 80% of Japan's oil supplies passed through the Straits of Hormuz making it one of the world's most strategically important waterways (Graz 1982: 49). With the founding of the Islamic Republic of Iran, hostile to Western influence in the area, Oman's strategic position with its territorial control of the Straits of Hormuz was highlighted and the strategic importance of the Sultanate to the West further increased.[4] In 1981 an American Staff Study Mission on US Security Interests in the Persian Gulf reported to the House Committee on Foreign Affairs that the Omani navy though 'small, ageing and slow' was 'doing a valuable and effective job of patrolling the shipping lanes in the strait' (quoted in Graz 1982: 184).[5] However the same report noted that: 'Responsibility for keeping open the Strait of Hormuz in the event of a serious regional conflict ultimately must be with the United States and the West.'

The 1980 US-Omani Agreement

In order to implement the Carter Doctrine the United States needed access to military bases in close proximity to the Persian Gulf to establish a secure location from which to conduct military operations. Bahrain had logistical disadvantages and Saudi Arabia would have political difficulties in openly allowing a US military presence. Facilities at the nominally British territory of Diego Garcia were improved but were viewed as inadequate as a forward staging area due to its distance from the Gulf (Rigsbee 1990: 72). A Pentagon official confided:

> We need to get much closer [than Israel] in the event of any actual military contingency [in the Gulf] and that's why we're going for forward basing in Oman. (quoted in Stork 1982: 12)

Oman offered a suitable point of access of the type the US was looking for. Negotiations for access to Omani facilities were intensified. By February 1980 the principal of an access agreement had been agreed: Foreign Minister Qais Al-Zawawi stated that Oman was interested in granting the US use of port and airport facilities under certain conditions although he maintained Oman would never allow foreign bases on it soil (Kechichian 1995: 147). The terms of the agreement were defined during a visit to Muscat in April 1980 by Reginald Bartholomew, Director of the Bureau of Political and Military Affairs and it was officially signed 4th June 1980 through an exchange of letters between US Ambassador Marshall Wiley and the Deputy Prime Minister for External Affairs, Qais Zawawi.[6]

US upgrading of military facilities in Oman

The details of the agreement have not been published but the main elements concerning the upgrading of airports, pre-positioning of supplies and access to port facilities on a prior approval basis are widely known (Kechichian 1995: 147; Rigsbee 1990: 76). The US gained contingent use and access to Omani air bases at Thumrait, Masirah Island, Sib and Khasab and naval bases at Salalah and Matrah (Joyce 1995: 115). In return the US undertook to pay for the modernisation and upgrading of the facilities and gave Oman a formal undertaking of support in the event of aggression against the country. The construction programme starting in fiscal year 1981 cost the United States $260.7 million 1981-1987.

US Military Construction in Oman 1981-1987 ($ millions)

1981	1982	1983	1984	1985	1986	1987	Total
85.5	80.7	60.4	28.6	2.3	0.0	3.2	260.7

Source: US Department of Defense. Fact Sheet: MILCON Program, Sultanate of Oman, Unclassified Pentagon Document, 9 January 1985. (Rigsbee 1990: 79)

Most of the construction was undertaken by the US Corp of Engineers although they wore civilian clothing to reduce the 'visibility' of the US military presence (Rigsbee 1990: 78). Three of the bases, Masirah, Khassab and Thumrait were chosen for development due to their remoteness from centres of population. Between 1981 and 1987 a total of $144.3 million was spent on upgrading Masirah allowing year-round use even in the monsoon season and making it an excellent centre for forward operations in a crisis. Khasab's location on the Straits of Hormuz seemed ideal for the rapid deployment force; however difficult communications made upgrading prohibitively expensive: work was only started in 1981 when $3.5 million was spent at which point no more money was spent. Thumrait was regarded as another possible base for rapid deployment operations as its isolation in the interior of Dhofar was attractive. Total military construction costs 1981-87 were $54.6 million designed to support the introduction of US Air Force Personnel (Rigsbee 1990: 82). Sib airport had the advantage of being capable of taking B52 bombers and as an existing international airport required less expenditure - between 1982 and 1985 $57.6 million was spent on upgrading. However it was feared that a large influx of foreign military personnel here could have negative consequences for the Qabus regime as it is located near the main centre of Omani population (Rigsbee 1990: 81).

US Foreign Military Sales (FMS) Program

A further aspect of the enhanced US-Omani security relationship which the agreement signified was the provision of military aid in the form of the Foreign Military Sales credit program. Under this program loans or even grants are made to foreign countries for the purchase of US military equipment and expertise. This started in the late 1970s but with the regional crisis of 1979 the amounts involved leapt upwards in 1980. Between 1977-1987 Oman received a total of $200.1 in FMS credits from the United States.

Foreign Military Sales Credits to Oman ($ millions)1977-1987

1977	1978	1979	1980	1981	1982	1983	1984	1985	1986	1987
.913	0.0	.059	25	25	30	30	40	40	9.14	0.0

Source: US Department of Defense, Office of Military Cooperation. Muscat: Briefing Book. Washington, D.C., Office of Military Cooperation, Jan.1988 (see Rigsbee 1990: 74-75)

In 1980 officials had to make a case before a Congressional Subcommittee that Oman, while its per capita income of $4000 placed it outside the category of a developing country, had other characteristics that allowed its classification as such and thus eligible for assistance on a grant basis under the Foreign Assistance Act of 1961 (see Graz 1982: 191-194). The sudden provision of extra credit in 1980 enabled the US to increase its military assistance and training and up its arms sales program. Six M60 tanks and an unknown number of TOW and Sidewinder missiles for Oman's Jaguar aircraft were sold in that year (Kechichian 1995: 150). Additionally, commencing in 1981 US training advisory field teams gave support to Omanis under the Defense Department's International Military Education Training Program (Rigsbee 1990: 83-85). However, the extent of the program remained relatively small as Britain pushed hard to remain the primary provider of training to Omani military personnel as was the case in terms of the supply of arms. The Americans were resigned to their secondary role in this regard although they believed that with the 'Omanisation' of the Sultanate's armed forces that US arms sales and training would increase (Kechichian 1995: 150).

Benefits for the US from the 1980 agreement

In logistic terms the agreement greatly strengthened US military capability in the Indian Ocean where the US was conducting a sea surveillance programme over Soviet ships. At the time the official public stance was that the facilities would be available in the event of a Soviet attack on the region but unclear as to the position in the event of an intra-Arab conflict in which American interests were threatened.[7] B52 bombers flown out of Guam could have landed at Masirah especially as the British government had refused them permission to land at Diego Garcia (Kechichian 1995: 149). The agreement allowed the US to stockpile supplies at three large depots as well as to use Masirah Island for flights bringing in equipment, food and supplies for the US fleet in and around the Persian Gulf (Kechichian 1995: 148). In short, the US had the opportunity to establish facilities fully compatible with US requirements for rapid deployment and to pre-position supplies ready for incoming 'over the horizon' forces from Diego Garcia in the event of a crisis (Pool 1994: 276; Cordesman 1984: 619).

The agreement was not a 'base accord' in the strict sense in that Washington had to officially provide advance notice of the landing and mooring of vessels entering the Sultanate. According to Sultan Qabus the US was to be granted access to Omani facilities only at the request of the Omani government or a majority of GCC states and in a case where a threat to Oman could not be repulsed alone (Kechichian 1995: 148). However, even before the official signing of the agreement the US used facilities at Masirah Island in April 1980 without prior warning or request for the ill-fated rescue attempt of US hostages in Iran (Skeet 1992: 88). This raises the question as to what degree of control the Omanis actually had over the base.

Benefits of the 1980 agreement for the Omani regime
The Omani motives for the agreement were varied (Kechichian 1995: 148). Essentially, Sultan Qabus saw his opportunity to extract from the US a security commitment in the context of uncertainty engendered by the regional crisis of 1979 and also to obtain US assistance in the modernisation of Omani military facilities - assistance which had not been forthcoming from the GCC.[8] Oman was the only Arab state that subscribed to the US view that Soviet Union and its allies were the main threat to the security of the region (Pool 1994: 276; Graz 1982: 175). While the main details of the agreement are well-known there is less public information about the side-letter to the agreement in which there is a formal undertaking by the US to support Oman in the event of aggression against the Sultanate.[9] Excluding President Truman's letter to Ibn Sa'ud this was the only case of such an agreement between the US and an Arab country until after the Kuwait War of 1991.

From the Omani perspective the agreement provided more than support for his regime. Specifically, it provided a 'low visibility' presence which reduced the political costs. The agreement stated that there were to be no American ground troops stationed in Oman and none in rotation through the Sultanate. It formally excluded an area of territory being used as a rest and recreation area. Muscat was concerned to keep the US presence as low profile as possible. Accordingly, military personnel were to wear civilian dress and little publicity was to be given to US military activities. Furthermore, US military exercises were to be staged away from populated areas (Kechichian 1995: 148).

As part of the negotiations the US also signed an agreement in August 1980 to set up a Joint Commission on Economic and Technical Cooperation and made further agreements to give assistance in fisheries development, water conservation projects and training of Omanis in the US. However, by the end of 1980 the Omanis were still awaiting the arrival of a team from the US Army Corps of Engineers promised for September to assess potential projects. The delay, due to Congressional constraints on expenditure, helped reinforce the Omani perception that the US did not live up to its security commitments.

Yearly, $5 million of Economic Support Funds appropriations financed the operations of the Commission, feasibility and design studies, technical assistance and training. In 1983 Nicholas Veliotis, Assistant Secretary of State confirmed to the Senate Foreign Relations Committee that a $10 million loan program had up to that point concentrated on water resources and in the following fiscal year 1984 would be focused on school construction (Skeet 1992: 85). What was the significance of this economic aid? Ian Skeet notes that, whilst no comparable process of scrutiny of foreign policy exists in Oman by which to assess official comment 'it seems incontrovertible...that Sultan Qabus saw that it was in his best interests to conclude an agreement with the US. The economic element was useful but only secondary. It was the military content that was important' (Skeet 1992: 88).

The development of the US-Omani relationship in the 1980's
With the advent of the Reagan administration the politico-military relationship was developed further. Despite public pronouncements, Oman encouraged the building and improvement of airfields as well as the pre-positioning of arms, equipment and fuel for use by USCENTCOM forces. Senior Omani officials asserted that whilst Muscat could not agree to the establishment of outright bases they would cooperate with the Western allies in order to meet their strategic responsibilities (Kechichian 1995: 151). Visits of high level US officials took place including former Secretary of State, Henry Kissinger, Chairman of the Senate Armed Forces Committee, John Tower and former President, Gerald Ford all of whom met with Sultan Qabus and Foreign Minister Al-Zawawi. A US General P.X. Kelly, Commander of the Rapid Deployment Force visited Muscat to check on logistical procedures. In January

1982 Senator Charles Percy, Chairman of the Senate Foreign Relations Committee spent four days in the Sultanate during which he discussed bilateral relations with Sultan Qabus. The following month Defense Secretary Caspar Weinberger visited the country. According to Omani sources he sought to 'acquaint himself with the capability of the Omani armed forces, the efficiency of the Omani soldier and his comprehension of the latest weapons and advanced equipment' (Kechichian 1995: 152).

Political links were further enhanced in 1983 after Sultan Qabus visited the United States at the invitation of Ronald Reagan and endowed a National Symphony chair for narrative music in honour of Nancy Reagan. He also expressed his confidence that the United States would indeed come to the assistance of the GCC states if requested to see off an enemy (Kechichian 1995: 152). In June 1983 Qabus affirmed that Oman still needed the back-up of the Access Agreement with the Americans despite the creation of a separate GCC Rapid Deployment Force. In December 1983 he conveyed his views on the Israeli-Palestinian situation to the President via Reagan's personal envoy, Donald Rumsfeld, who also held much noticed talks with Major General 'Ali Majid Al-Ma'mari. This facilitated the visit to Muscat in March 1985 of Lieutenant General Robert Kingston, commander of USCENTCOM and Major General David Watts, Director of Logistics and Security Assistance for USCENTCOM. They served notice that Washington had nearly completed building and modernising sites in Oman for use by their force in the event of a crisis. These upgraded facilities would support tactical airlift operations, MAC (Military Airlift Command) operations, and pre-positioning of Air Force war readiness material assets. A senior military official asserted that 'Oman had become what we had hoped Egypt might be,' while a State Department official maintained that 'we could never secure the kinds of access in Saudi Arabia that we have negotiated in Oman' (see Kechichian 1995: 154). One aspect of this access was the opportunity to conduct invaluable training exercises to practise rapid deployment.

US-Omani Military Exercises

The 1980 Agreement had laid the foundations for military to military contacts in which joint exercises were the main focus. They were of great value in testing the effectiveness of the upgrading work and due to censorship of the media in Oman could take place without generating publicity in Oman (Rigsbee 1990: 86). The Saudis reportedly offered Oman $2 billion in development aid to reduce its military cooperation with the US and to cancel the Operation Bright Star 1 Exercise.

The first exercise 'Operation Accurate Test' took place in February 1981; designed to test communications equipment for the RDJTF in the environmental conditions of the Persian Gulf it was deemed a success. In December 1981 Bright Star involved 960 marines practising amphibious landing on the Dhofari coast Operation to demonstrate American intentions to help safe-guard the security of the oil-producing states of the Gulf in an exercise in which a total of 6000 Army, Marine, Air Force and Navy Personnel took part. The duration of the exercise was shortened to forestall Oman's Gulf partners objections and as a result of the concerns of British advisers fearing a loss of influence (Kechichian 1995: 151). Oman also participated in the annual US exercise in South West Asia code-named 'Jade Tiger' and 'Operation Bright Star 2' exercise which took place in August 1985. However, the US was involved in more than just exercises during this period.

US military deployment

In the 1980s facilities in Oman were used by the US in the prosecution of a number of military operations, primarily in relation to the Iran-Iraq war. In February 1981 a small contingent of US Army and Air Force Personnel set up a temporary communications centre in the Sultanate to monitor airborne surveillance of the Straits (Kechichian 1995: 150). One writer reports that early in the Iran- Iraq War the US received intelligence reports that Iraqi helicopters were preparing to commandeer Omani and Saudi Arabian facilities to launch attacks on Iranian bases across the Gulf as well as Iranian installations on three Gulf islands. The Saudis signalled to Washington that they expected prompt military help from the US (see Bradley 1982: 106). In February 1984 the Supreme Defense Council in Tehran allegedly decided to occupy and fortify Goat Island. The commander of the Omani army, a British general let it be known that Oman could probably resist a determined Iranian invasion for less than 48 hours. The US promptly reaffirmed the Carter doctrine and no attack or invasion took place (Cooley 1991: 132).

In the 1980s US naval P-3 surveillance aircraft 'transited' at Masirah Island and also occasionally at Sib, allowing them to maintain surveillance over the Gulf of Oman area, including Iranian naval vessels, resulting regularly in Iranian protests to Oman (Eilts 1988: 27). In October 1986 a USCENTCOM briefing team visited Muscat and reviewed regional military threats and capabilities. At this point the Iran-Contra link was surfacing in public (Halliday 1987: 6). The Persian Gulf area was just as vital an arena for the application of the Reagan Doctrine: Americans claimed that Oman was an invaluable staging area for the supply of the CIA supported *mohaddejin* in Afghanistan (Kechichian 1995: 154). In April 1987 Vice President Bush returned to discuss regional developments and Gulf security. Following talks in June 1987 between the Chairman of the Joint Chiefs of Staff, Admiral William Crowe, and Senators John Glenn and John Warner, Oman granted US overflight rights for vital operations during the Kuwaiti tanker reflagging operation. In April 1988 US naval aviators launched attacks on targets in the Straits of Hormuz. In June 1988, USCENTCOM Commander General George Crist and US Assistant Secretary of State, Richard Murphy visited Oman again to discuss bilateral military relations. In November 1989 the new US CENTCOM Commander General Norman Schwarzkopf met with the Commander of Oman's Land Forces, Major General Khamis bin Hamid Al-Kalbani and exchanged views on the Sultanate's defence posture (Kechichian 1995: 156-157).

The 1985 renewal of the agreement

The 1980 Access Agreement had stipulated a five-yearly review the negotiations for which proved more difficult than expected and generated considerable ill-feeling (Eilts 1988: 34). Essentially, the Omani side sought to strengthen the conditions of access (the secret use of Masirah for the attempted rescue of US hostages in Iran was a sore point) whilst the US military negotiating team took the line that as the US had paid for the upgrading of the facilities they should have unconditional access to them (Skeet 1992: 88). Accordingly, US Department of Defense lawyers sought to obtain 'status of forces' provisions which in the words of a former American diplomat 'would have made these Omani facilities virtually American bases' (Eilts 1988: 33). Despite the difficulties, sufficient coincidence of interest between the countries existed so that the agreement was eventually renewed with US personnel perquisites at Omani military sites curtailed and advance Omani approval conditions for American usage of facilities tightened. Final agreement on conditions for pre-positioning US military supplies was also reached (Kechichian 1995: 154).

In the mid-1980s strains in the Omani-American relationship focused around three issues relating to the negotiations. The first, as mentioned above, was the issue of US access without Omani permission. The second was over publicity. Various reports in the American media highlighted the involvement in Oman of ex-CIA officials; furthermore the Pentagon was wont to give publicity to joint US-Omani military manoeuvres.[10] Thirdly, there were considerable tensions over the presence of the British officer, General Watts - the Omani Chief of Staff - at the head of the Omani negotiating team. The American military assumed that the British government was 'pulling the strings' behind the scenes (Skeet 1992: 89). This raises the question: what was the nature of the British-Omani relationship in the 1980s - what had changed and what had remained?

Britain's relationship with the Sultanate in the 1980s

The British withdrawal from Masirah Island in 1977 marked the abandonment of Britain's commitment to act as the 'ultimate guarantor' of the security of the Qabus regime against external attack. As has been seen developments at the turn of the decade led the US to assume this role. The Americans was willing to do so and the Omanis, aware of the limits to Britain's resources, were keen to enlist US guarantees of support and assistance in the modernisation of its military infrastructure. However, Britain's long-standing and wide-ranging relationship with Oman meant that it maintained a presence and still exerted influence in a number of ways. These can be identified as the broad commercial, cultural, and educational contacts, the role of British advisers to the Sultan and the command structure of the Omani armed forces, police and intelligence service and government ministries. These all reflected the long standing British-Omani politico/military relationship which can be clearly identified by focusing on joint training exercises and arms sales in the 1980s. In many of these areas the British presence in the 1980s could be contrasted with a negligible US role.

Oman was an extremely lucrative market for Britain. A quarter of Oman's imports came from the UK - nearly four times the amount from the US. Conversely, the UK bought only one per cent of the Sultanate's exports, in contrast with six per cent for the US. Britain therefore derived considerable benefit to its balance of payments from Oman resulting from the $1 billion in annual export earnings (Anthony 1987: 188). In contrast, the US did not penetrate deep into the Omani market except in areas connected with the Defense and Access Agreement (Skeet 1992: 89). These well-established commercial connections were reflected in the tendency of wealthy Omanis to send their children to schools in England and also to own property there. This educational link also held in the military sphere: training abroad for the Omani armed forces took place primarily in Britain (Anthony 1987: 191).

This was hardly surprising, reflecting as it does Britain's long involvement with the Sultanate. Oman's armed forces have been described as a 'miniature version' of the British army, indicating their build up by Britain in the decades since the 1950's. Britain sold arms and provided the basic structure of technical, personnel, training and staff appointments - officers who were seconded from the British army or contracted directly to the Sultan's Armed Forces (Skeet 1992: 99). In 1980, following visits by Foreign Secretary, Douglas Hurd and Defence Minister, John Nott, additional British officers were transferred to serve with the Omani armed forces. In 1981 Prime Minister Margaret Thatcher and Sultan Qabus agreed to appoint General Sir Timothy Creasy, the former commander of British Land Forces, as Chief -of-Staff of the Omani Armed Forces for a two year period. In 1982 out of a total number of Omani Air Force officers of 350, 200 were British. Similarly, in the army there were 32 officers seconded and 130 British 'contract officers'[11] (Cordesman 1984: 611). Until 1987 the Chief of Staff was British, the last one being Lieutenant General John Watts.[12]

In 1982 an Omani became commander of the police; however it remained dominated by expatriate officers as did the secret police, the Oman Research Bureau (Allen 1984: 7-8). In the 1980s the head of the Omani foreign intelligence department was an ex-M16 officer Reginald Temple, appointed on his retirement from the British intelligence services in 1979 (Block 1983: 259). An interesting case of British influence in the Omani government ministries is that documented by Fred Halliday (1987a: 196). It concerns the activities of a certain Tony Ashworth who, in the early 1980s, continued to work in the Omani Ministry of Information where he had been 'seconded' in 1974. Halliday argues that there was no case in which it was 'clearer how the British in Oman used their Arabian client for ventriloquy and deception.' Another case was that of the British Corporation, AirServices, the major consultant to the Omani Ministry of Defence, a link which both reflected, and was strengthened by, the order of British Aerospace Tornado jets in 1985 (Allen 1987: 118).

A further source of perceived influence were the British advisers to Sultan Qabus. Hermann F. Eilts, a former US ambassador to Saudi Arabia, put it like this:

> Oman does receive some criticism from its fellow GCC states for its continued heavy dependence on the British. The sultan is surrounded by British advisers who, presumably with his concurrence, control all access to him, especially during the six months of the year that he spends in Salala. To be sure, they are there entirely at the sultan's pleasure, yet their influence, real or imagined, projects an image of British dependency. (Eilts 1988: 32)

Ian Skeet writing at the beginning of the 1990s maintained that this relationship with the British was unlikely to change at least whilst Qabus remained in power:

> His personal experience of Britain and the British has given him confidence in their advice and judgement. This has occurred at many different levels, from the friendships that he has with members of the Royal Family, the prime minister and ministers, through to the military, diplomats, bankers and ordinary professional people. This has given Britain a preferred position amongst foreign countries, a position which is reflected by large numbers of Omanis from a broad spectrum of experience and activity who have personal links with Britain. (1992: 99)

A further source of British influence certainly applicable to Qabus is that made by John Duke Anthony:

British foreign affairs practitioners in general, and 'old British Arabian hands' in particular, unlike their counterparts on the US side, continue to derive subtle influence due to the fact that more than a few of their number were intimately involved in the accession to power of a majority of the incumbent GCC heads of state. (1987: 190)

Essentially, all the above points have to be placed in the context of Oman's historical political and military relationship with Britain as examined in earlier chapters. In the 1980's these two aspects were expressed in the sale of arms to Oman and in the conduct of joint military exercises and training in Oman.

Britain remained Oman's principal supplier of arms in the 1980s.[13] These arms sales were facilitated by the provision of export credit, as shown below.

UK Export Credits for Arms Sales to Oman 1980-1989 (Total: 486 million pounds)
(£ million and percentage of total cover each year)

1980/81	1981/82	1982/83	1983/84	1984/85	1985/86	1986/87	1987/88	1988/89
£ %	£ %	£ %	£ %	£ %	£ %	£ %	£ %	£ %
305 100	62 94	61 15	0 -	4 10	17 22	37 56	0 -	0 -

Source: World Development Movement, *Gunrunners Gold* (1995:22).

This provision of export credit was a political decision in which large tranches of export credits were provided for arms sales which were perceived as cementing the British-Omani strategic relationship. They often generated substantial disagreement within the British government from the Treasury which came into conflict with Ministers, including Prime Minister Thatcher, and Ministry of Defence officials who were enthusiastic about large arms sales. An example of this was the battle over the sale of patrol boats. Robin Fellgate, a former senior Treasury official dealing with defence, argued at the time that this sale 'would have entailed increasing ECGD's exposure to the Omani market in a manner to which Treasury Ministers were opposed.' Ultimately these considerations were overruled from the top and export credits extended, 'partly for economic reasons and jobs in a particular area of Britain, but I think at least as much for wider political reasons, the bilateral relationship with what, after all, was an ally country' (World Development Movement 1995: 21).

British arms sales to Oman developed throughout the 1980s within this context of the politico-military relationship. In 1980 Oman placed an order at a cost estimated at over $140 million with British Aerospace for 12 Jaguar strike aircraft (effectively doubling its fleet of Jaguars) as well as Rapier Blindfire missiles. In November of the same year an agreement was signed to allow for the refuelling of Royal Navy ships at Mina Qabus.

British arms sales developed throughout the 1980s within this context of the political-military relationship. In 1980 Oman placed an order at a cost estimated at over $140 million with British Aerospace for 12 Jaguar Strike Aircraft (effectively doubling its fleet of Jaguars) as well as Rapier Blindfire Missiles. In November of the same year an agreement was signed to allow for the refuelling of Royal Navy Ships at Mina Qabus (Kechichian 1995: 133). Britain still had the edge on its Western competitors in Omani defence procurement; an example was the contract for armoured vehicles for the army. French and British bids were alike technically and on price: the contract went to the British firm partly due to the Sultan's conviction that it was more efficient to buy mostly from one source and also for reasons of sentiment accruing from the Dhofar campaign. A British officer holding senior rank in the SAF commented, 'Blood, sweat and tears we shed together in those days. That created an emotional bond that is difficult to break.'[14] Following the visit of Defence Secretary, Michael Heseltine to Muscat in October 1985 the first export order for Tornado air defence variant aircraft was placed by Oman at a cost of $350 million.[15] This deal indicated the continuing involvement of Britain with Oman in the military sphere which was also reflected in manoeuvres and deployment.

British manoeuvres and deployment in the 1980s
The SAS were regularly present in the Sultanate where they trained the Sultan's Special Force[16] and conducted their own exercises. In 1981 a fifty strong company of SAS soldiers, in Oman on training, were sent to Salalah by 'Omani' intelligence to put down a rebellion which turned out to be non-existent.

The reporter for the Times explained that the SAS was not even supposed to be in Oman that year, indicating that the force was there on a regular basis (Block 1983: 140). The military links between Britain and Oman were exemplified in 1986 with the conduct of Operation Swift Sword.[17]

This exercise lasted from 16th November to 8th December 1986 and was the largest British deployment in the Gulf until the Kuwait crisis of 1990. It involved 4750 British serviceman as well as units from the Sultan's Armed Forces. The exercise, at a cost of 4.1 million pounds, was designed to test Britain's capacity to operate in out-of-area contingencies and to test some of the lessons of the Falklands Campaign. The scenario was that the eastern oilfields of Oman are occupied by a hostile force and Oman turns to Britain for help. Using Masirah Island as a forward base, British forces, using amphibious landing and parachute drop tactics, repulse the forces of 'Fantasia'. Also practised was the 10 hour non-stop flight to Masirah by six Tornado jets with in-flight refuelling from VC-10s and the RAF's new tanker, the Tristar. Lieutenant-General Sir Michael Gray, the on-the-spot commander of the British forces admitted that the heavy British 'infiltration' of Omani forces made Swift Sword easier than other joint exercises. Press reports at the time noted that self-interest and a web of confidential defence agreements meant that neither British or Omani government officials would rule out such a fictitious scenario from actually occurring in which British planning for rapid deployment would be put to the test. This planning had its origins in the Nott Defence Review of 1981 (before the Falklands Campaign) which called for the creation of a rapid deployment force, composed of an airborne and seaborne brigade, and similar in concept to those of France and America.

This kind of exercise facilitated the 1987 'Armilla' naval deployment to safeguard the passage of oil tankers through the Straits of Hormuz during the Iran-Iraq war. This operation was supported by RAF Nimrod maritime reconnaissance planes operating out of Seeb. British minesweepers routinely made use of Omani ports (Kechichian 1995: 133).

Anglo-American tensions: competition and cooperation
From the above it is evident that in the 1980s the Omani-British relationship remained strong and that Britain still continued to

exert considerable influence in the Sultanate. So whilst the significance of the US-Omani Access Agreement was of great importance it should not be interpreted as the 'overnight' departure of the British. The British reluctantly came to accept the US presence but pushed hard to maintain British interests in Oman, commercial and military. Accordingly, Margaret Thatcher assured President Reagan that America could rely on Britain's full support in the Gulf but at the same time opined to her compatriots that it would not be in their interests to let the Americans any further into the Sultanate (Anthony 1987: 188). For example, Hermann Eilts notes that controversy arose when some British advisers to the Sultan sought to limit US access to American-financed Omani facilities (Eilts 1988: 28). In certain US military circles this was all seen as British 'obstinacy'; this 'obstinacy' undoubtedly reflected the resentment at increased US competition in a state which, with the British withdrawal from the Gulf, represented the last major bastion of predominant British influence in the area. The outcome of this was that the 'visible' US presence in the Sultanate in terms of US military personnel and US nationals working there could, in the mid 1980s, still be characterised as 'small beer' by John Duke Anthony (1987: 187). He notes the various arguments put by both sides and the tensions it engendered. However, he then goes on to detail a substantial record of Anglo-American cooperation reflecting a mutually beneficial division of labour. Furthermore, Eilts notes that Britain is able to support the Qabus regime in areas which the Americans would find more difficult, for example, counter-insurgency and dealing with internal rebellion and dissent (Eilts 1988: 33).

The two countries cooperated to improve 'Omani' maritime surveillance capacity, integrate the new British consignment of Jaguars into US-developed facilities on Masirah and held periodic joint consultative sessions in London and elsewhere. John Duke Anthony assesses that Britain accommodated basic US security needs and interests which in turn was reciprocated. British military personnel serving with the Omani armed forces were briefed at the US Central Command headquarters. The US also arranged for tours for Omani air force officers and their British advisers of US arms manufacturers such as McDonnell-Douglas and Nyrop. Furthermore, a defence contract relating to Oman that would normally have gone to a US company was apportioned to a British one (Anthony 1986: 191).

In summary, Britain and America cooperated on issues relating to shared interests in overall Gulf security whilst competing for influence in the Sultanate. The Americans perceived that British influence would gradually decline and were happy to assign some aspects to British management such as internal security. By the same token the British could not resource such commitments as defence guarantees and were relieved to have this burden lifted from them. The Americans were also aware that some of the failure to make greater inroads into the Omani market was of their own making although various military strategists and US armament manufactures riled at the British attempts to restrict their presence in Oman and its markets. Ultimately, the Pentagon military planners were delighted to have secured such 'breakthroughs' as the access to Omani facilities.

The development of the Omani state in this period and the impact of Western strategic interests on it will now be discussed.

6.1.3: The development of the Omani economy, political system and military

The development of Western strategic interests in Oman reflected Oman's integration into the world capitalist state system. A number of points can be made concerning the consequences of Western involvement for Oman relating to the Omani economy, society and political system. The integration of Oman's oil dominated economy[18] into the world capitalist system meant that it was exposed to the fluctuations of the international oil market. Oil provided the major part of Omani finance although since 1980 it has transferred a proportion of the revenue into a State General Reserve Fund (SGRF) to offset dependence on yearly income (Skeet 1992: 103). Oman was particularly hard hit by the collapse of the oil price in 1986 and as revenue remained relatively static thereafter, the squeeze was on development expenditure. However, this was not implemented across the board. The breakdown of expenditure by ministry in Omani Five year Plans shows that Western defence of Qabus' regime had another pernicious consequence. The main growth area was the royal *diwan*, always the most difficult cost centre to control. From 1981- 1985 the *diwan* was responsible for 12 per cent of all expenditure and 13 per cent of civil recurrent expenditure. In 1988 the *diwan* was responsible for one third of development expenditure and its share of recurrent expenditure had risen to 14 per cent. In terms of combined development and recurrent expenditure the diwan had become larger than any other ministry, spending in 1988 RO140 million presumably on ever more lavish palaces and the like (Skeet 1992: 104).

In such lavish consumption the Sultan was undoubtedly supported by his British advisers and friends who benefited accordingly. One such case was the awarding of a £300 million contract in the construction of Sultan Qabus University to the British firm Cementation International which happened to employ Mark Thatcher, the Prime Minister's son, as a consultant. This followed the visit by Mrs Thatcher to Oman in 1981.[19] In 1984 a Sunday Times investigation established that Dennis Thatcher was a co-signatory to the account through which Mark Thatcher would receive his remuneration.[20] The Export Credit Guarantee Department handed over all its papers relating to the affair to the House of Commons Public Accounts Committee.[21] However, the inquiry was effectively limited by the Prime Minister's refusal to say actually what she did discuss in Oman and by limiting Mark Thatcher's exposure to the press before spiriting him off to the USA.[22] The Prime Minister saw no conflict of private and public interest and asserted she was 'batting for Britain'.

In the political sphere Qabus remained an absolute ruler and showed little enthusiasm to widen participation from his inner circle. He retained the prime ministership, and the direction of finance, foreign affairs, and defence and continued to directly administer Dhofar, Musandam and Muscat. He kept a close watch on petroleum and commercial affairs through his cabinet appointees. These areas were dominated by a group of Al-Sa'id family members, long-time business associates and expatriate advisers, together known as the Muscat Mafia. Prominent among the Mafia were Qabus's first appointees such as Thuwaini bin Shihab Al-Sa'id, Hamad bin Hamad Al Bu Sa'id and some more recently appointed officials. This latter group included Fahr bin Taimur Al-Sa'id, deputy prime minister for defence and foreign affairs; Fahd bin Mahmud Al-Sa'id, deputy prime minister for legal affairs; Qais Abd al-Munim al-Zawawi, minister of state for foreign affairs and deputy prime minster for financial affairs and his brother Omar, a personal adviser, the son of Zubair bin Ali,

Sultan Sa'id's one-time minister of justice; and Sa'id Ahmed al-Shanfari, a member of the merchant family which has most strongly supported Al-Sa'id control of Dhofar (Allen 1987: 85). Additionally, there were various 'freelance' expatriate advisors, both American and British, whom Qabus had brought in after the 1970 coup (Halliday 1987: 194). Qabus tended to isolate himself and paid no attention to those areas of government in which he had little personal interest and in this respect was like his father.

Creation of the State Consultative Council

In 1981 Qabus set up the State Consultative Council (SCC) (see Eickleman 1984, Peterson 1988 and 1984). Preparations for the SCC itself dated from 1980. The Sultan requested several ministers to discuss how broader formal consultation might take place in Oman. According to participants they considered such topics as what "democracy" might mean in the context of Oman, representation, a parliamentary versus a consultative body, and even the possibility of voting. Clearly a major decision was being considered, but the discussants were given no specific information beyond their initial mandate and no feedback.

Although Muscat officialdom takes pride in knowing of developments in the pipeline before they are officially announced, in the case of the SCC almost complete secrecy was achieved. Only senior members of the Royal Family and those sections of government involved in the drafting of the SCC and selecting the delegates had knowledge of the new developments before the event (Eickleman 1984: 55).

The concept of consultation (*shura*) with its Islamic connotations, was an integral element in the Ibadhi Imamate but the newer Sultanate, based on the Al Bu Sa'id dynasty, had never developed a tradition of consultation, let alone formal representation. The council was made up of 43 members initially but was expanded to 55 in 1983. The original SCC committee was responsible for selecting the members and sending their names to the Sultan, who accepted every nominee for all three SCC sessions. Only the SCC's president was directly chosen by the Sultan; the president always held the rank of minister because he had to have direct access to the Sultan.

Nineteen members (including the president) belonged to the government, comprising the 11 under secretaries of the social service ministries and seven other nominated officials. The

Chamber of Commerce elected 19 candidates, from which the SCC committee chose 11 members. Each of the Sultanate's seven geographic regions was represented by a varying number of members according to its population size and development needs; the number ranged from seven for the Batinah coast to two for the Musandam enclave. Despite the manner of their appointment, these 25 members officially represented all of Oman. The member of the SCC guiding committee from a particular region (or the one most familiar with that region) was responsible for choosing a list of 12 candidates, from which the whole committee selected the region's representatives. During the first session, the 44 members included 24 Ibadhis, 13 Sunnis and 7 Shi'a. Twenty two had received some modern education, with six having attended university; their average age was 47 (Peterson 1988: 103-104).

Despite all this elaborate preparation, the SCC had the most restricted national council mandate in the GCC. In part this derived from the infrequent, highly formal nature of its meetings. Only three sessions were held each year; each session lasted only three days until 1985, when the period was extended to five days or a week. As originally conceived, all meetings were held *in camera* and the council's competence restricted to economic and social matters. Because the SCC is not in session most of the year there was little scope for discussion and debate. Consequently, if a member wished to raise an issue during the 48-49 weeks the SCC was not in session, he had to submit a letter to the SCC's executive committee (composed of president and his two deputies as *ex officio* member, plus another five members elected by the council). This committee could then pass the matter on to the appropriate standing committee, which returned its recommendation to the Executive Committee, which added its own recommendation and sent it to the appropriate ministry. The committees have met much more regularly than the SCC as a whole. Eickleman quotes one SCC member as explaining that 'the committees are where our recommendations are cooked' (1984: 64). By the time issues were discussed in the full quarterly meetings, the major lines of recommendations had already been decided (Peterson 1988: 105).

The mixing of government and non-government members raised the question of conflict of interest, not only in regard to the under-secretaries but also to the president. Because the president was the head of the SCC for only two years, he had no real stake in the consultative process. Because he was a minister, both by virtue of his personal rank and by past and future positions, he was more a member of the government than a watchdog. Another area of conflict of interest arose from the tendency of some ministers to use their official positions to advance their personal business. How could a president support measures of personal accountability among officials when it might involve him and his past and future colleagues, it was asked. The representational nature of the SCC could be questioned as well, given the secretive nature of the selection of its members.

It was difficult, therefore, to determine whether the formation and activities of the SCC contributed to the legitimacy of the state. In a sense, the SCC carved out a modest niche through the petitions submitted to it by individuals and groups of citizens, who also questioned members from their region. The exclusion of such areas of government activity as defence, foreign affairs and oil from the council's competence was defended by the government on the grounds that the SCC was too new to entrust it with such sensitive matters. Beneath it all ran the knowledge that Oman, far more than its GCC neighbours, was a one-man monarchy whose authority was virtually unchallenged by the ruling family or merchant families or even the cabinet. One area in which the council could conceivably have provided a benefit was discussion over the question of succession, but this was the most sensitive area of all. Peterson commented: 'It is to the sultan's credit that he established the SCC and has pushed for its acceptance within the Omani political system, often against the reluctance of other family members and ministers' (1988: 108). Although it was outwardly a representative body the council was, in practice, very much controlled by the Sultan through the power of appointment. Calvin Allen, writing in the mid 1980's commented:

> ...[the council] has been dominated by Al Bu Sa'id loyalists, the Muscat commercial community, and traditional elites from the interior. The newly appointed president, Salim bin Nasser Al Bu Saidi, is a member of the royal family. There appears to be little desire to turn the council into an elected body, and Qabus seems very reluctant to introduce any form of democracy into the country as demonstrated by the abrogation of the rural councils. (1987: 86)

This abrogation of the elected rural councils in 1985 by Qabus was hardly a 'step towards political participation'.[23]

The Omani Military

In the military[24] sphere Qabus refused to put a time frame on complete 'Omanisation' of the military and in this he was supported by the British (Allen 1987: 88). On the appointment of the General Sir Timothy Creasy as Omani Chief-of-Staff in 1981, a senior British adviser, commented, 'when you have a family of children you don't consult with them until they've grown up a bit' (see Kechichian 1995: 133). In foreign policy terms Qabus pursued a number of independent initiatives, amongst others establishing diplomatic relations with the Soviet Union in 1985.[25] However, Oman relied on the 'umbrella' of the protection of the Western allies in the eventuality of any serious threat to its security. With the effective end of the Cold War and cessation of hostilities between Iran and Iraq in 1988 it might have appeared that such threats had receded. However, this was only the calm before the gathering storm. The events of the early 1990's are examined in the next part of this chapter.

6.2.1: The international context since 1990

The key developments in the international context since 1990 were the regional threat to Western interests posed by Iraq and its invasion of Kuwait in 1990, the resulting Western military campaign and evolution of a dual containment policy. The election of George W. Bush brought to office an American administration with officials who thought in terms of 'regime change' in Iraq even before the events of September 11th 2001.

The United States, the Gulf, and Iraq: preparation for 'middle intensity conflict'

It might have been thought that with the end of the Iran-Iraq war and the demise of Cold War tension that both a regional and global source of potential conflict had been removed from the Persian Gulf. However such a surmise would ignore the remaining problems for Saddam Hussein's regime which remained despite the defeat of the Iranian threat and the acceptance by Khomeini of the 'poisoned chalice' - the UN cease-fire resolution. In the aftermath of the Iran-Iraq War Iraq was in a parlous state and required funds to rebuild its war-shattered economy. It was widely perceived that Iraq had conducted its campaign against Iran with the financial backing of Kuwait and Saudi Arabia. The Saudis and Kuwaitis were fearful of an expansion in influence of Iranian-style Islamic fundamentalism which threatened the legitimacy of their ruling houses - autocratic monarchies.

Furthermore, Saddam Hussein, indeed all governments of Iraq, had a number of special grievances against the Kuwaiti government, resulting from the geopolitical position. The most long standing was the claim that the Emirate was the 19th province of Iraq separated by the machinations of British imperialism in the settlement after World War One. Thus, Iraq had never relinquished its claim even after it accepted the military limits in the Kuwait Crisis which followed Kuwaiti independence in 1961 (see Chapter 5). A further grievance of this nature was the refusal of Kuwait to cede sovereignty of two islands at the mouth of the Shatt al-Arab waterway Bubiyan and Warba. This meant that Iraq's sole access to the Gulf was restricted to the port of Umm Qasr: possession of the islands would have facilitated the development of a petrochemical industry there (Yapp 1996: 502).

On the oil front there were two points of dispute. Firstly that Kuwait was extracting more oil than it was entitled to from the Rumallah oil field in the neutral zone. Much more serious was the Kuwaiti exceeding of production quota which was keeping the price of oil low. This, Tariq Aziz maintained, was an act of war against Iraq, which was losing $1 billion in foreign exchange earnings a month as a result; had the situation continued for another month Iraq would have gone bankrupt.[26]

In these circumstances, Saddam Hussein ordered the Republican Guard to move south towards the border with Kuwait. His perception was that the US, after Vietnam, would not intervene. This perception was confirmed by a discussion with US ambassador April Glaspie on 25 July 1990, in which she told the Iraqis that the US would not excuse the use of force but she had no authority to go further. Given the subsequent US response this meeting has been seen by some as evidence of a US conspiracy to lure the Iraqis into Kuwait in order to smash them militarily. However, for David Mack, Director of Gulf Affairs at the State Department in 1990 the idea was absurd: 'the idea that April Glaspie with no instructions to do so could have told Saddam Hussein "if you send one tank across the border my President will send a half a million US men and women and kick your butt back across into Iraq" - well, she would have been laughed out of the room.'[27]

That said, the United States had been preparing for a war of this type for some time:

> For the USA this war - or a variant of it which would inevitably take place in the Middle East, with control over oil as the trigger - was one Washington had been preparing for even as the arms trade with Iraq flourished in the late 1980s. In 1988 the US Commission on Integrated Long Tern Strategy underlined the new threat to the USA of strong regional powers with large well-equipped armies. As any threat from the Soviet Union disappeared with the end of the Cold War, in the early months of the Bush Administration, Middle Intensity Conflict became the preoccupation of the planners. The US military began to prepare itself to face conflicts with what President Bush himself called 'renegade regimes' in the Third World. Spelt out by Defense Secretary Richard Cheyney in secret planning documents for the period 1992-97, Middle Intensity Conflict was clearly targeting Iraq and Syria. (Brittain 1991: 9)

The Iraqi invasion of Kuwait: the first post-Cold War crisis

Tensions were eased by Egyptian President Hosni Mubarak's visit to Iraq when he received Saddam's assurance that he had no intention of invading Kuwait but was merely seeking to exert some pressure. However, in the weeks before the invasion the US national security establishment received intelligence suggesting that something serious was underway. On the early morning of August 2 1990 intelligence photos were received which showed the Iraqi tank encampments empty: the tracks were going south in the direction of Kuwait. The Iraqi invasion of the Emirate had begun.

Iraqi control of Kuwait was quickly established, the Emir eluding capture with minutes to spare. Iraq now controlled one fifth of world oil reserves which was deemed a threat to US vital interests: 'the notion of Iraq, which was an oil powerhouse in itself acquiring the Kuwaiti resources and then perhaps being able to dominate OPEC was a tremendous danger.'[28] A move towards the Saudi border seemed to indicate the possibility of a bid to seize the eastern oil fields of al-Hasa province which would have increased the Iraqi control to 2/5 of world oil.

This was the first post-Cold War crisis, a test of the New World Order which President Bush had declared. Initially, American policy makers discussing what the appropriate response to the invasion was considered whether the US 'could live with the Iraqi occupation.' After this period of deliberation and emboldened by Margaret Thatcher's advice President Bush declared that this 'aggression will not stand.' Operation Desert Shield swung into action. The Americans elicited support both diplomatic and military. In the UN, with the Russians willing to cooperate with the US, a resolution condemning the Iraqi occupation was passed without serious opposition. Only Jordan and the Palestinians supported Iraq. Of vital importance for the success of the military operation was the willingness of Saudi Arabia to support US efforts against Iraq by providing access to Saudi bases.

Operation Desert Shield involved the dispatch of a vast amount of military supplies and troops from 33 countries in all, but principally the United States. Saddam Hussein was given a deadline to withdraw from Kuwait and Iraqi assets were frozen and sanctions installed. After the failure of negotiations the 15 January deadline passed and the military operation moved into Desert Storm. The first part was the extensive bombing of Iraqi air defences, communications and military installations and subsequently Iraqi troops. Following diversionary tactics a surprise land assault from the western desert which swept round towards the Euphrates to cut off the Iraqi troops in Kuwait. The retreating Iraqi army was caught in a 'turkey shoot' on the road to Baghdad.

Sanctions and Dual Containment
Following the expulsion of the Iraqis the UN maintained the programme of sanctions which were to stay in place until the destruction of Saddam's arsenal of weapons of mass destruction had been supervised; an unofficial goal seemed to be the end of Hussein's regime. This was in the context of a US policy of dual containment which sought to isolate both Iraq and Iran internationally, fully implement sanctions against Iraq in the belief that it would lead to the fall of the regime there, and to pressure Iran

to change its foreign and domestic behaviour.[29] In the aftermath of the Kuwait War US power was untrammelled. The United States had demonstrated that only it could defend the oil monarchies; ideas of Gulf self defence or European leadership were illusions. The US concluded defence agreements with five of the six GCC states and an extensive informal defence cooperation with Saudi Arabia (Dunn 1996). In 1995 the US 5th Fleet was established with its headquarters in Bahrain from where periodical bouts of 'sabre rattling' with Saddam took place as the Iraqi leader sought to test the limits of his freedom of manoeuvre and to exploit strains in the coalition.

For the citizenry of the GCC the invasion of Kuwait highlighted the fact that despite the spending of billions of dollars on arms the Gulf monarchies still required American troops to defend them (Gause 1994: 89). A further impact of the Kuwait War was renewed domestic demands in the Gulf states for political liberalisation; these states, caught in the intense international media spotlight were the subject of Western media calls for democratisation. The Omani experience of this phenomenon is examined in the final part of this chapter. The role of Western strategic interests in Oman in these operations is the focus of the next section.

6.2.2: Western strategic involvement in Oman since 1990

In this section we consider British and American use of facilities in Oman during the Kuwait crisis and subsequent use in training exercises and the War on Iraq.

British and American use of Omani facilities during the Kuwait crisis

Oman played an essential role for the coalition forces during Operations Desert Shield and Storm and the improvements which had been carried out during the 1980s proved their worth. Although little information has been made public Joseph Kechichian comments that senior US officials have verified the vital link that Oman provided at an early stage of Operation Desert Shield before supplies could be flown from the US (Kechichian 1995: 157). The US Airforce in particular benefited from the use of pre-positioned supplies at Thumrait which saved the US the equivalent of 1,800 C-141 airlift sorties, thus increasing the quickness of the US build up during Operation Desert Shield

(Cordesman 1997: 204). Furthermore, Oman gave political support to the effort against Iraq. In August 1990 Oman initiated a resolution at the Cairo League of Arab States meeting, condemning the Iraqi invasion of Kuwait. At the same time, the Omani foreign minister travelled to New York and Washington to discuss the effectiveness of the UN sponsored international coalition force against Baghdad. Despite this major preoccupation and at a time when it was difficult to anticipate what political outcomes might result from a defeated Saddam Hussein, Oman and the United States were also involved in the renewal of the ten year old "Facilities Access Agreement". Negotiations resulted in a new agreement extending US access after December 1990; a side letter on excess defence articles was appended to the accord subject to bilateral military arrangements (Kechichian 1995: 157).

Between December 1990 and February 1991, Oman participated in Operations Desert Shield and Storm by deploying troops to Saudi Arabia, granting US access to its air and seaport facilities, and authorizing a drawdown of pre-positioned equipment to support US forces in the Kingdom of Saudi Arabia. During the opening stages of this conflict Omani troops were the only GCC force able to communicate effectively with Western forces due to similarities in equipment and procedures according to Omani officials.[30] US air transport planes came into Sib at the rate of one an hour.[31] A much publicised practice amphibious landing in Oman was relayed to the world on CNN and served as a bluff to Saddam Hussein who expected a seabourne assault on his positions in Kuwait rather than the sweep in from the western desert.[32] Kechichian argues that 'simply stated, the West in general and in the United States in particular could not have achieved their success in the liberation of Kuwait were it not for the pre-positioned equipment in Oman'(Kechichian 1995: 158). This was personally acknowledged by General Norman Schwarzkopf when he visited Muscat in March 1991; he emphasized Muscat's support during the early stages of the conflict before major US reinforcements could arrive in theatre.

British forces also used the Omani facilities in their part of Operation Desert Storm: Operation Granby. Britain benefited from its long-standing links and good military relations with the sultanate's forces. As with the plans for dispersal of nuclear bombers in the 1960s Omani bases enabled Britain to achieve its strategic goals. The following extract illustrates the way in which Omani bases facilitated training and reconnaissance in the deployment following the invasion of Kuwait.

> The Jaguar wing led by Wing Cdr Jerry Connolly and its attendant fleet of transports left Coltishall early on 11 August. After a stopover in Cyprus they proceeded to the Gulf then flew south to Oman - landing at the desert airfield of Thumrait, 40 miles inland of the coastal town of Salalah.
> There were good reasons for this move so far south as 6 Squadron, Jaguar Pilot Flt Lt Dick McCormac explains: "The Omani air force had Jaguars as well, we did training missions with them and they were pretty good to us down there. It was of mutual benefit. They used to simulate air threats against us, bouncing us on training missions."
> Also sent to Thumrait was one of four teams despatched from the Mobile Servicing Section, based at Brize North, whose job it was to refuel aircraft. "Because we're a mobile section my bags are packed the whole time" states Sergeant Jim Carr. But we didn't know where we were going til we landed . The VC10 Captain said 'Welcome to Thumrait. the time is eight o'clock local time - that was a shock to the system. The Americans were already there and were very helpful in lending us ground refuelling equipment. The next day the Hercs and VC10s started pouring in. We had to refuel them at three different locations, the four of us, working 18 hours on, having a short break, then back to work again. (Charles Allen 1991:6-7)

By the third week of August Operation Granby was in full swing; all the machinery of support command was generating the personnel, the equipment and the organisation required to enable strike command to get a second wave of aircraft to the Gulf and bring a third wave to combat readiness. A Nimrod detachment had already been dispatched to Oman to support the UN naval blockade on Iraq (Charles Allen 1991: 10). The operation of the Nimrods in the area was already well established: an officer involved comments 'for the previous eight years we'd been sending Nimrods to Oman as part of a deployment known as the Magic Roundabout. Its primary role was to have a British presence there to support the Omanis' (Charles Allen 1991: 26). For one officer, Squadron Leader Sean McCourt, the operation revived memories of an earlier attempt to counter an Iraqi invasion of Kuwait: 'when I first joined as a young airman in 1960 I was involved in a similar operation when British troops actually went into Kuwait in Britannias and Comets. They went in and prevented an invasion by Iraq. So I was only surprised that we didn't get involved more quickly' (Charles Allen 1991: 26). In the aftermath of the war access to bases in Oman remained an important Western strategic interest to enforce the policy of dual containment.

Western military involvement with Oman since the Kuwait War

Oman renewed its Access Agreement with the US in 1995 and retained its importance to US military policy in the region; some 20% of US pre-positioned supplies in the Gulf are in Oman - mainly at Masirah, Sib and Thumrait. US ships regularly resupply in Oman and the US has an electronic surveillance centre in Oman which plays an important role in monitoring Iran. The US and Britain have a joint venture contract for some of the facilities in Masirah (Cordesman 1997: 204). Oman also continued to work closely with Britain; there are roughly 500 British officers and NCOs seconded or contracted to the Omani forces. British officers play a major role in training the army, and some 80 British officers are seconded to the Omani air force. The crew training for Oman's new Muheet-class frigates is carried out by the Royal Navy's Flag Officer Sea Training. British SAS personnel have trained the Omani anti-terrorist and assist in surveillance of the border with Yemen. British forces also make frequent use of Omani facilities, have an intelligence post near Muscat, and use the Omani base at Goat Island in the Strait of Hormuz and a new intelligence post at Qabl in the Musandam Peninsula for a variety of functions (Cordesman 1997: 205). During the 1994 Yemen civil war, Oman and British military intelligence benefited from the close ties between the two establishments.[33] Despite the ostensible 'Omanisation' some 65 British officers, including a General-Major, Jeremy Phipps, continue to serve on official secondment. In addition Sultan Qabus continues to rely on a small group of British advisers. These include RAF Air Marshall Sir Erik Bennett, Timothy Landon listed as a counsellor at the Omani embassy in London and Timothy Ashworth still reported to be controlling censorship in the Sultanate (Jones and Stone 1997: 10). France signed two military cooperation agreements with Oman in 1989, and now trains part of the Omani Navy. Oman conducts joint exercises with British, French, and US forces. The joint Kunjar Hadd Exercise - held in April, 1995 - was part of an annual series of exercises involving Omani, British, French and US units. One particular large-scale exercise acquired a particular significance following the events of September 11 2001.

Operation Swift Sword II

Operation Swift Sword II had been planned long in advance to take place in October 2001 but following the September 11 attacks on New York and Washington acquired added, unforeseen significance. The British Defence Secretary, Geoff Hoon, had tried to cancel this exercise on the grounds of the £93 million cost but he was overruled by Prime Minister Tony Blair following complaints by the chiefs-of-staff led General Sir Charles Guthrie. Operation Swift Sword II involved 24,000 troops, nearly a quarter of the army, RAF fighters and transport aircraft, special forces and the largest taskforce since the Falklands War.

Following the September 11 attacks on New York and Washington the deployment of British military forces to the region in the following month proved useful both in highlighting shortcomings in existing equipment and for providing a springboard for British operations in Afghanistan to remove the Taliban regime which refused to expel Osama bin Laden and other members of Al Qa'ida. The exercise showed up a number of problems in British army equipment, specifically the Challenger Tank, which had been designed to operate on the plains of North West Europe rather than the deserts of the Middle East -its engines were unable to deal with the desert sand. One of the submarines involved in Swift Sword II, HMS Trafalgar, fired Tomahawk missiles against targets in Afghanistan at the start of the military campaign to bring about regime change in Afghanistan. SAS soldiers took part in the Oman exercise and from there went to Afghanistan.

In the aftermath of 9/11 the US president George W. Bush declared a 'War on terror' and identified an 'axis of evil' consisting of Iraq, Iran and North Korea. The US National Security Strategy 2002 emphasised the need for pre-emptive action which could include regime-change in Iraq as a rogue state. Osama bin Laden proved elusive and Al Qa'ida continued strikes against 'soft' Western and Israeli targets in the form of Bali and Mombassa attacks against tourists. The Bush administration with support from Tony Blair continued with military preparedness for operations against Iraq. In early January 2003 the US dispatched B1 Bombers to bases in Oman.[34] The deployment of British forces to the Gulf now became the largest since the Malaysia operations of the 1950s and from March to April 2003 the United States and Britain undertook military action to remove Saddam Hussein and his regime from Iraq. Oman along with other members of the Gulf Co-operation Council insisted that Iraqis should run the affairs of their entire country following the removal of the regime of Saddam Hussein from power.[35] The leaders of the six Gulf Arab states decided to ensure that their security chiefs would meet on a regular basis to cooperate and coordinate measures concerning regional security. It was reported that the leaders concluded that Islamic insurgency groups have targeted all of the GCC states for attacks. Following the May 2003 Riyadh bombings Western embassies in Oman issued warnings to their nationals of the increased threat – in common with the rest of the Gulf region - of a terrorist attack in Oman.

6.2.3: Oman since 1990

In this section we examine the impact of the Kuwait and Iraq wars on Oman. In foreign policy terms to what extent has Oman been able to maintain its independent foreign policy positions which have often isolated it within the Arab world and the GCC? In the domestic arena the key features that emerged from the Kuwait and Iraq wars was the pressure in the Gulf to 'democratise' in some form - the nature of Omani constitutional development is analysed and the response of Islamist movements discussed. A further concern is to identify the impact of the form of development that has taken place in Oman in the last three decades. Is it sustainable both in human and natural resource terms and what are the challenges of the approaching post-oil era for Oman?

Oman and its foreign policy: an independent actor
In the aftermath of the War for Kuwait, Qabus chaired the GCC Higher Committee on Security that sought to investigate what kind of security arrangement might be adopted for the region but his efforts came to naught. His proposal to create a 100,000 man GCC army, which could become a first shield against potential aggressors, remained in committee. Qabus concluded that a lot more must be done to change preconceived security notions among senior GCC leaders. Disappointed, Qabus instructed his negotiators to move ahead with Western powers, including the United States, in planning future contingencies. Still, he instructed them to insist on being treated equally regardless of existing problems, to maintain a degree of pragmatism and continuity in the Sultanate's foreign policy. Muscat signed a Facilities Access Agreement with Washington in 1980 because of its perceived long term interest even though this was unpopular in the Arab world. Then as now, it strove to delineate intrinsic interest and to persuade Washington to stand by its allies (Kechichian 1995: 158). These independent foreign policy positions were backed up by a continued high level of expenditure on military hardware. Oman imported a total of $180 million worth of arms during 1992-1994, $20 million coming from the US, $150 million from the UK. Since the Kuwait War Oman has signed a total of $600 million worth of new agreements during 1991-1994, all with major West European countries. In the same period a total of $300 million worth of major new arms deliveries took place (Cordesman 1997: 172). Such arms expenditure was proving to be a real burden to Oman's economy to make many analysts, including the World Bank to question whether it is sustainable. This issue will be considered after we examine the impact of the Kuwait War on Oman's political development.

The impact of the Kuwait War on political development in Oman
In the wake of the Kuwait War leaders of Arab regimes were alarmed by renewed domestic demands for liberalisation which were reinforced by Western media calls for democratisation, particularly with regard to the Gulf states. Claiming the exigencies of national security, states were able to resist these pressures in the immediate aftermath of the war. Subsequently some states developed some institutions of 'consultation' with-

out yielding any significant power; advisory councils were created or expanded in the UAE and elections for the National Assembly in Kuwait were held in October 1992 (Faour 1993). In Oman Sultan Qabus announced the Oman Consultative Council: the US was the only global power that was able to play the role of powerful external ally and with the US presence in the Gulf there was an indirect pressure to democratize (al-Haj 1996: 571).

1991: Omani Consultative Council - Majlis al-Shura

As we have seen in chapter five the Sultan's regime was subject to intense military and ideological pressure during the Dhofar rebellion of the early 1970s. With the defeat of the rebellion, overt political opposition all but disappeared. The regime has encouraged an apolitical ethos since that time, built on commitment to economic and infrastructural development under the leadership of the Sultan and a self-consciously technocratic governing elite (al-Haj 1996: 560). The outcome was a political situation that was either tranquil or dull depending on one's perspective. It was therefore a surprise when the Sultan announced the Consultative Council - there was no great public demand similar to public petitions in Saudi, Bahrain and Qatar - this was a political initiative from the top of the political system. It was explained by Sultan Qabus and other government sources as the natural evolution of the State Consultative Council experiment, unrelated to the regional ferment set off by the Gulf crisis. Perhaps the timing of the announcement was affected by the crisis, but it appears that the changes had been in the Sultan's mind for some time (Gause 1994: 113). Gause sees two aspects as worth noting; firstly, the selection process was innovative and, secondly, it enjoyed greater powers than its predecessor - ministers can be questioned in the fields of health, education, housing - but not defence or foreign affairs.

Social composition of the Omani Consultative Council

The names of the OCC members indicate that they come from prominent tribes, the urban notability, the business community including traditional and new merchant families, and from the emerging educated elite whose members come from poorer families with tribal or merchant backgrounds. Tribal identification played an important part in the nominations for members to this council (Crystal 1996: 269). The merchant families of Oman, as well as those of other GCC states, have always been in alliance with the ruling families because of shared mutual interests. Thus, while the Sultan has needed the merchant families in the past to provide him with financial resources to run the state, the latter have sought the Sultan's help to ensure their security and protection (al-Haj 1996: 564). Crystal argues that oil merchants have in effect, 'renounce[ed] their historical claim to participate in decision-making. In exchange, the rulers guaranteed them a large share of oil revenues. Where economic elites once entered politics to protect their economic interests, after oil, merchants left the realm of formal politics to preserve those interests' (Crystal 1990:1). For Al-Haj the OCC has proved to be a stabilising institution because it has provided an element of increased political participation in line with the Ibadhi tradition of shura. He feels it is possible that Sultan Qabus will expand the council's authority in the future and that political participation will increase rapidly in the coming decade.he OCC has proven to be a stabilizing institution in the country because it has combined elements of increased political participation within an Islamic framework that is in congruence with Ibadhi tradition. It is quite conceivable that Sultan Qabus may expand its authority in the coming years, and that political participation will increase rapidly in the coming decade (al-Haj 511).

However, other groups in Omani society were plotting to increase their participation without waiting for it to be handed to them by the Sultan. His postponement of this 'stage' is comparable to Sa'id bin Taimur's remarks that his people were not ready for economic development yet.

The arrest of dissidents in 1994

In August 1994, in an unusual press release, the Omani government announced that the security services had uncovered a secret organisation that was using Islam to cause civil unrest and national disunity in the county. The organisation was said to have more than 200 members, all of whom had been arrested by the authorities for questioning in May 1994. Members of this organisation included the former Omani ambassador to the United States (Riphenburg 1998: 107). *Al-Omania*, the official news agency of Oman, emphasised that the organisation had external connections, both financial and organisational and government sources mentioned that the detainees were political activists belonging to the Muslim Brotherhood. Those sources added that the individuals arrested were members of a highly sophisticated and secret Islamic organisation which had attempted to overthrow the regime in Oman and put an end to its new representation experience. Furthermore rumours suggested that the detainees had weapons and communication devices and that they were linked to foreign agencies (al-Haj 1995: 566).

The government played up the Islamist nature of the plot, according to unofficial sources consulted by the *Gulf States Newsletter*. In fact, the 40 to 50 hard core of the roughly 250 plotters were mainly concerned about questions of nepotism and corruption. In particular, there was anger that the traditional distinction between politics and business was breaking down. Merchants who were losing out believed that certain ministers were abusing their positions of power and enriching themselves.[36] The strengthening of the Omani autocracy had been evident for a while. Although the elections to the OCC gave it a democratic veneer, at least in comparison to the appointed *majales* in other GCC states, the institution was no more than a sounding board for the government although at first it was also a forum for the expression of nation-wide administrative grievances. Ministers who were publicly humiliated on television subsequently denied the council information, imposing tight restrictions on access and thereby rendering the Council. In the same way the annual meet-the-people tour was initially a useful way of identifying local failings of the administrative bureaucracy. However, powerful senior ministers who did not like to be admonished in front of the Sultan have since made this event a stage-managed event with carefully screened participants powerless.[37]

None of these processes however provide a communication channel on controversial issues to the powers that be. In the Omani political system power is centralised and decisions forever pushed upwards. The final decision on most matters always rests with the Sultan. Furthermore, he seemed unable to curb the ambitions of some of his ministers: the *Economist* reported that some ministers originating from Dhofar had, for every government office, created duplicate staff in Dhofar.[38] Since the top leadership is protected from serious protest by an effective and pervasive internal security apparatus, there remains little opportunity for popular expression of dissent or disagreement.[39] The next initiative from the top of the Omani political system came in 1996.

Oman: A Hereditary Sultanate

In November 1996 during his 'meet-the-people tour' Sultan Qabus announced a new constitution for Oman, the Basic Law. As with the State Consultative Council no information on this new constitution had been released during its period of planning (Siegfried 1998: 62). Sultan Qabus promulgated the state's first written constitution describing the system of government as a 'Hereditary Sultanate'. The constitution stipulates the establishment of a supreme judiciary council and forming an institution called the 'Council of Oman' which is made up of the Consultative Council and the Council of State which will be formed soon. The constitution allows the creation of 'organisations on patriotic grounds' but not political parties and bans 'military or secret groups or those which have activities hostile' to the government.[40]

Siegfried (1998) points out that the term *nizam asasi* is used rather than *dustur* which has connotations of the European dominated constitutional arrangements which had been introduced in the Middle East. The nation (*watan*) is strongly stressed and Qabus as an embodiment of this national unity is used as an explicit symbol. There is no reference to God or the people as holder of this sovereignty - the Sultan is sovereign independently (Siegfried 1998: 84). The power of the Sultan is described in detail in Article 42. He alone is responsible for the integrity of Oman, its internal and external security, and the rights and freedoms of its citizens. Article 42 allows him to take any powers necessary for the defence of these values (Siegfried 1998: 75). Nicholas Siegfried concludes that with regard to the participation of the population the decree is not innovative and further inclusion is not enhanced by the constitution. Qabus has merely confirmed his politics up to now - that of an enlightened despot (Siegfried 1998: 86). In many respects the document has an ideological function. It seeks to create the idea that the Sultan is the embodiment of the Omani nation and unity when in fact the sense of Omani identity is based on factors other than the existence of the present ruling dynasty.

With regards to the issue of succession Article 5 says that the successor must be a male descendant of Sayyid Turki bin Sa'id bin Sultan and "a Muslim, judicious, of sound mind and legitimate son of Omani Muslim parents." Article 6 rules that "the Ruling Family Council shall within three days of the throne falling vacant, determine the successor to the throne." If the Council is undecided, "the Defence Council shall confirm the appointment of the person designated by the Sultan in his letter to the Ruling Family Council." Possible successors include Sayyid Fahd bin Mahmud, deputy prime minister for cabinet affairs, and three sons of Tariq bin Taimur, Sultan Qabus's deceased uncle (O'Reilly 1998: 83). Whoever the successor is they will confront in the not-so-distant future the problem of how to sustain Oman's development.

Development in Oman: is it sustainable?
How sustainable is the development which has taken place in Oman since 1970? Serious problems are the dependence of the economy on oil and gas, lack of investment, depletion of water resources and the approaching exhaustion of oil reserves.

The issue of diversification
The Omani government is conscious of Oman's dependence on oil and gas and plans to diversify the economy as part of it s 1996-2000 development plan. The government plans to reduce the oil sector's share of the GDP from 35% to 32% during 1995-2000. It also plans to cut the share of government spending of the GDP from 23% to 11%, while it raises the share of commodity production from 12% to 16% and of other services from 40% to 42%. Cordesman (1997) believes that these plans are credible in broad terms but that on closer scrutiny there are obvious problems. At present, Oman's non-oil sector is heavily oriented towards services - only some of which contribute to development and true economic growth. Agriculture and fishing have declined in importance in recent years to only about 3.3% of the GDP, and little progress is really planned to increase the share of mining - which is only 0.26% of the GDP. Manufacturing is only about 5% of the GDP. The service sector accounted for 54% of the GDP in 1995 and Oman's current plans indicate that it will still be 53% in 2000. Government services accounted for 13% of the GDP in

1995 and will still be 11% in 2000. The Government sector has grown in recent years despite budget deficits and Omani sources indicate that the government sector grew from 16% if GDP to 19% in 1993 (Cordesman 1997: 159).

The 1994 World Bank Report on Oman

In January and February 1993 a world bank team of five researchers produced *Oman: Sustainable Growth and Economic Diversification,* a 224 page report on the financial policies being pursued by Oman. This report was made public in May 1994 and summarised in an article in November 1994 in the *Financial Times.*[41] The *Financial Times* highlighted the World Bank's view that the financial policies being pursued by Oman were not sustainable. It noted that many of Oman's underlying structural weaknesses are shared by its neighbours and partners in the Gulf Cooperation Council. However Saudi Arabia, Kuwait and the UAE hold 40 per cent of the world's known oil reserves and are not faced with the same immediate and critical choices as Oman, thanks to their larger 'cushion' of capital derived from their far greater oil reserves. Because all six share the same type of hereditary and autocratic monarchical systems, instability in one, Oman for example, could easily spread to one or more of the others. The bank was particularly severe on the scale of Oman's repeated budget deficits, current expenditure trends and the decline in investment, all of which feature - sometimes to a chronic extent - in the other five GCC countries. If these and other problems are not corrected, and the reforms proposed ignored, Oman is heading for a 'major economic and social upheaval' as the oil and gas era comes to an end and Omanis are 'forced to give up accustomed standards of consumption.'

The report amounted to an indictment of the Omani government's management of the economy, particularly in the ten years prior to the report when many key ministers had held the same jobs. The bank's analysis also represented a comprehensive rebuke to officials at all levels who had developed the 'plausible and positive platitude' almost to a fine art form, even when confronted with unpleasant realities. The bank commented: 'Oman's oil and gas wealth, being depletable, is analogous to a large inheritance...Oman, like most neighbouring oil and gas producers, is currently spending an excessive proportion of the proceeds of extraction on current consumption. In other words it is consuming its capital at a rapid rate.'

The World Bank report catalogued serious problems in the Omani economy. They included a persistent top-heavy government role in the economy and state budgets over-stretched by bloated government expenditures, notably on defence and internal security (among the highest in the world with an average 33 per cent of budget expenditure for the last 14 years and now 23 per cent of GDP) and civil service salaries.[42] There was no consistent foreign and domestic investment strategy for when oil reserves taper off. The real exchange rate was overvalued in relation to what would be consistent with higher (and more desirable) national savings rates. Efforts to diversify into manufacturing and other non-oil industries were failing because of current public expenditure/savings policies. The state's reserves and contingency funds were being misused and there was no appropriate tax structure and realistic charges for public services.

Furthermore, the Omani government held ill-conceived notions about the role and cost of expatriate labour and consequently distorted the market when it sought to employ Omani nationals at uneconomic rates. The Bank perceived there was a failure to alert Omanis to the reality of the country's fiscal position, to the inadequate rate of saving and to their own unrealistic consumption and employment expectations. This was combined with bureaucratic inertia and lack of financial discipline by ministers over their own budget allocations. Other problems identified were out-of-date and cumbersome legal frameworks, lack of a self sustaining private sector and an investment framework to attract foreign capital, and lack of a role for private banks in medium and long term financing. There was a need for more entrepreneurial, competitive and less 'rent seeking' (cash income for no effort and minimal risk) attitudes among Omani nationals.

The growing incidence of some of these structural economic weaknesses and the concomitant political risks which the government of Oman was courting by ignoring them was demonstrated by the protests which led to the arrests of Islamic activists in 1994. Although oil prices have recovered from the lows of 1986 and 1988, they have remained apart from a brief period during the Kuwait War below $18 a barrel. The World Bank Report stated that: 'Even now, the Omani government has made only a partial expenditure adjustment to the stagnation in its oil revenues. In consequence, its financial position has deteriorated and continues to do so.' This the report said was apparent in an almost unbroken string of deficits since 1981 (an annual average deficit of $871 or 23.4 per cent annually over budget revenue during the 11 year period); declining contributions to the State General Reserve Fund (SGRF); a substantial rise in external debt; increased recourse to borrowing from the domestic private sector; and a massive recent accumulation of negative changes in the governments accounts and the virtual disappearance of net government financial reserves. The deficits have been the result of an exceptionally high level of defence and national security expenditures, coupled with continued strong growth in civil recurrent expenditures. The use of the SGRF as an oil revenue stabilisation fund has pre-empted its potential as a vehicle for long term public savings and investment. One of the report's key recommendations was that Oman make major cuts in its military spending to compensate for the loss of oil revenues (Cordesman 1997: 168).

The article in the *Financial Times* caused considerable irritation to Omani officials. They accused the newspaper of focusing on the bank's criticisms of the Sultanate whilst ignoring the more positive aspects. The Omani government reacted swiftly to the criticism. Oman's Minister of State for development planning, Muhammed bin Mousa al-Yosef, said 'We have already initiated a strategy of action which is based on public sector deficit reduction.' World Bank officials responded by assuring the Omani government that they thought the article ignored the progress the Sultanate's government had already made, reiterating the fact that the report had been commissioned by the government itself. Although the original *Financial Times* article was censored in Oman, the rebuttal was widely reported in the Sultanate's newspapers. Privately many Omani businessmen were pleased that the report was discussed so publicly. Despite the World Bank's reassurances to the government, the report raised some sensitive issues which had not been raised before in such a public manner. They pointed out that for some years Omani businessmen had complained about monopolies enjoyed by government ministers, excessive bureaucracy and government interference in business. Many hoped it would spur the government into taking rapid corrective measures.[43]

A few weeks after the *Financial Times* report, Muhammed bin Mousa al-Yousef, speaking at an investment conference in Muscat, gave a brief preview of the next five year plan, which covers the period from 1996 to 2000. He said that the plan would concentrate on creating a macro-economic framework and development policies which would act as an incentive for the private sector to take the lead in development and diversification. The *Gulf States Newsletter* commented: 'the government is making significant steps to come to grips with its structural deficit but whether it will really be able to cut into the fat remains to be seen. At the same time, the country faces problems with motivating its people to switch from their cushy government jobs into the harsh private sector'.[44] There were other problems which the Omani government sought to address, such as the lack of investment in Oman and depletion of the water and oil reserves.

The problem of investment
In a speech in 1995 Sultan Qabus sought to encourage Omanis to invest in Oman. During his speech he said that 'only 6% of the capital available in the Arab world...is invested in their countries...and the rest is abroad.' This, he said, was very unsatisfactory and he commented that he would like to see Omanis investing considerably more in Oman. This is necessary because Japan, the world's largest creditor nation, has been reluctant to invest substantially in Oman. In late 1994 a large Omani delegation visited Japan to try to promote investment in the GCC. The chairman of the Omani Chamber of Commerce and Industry, Sheikh Yaqoub bin Hamed al-Harthy disclosed in an interview with the UAE newspaper *al-Khaleej* that the Japanese had said during the talks that they were worried about investing in Middle East countries because they lacked cheap and qualified labour, and had limited markets. He said that he was not hopeful that significant Japanese investment would be attracted to the Gulf.[45]

The political stability of Oman, as in any other country, is a factor in the decisions of banks to invest. An insight into the concerns of Japanese banks when considering an investment in Oman is found in a request for a political risk analysis in January 1994 from the Industrial Bank of Japan to the International

Institute for Strategic Studies, London. This requested a risk assessment with responses to the following four questions.

(1) Would it be right to assume that the Sultan will have no natural heir? What would be the succession process: who are the likely candidates; what is the prospect thereby for a stable policy-making and outlook?

(2) What is the state of the border disputes with Yemen and UAE (any others?)? Are the resolutions for peace liable to be lasting?

(3) Are there opposition forces lurking at all in the country, perhaps in the form of tribal rivalries? Again, what are the underlying prospects?

(4) Which country/ies have most influence on Oman, commercially and politically, and how might the picture change?

This gives an indication of the Japanese bank's perception of possible causes of political instability; if they feel that the risk is too high it would sway them against an investment decision. This, according to a Foreign Service Officer for the US State Department, has also been a factor in US companies not being so keen to invest after Iran. In contrast British companies were not so afraid with their greater experience of the region.[46]

Future Developments in Oman
In the future the Omani regime will face the reduction in a number of natural resources such as oil and water which will bring a political challenge. Oman, traditionally had the greatest water resources and hence agricultural potential of the Arab Gulf states; the present Omani generation has grown up in the era of oil revenues. As Riphenburg puts it: 'the major political issue confronting the regime is how to deal with the politics of rising expectations in a climate of diminishing resources' (1998: 2).

Water and 'geo-constants' in Oman
If the Omani government was thinking ahead on how to reduce the state sector it also faced a problem in its development poli-

cies with regard to a natural resource which will increasingly be the most important in the Middle East: water. The depletion of aquifers means the loss of a resource which, in the next century, will be a more contested resource in the Middle East than oil according to some analysts (Bulloch and Darwish 1993). The depletion of Oman's water resources is a major problem. Oman has only about 0.43 cubic kilometres of internal renewable water resource, which is low, and which amounts to about 1333 cubic meters per person. Even though Oman receives rain from the Indian Ocean monsoons, some 70% of its annual rainfall of 100mm evaporates without affecting the soil. It comes as no surprise, therefore, that Oman has begun to deplete the water resources from its wells in the Batinah Plain, its most fertile region, and may be depleting the water resources of the Salalah Plain. Oman has used its fossil water by over pumping its aquifers. Oman has tried to solve this water problem with retention dams that will force the water into the soil, and by repairing the 1000 year old system of underground aqueducts that once provided water in Oman's interior. Desalination is too expensive to be a solution to meeting anything other than civil and urgent industrial needs and Oman currently allocates nearly 94% of its natural water on agriculture versus 3% for domestic needs and 3% for industry (Cordesman 1997: 163).

Furthermore, Oman's rapid increase in population is causing its natural water resources per capita to drop sharply.[47] The World Resources Institute and World Bank estimate that Omani natural per capita water resources fell from 4000 cubic meters in 1960 to 1,333 cubic meters in 1990 and will drop to 421 cubic meters in 2025. Consequently, Omani water policy is a problem that needs more government attention. Unless Oman receives outside development aid to help it with water, it will become increasingly dependent on food imports and may find it steadily more difficult to create jobs (Cordesman 1997: 163). Such problems stress the continuing importance of what Bowen-Jones (1987) terms geographical constants or geo-constants as constraints on Oman's development, of which the characteristics of groundwater is one. In contrast to the view that holds that while, such constants may have operated in the past, they are no longer so important today he argues that 'the relationships between man and some fundamental geo-constants, it is true, may not be as simple or as direct today as once they were, but they do exist and are ignored at our peril' (Bowen-Jones 1987: 119). The depletion of groundwater resources are not the only resource facing depletion: the resource on which all Omani development has been based is also running out - oil.[48]

Towards the end of the oil era in Oman
Omani oil revenues declined steadily in the 1990s and continue to do so in the first decade of the new millenium (Allen and Rigsbee 2000: 226). The cessation of oil production in Oman will break up the unstated compact between rulers and merchants in Oman in which the merchants withdrew from direct input into the decision-making process if the rulers allowed the merchants to make money. The death of Qabus or his incapacitation, which almost happened in the car crash in 1995 which killed Qais Zawawi, could also throw Oman into turmoil. Political loyalty in Oman is very much to Qabus personally rather than to Al Bu Sa'id ruling family.[49] Eickelman has commented:

> Younger Omanis acknowledged a pervasive governmental respect for Islam, but perceive a de facto separation of religion and state despite a vigorous programme of constructing new congregational mosques bearing the name of the ruler throughout the country. Indeed, the Qabus mosque in Nizwa is built on the site of the congregational mosque in which imams were formerly selected. The Sultan's National Day speeches and others make only general references to 'our heritage' (*turathuna*), not to the rich stock of Qur'anic imagery that is a pervasive part of the political process elsewhere. Yet government sensitivity to the potential influence of religion upon contemporary politics is recognised. After the Grand Mosque siege uniformed police were posted outside Nizwa's congregational mosque leading one religious scholar to comment 'the government now knows so little of what we think in the interior that they believe we want the Imamate restored'... At the level of the influence of Islam upon national politics, there is a decided lack of enthusiasm for the principle of monarchic rule, but support for Qabus as a moderate ruler. (Eickelman 1986:46-47)

Thus the death of Qabus could lead to a new phase in state formation in Oman. Sultan Qaboos addressed the issue of succession in the 'Basic Statute of the State' promulgated in November 1996. Chapter One of the Basic Law establishes that the Omani government will be based on sultani (royal) succession of the male descendants of Sayyid Turki bin Sa'id b. Sultan. The future sultan must be a Muslim and the legitimate son of Omani parents. When the throne becomes vacant the Ruling Family Council is required to meet within three days to determine a successor to the throne. If the RFC fails to choose a successor in three days the defence council is constitutionally obligated to confirm the individual designated by the sultan as his successor. The major issue is whether the RFC is obligated to approve the sultan's choice of successor. According to the Minister of Information Abd al- Aziz al-Ruwas the answer is no. If the RFC is of the opinion that another candidate is more qualified than the designated successor, the RFC may select that individual. The defence council is not constitutionally permitted to overrule this decision. A secondary issue is the the role of the defence council, which upon the death of the sultan summons the RFC into session, rather than either the Majlis or the Council of State as the legitimizer of the sultan. One can well imagine the undue influence of the defense council as the RFC meets under its watchful eyes and protection. This is obviously a system in marked contrast to either Al-Sa'id historical practice or the Omani Ibadhi tradition. (Allen and Rigsbee 2000: 222). Qaboos has reportedly designated two members of the family as acceptable heirs, and their names have been sealed in envelopes and deposited in two secret locations. He will not name a crown prince. The names have remained secret and are cause for much speculation. The most likely candidates are one of the sons of Qaboos's uncle, Sayyid Tariq bin Taimur: Sayyid Haitham bin Tariq, the secretary-general of the ministry of foreign affairs, Sayyid Shihab bin Tariq, Commander of the RNO, and Sayyid Asad b. Tariq, the former commander of the Sultan's Armor and now director of conferences. It is rumoured, however, that more conservative elements of the royal family might object to one of Tariq's sons being designated successor owing to Tariq's activities during the suppression of the imamate in the late 1950s, his supposed sympathy with leftist guerillas in the early 1960's, and his removal as prime minister by Sultan Qaboos in the 1970s. Consequently, other names have been suggested: Thuwaini bin Shihab Al-Sa'id, deputy prime minister for cabinet affairs, and Sayyid Faisal bin Ali Al-Sa'id, the long-time minister of national heritage and the family member with the strongest backing of the religious elite (Allen and Rigsbee 2000: 222). However, the Western attitude to Oman will remain the same. The West is not that concerned about Oman's oil which is insignificant in comparison to the Saudis and Kuwaitis whose reserves are still expected to last another 100 years. Therefore Oman's geostrategic importance would remain even after oil in Oman has been exhausted. In the event of political instability following from the exhaustion of Omani oil reserves the West will keep a close eye on developments and the status of its strategic interests there. It is clear that the US and the British could not easily contemplate an unfriendly government in Oman. Therefore, if domestic instability in Oman were to threaten Western interests it is quite possible that a Western intervention of some kind would seek to avert an anti-Western government from gaining and consolidating power in Oman.

Conclusions

Conclusions can now be drawn to the three central research questions posed at the beginning of the study.

State formation in Oman since 1920: from informal empire to contemporary state

The first research question asked what have been the most significant factors in the historical process of state formation in Oman in the era of modern Middle East politics? It is first possible to summarise the four periods of state formation since 1920 identified in this study which constitute 'Oman's odyssey'.[1] Located on the remote mountain range of south-east Arabia a distinctive form of social organisation developed optimising the sparse water resources available to it. Through the institution of the Imamate this tribal society was able to achieve a periodic unity and benefit from the opportunities of maritime trade in the Indian Ocean. Subsequently, these trading polities situated on the coast, concentrated on the opportunities to accrue wealth and neglected the tribal politics of the interior, resulting in civil war and the frequent intervention of outside powers. This pattern of politics was disrupted by the impact of capitalism through its agency of British imperialism whose foremost concern was safeguarding the route to India. Starting in 1798 the sayyids of Muscat became progressively enmeshed in the security sphere of the British Raj which had no intrinsic interest in the Arabian peninsula, but was merely concerned to ensure that the coastline remained secure from internal disruption or rival great power intrusion. This was based on strategic considerations which ultimately related to the very real importance of India to the British economy. British imperialism played a decisive role in the nineteenth century in disrupting the Omani maritime economy. In this process the coastal based Sultanate's sources of wealth were steadily eroded with the resulting internal weakening of the Sultans' position and corresponding financial and military dependence on the Indian merchants and Government of India to repulse the attacks by the Imamate from the interior. These attacks culminated in the siege of Muscat and its defence by the Indian Army 1913-1920.

In 1920 the Government of India in accordance with its policy of promoting security on the Arabian littoral brokered the Treaty of Sib which led to a de facto separation of the Imamate in the interior from the British-backed Sultanate on the coast. The administration of the Sultanate was restructured by British officials in the hope that it would become less reliant on the Government of India. In accordance with the 'traditional' strategic interest of protecting the sea-routes to India there was only a concern with peace and stability on the coast - there was no concern with the Arabian Peninsula intrinsically. In the 1920s new strategic developments began to erode this strategic position: the arrival of the air age to Arabia and the first intrusions of the oil era. The first of these did not challenge the traditional preoccupation with the coast - the air routes all ran along the littoral. However, the second development did: the initial oil prospecting of the 1920s foreshadowed the greater probes of the next decades.

The discovery of oil in Bahrain in 1932 heralded a new phase of the incorporation of the Arabian Peninsula into the capitalist world market and its state system as it required the creation of capitalist property rights where previously tribal rights had held sway. The oil companies required 'sovereign' rulers who held sovereignty in clearly defined areas. This would allow the oil companies to sign legal agreements with the rulers granting concessions to first prospect for and then extract oil resources. There were many competing contenders who sought recognition as such 'sovereign rulers'; the oil company was essentially ambivalent as to which ruler became 'sovereign'. British strategic interest required that the government sought to ensure that British oil companies be awarded these concessions. It was to be British strategic policy in the Persian Gulf as a whole that mediated the eventual outcome of this process; the entire position in the Gulf - most notably its access to Kuwaiti oil - was seen as depending on continuing to back the rulers with which it had a relationship: relationships formed during the nineteenth and early twentieth century. Thus, in 1955 the Sultan of Oman's military forces, first created in the 1920s by Britain, were expanded with finance from the oil company and occupied the interior of Oman to effectively end the twentieth century Imamate and establish a unified Sultanate of Muscat and Oman as a sovereign *rentier* state with Sultan Sa'id bin Taimur as its client ruler. This process took place in a particular international context: regionally, of Anglo-American rivalry over oil in southeast Arabia, but globally, in an emerging cooperative division of labour in the Cold War conflict with the Soviet Union in which Britain progressively became the more junior partner as it retreated from empire.

In the period 1956 to 1977 British military involvement ensured that the 'sovereignty' of the Sultanate was maintained against two principal challenges to unity: the Imamate resurgence of 1957 and subsequent Jebel Akhdar conflict, and then the Dhofar rebellion. Without external military intervention the unified Sultanate of Muscat and Oman would have crumbled and, given the ideological climate of the time, been replaced by an Imamate of Oman and then a 'Peoples Republic', certainly in Dhofar and possibly in the north, threatening the entire post colonial state system the British were attempting to erect. Instead, the massive military intervention and the restructuring of the Omani military were accompanied in both cases by British instigated 'development'. In the first case, after the Jebel Akhdar war the British sought to pressure Sa'id into instituting various schemes for economic and social development. In the second case, the British allowed Qabus to take power and take advantage of the opportunities for oil based 'development' which ultimately allowed the suppression of the rebellion and British withdrawal in 1977. This marked the end of British 'informal empire.' This represented the maturation of possibilities for an Omani *rentier* state created by the unification of the 1950s, in which the British had acted, in Bierschenk's phrase, as a 'mid-wife' (1989: 218).

The final stage examined was that of the contemporary state. Here Western strategic involvement, American and British, was geared to planning for rapid deployment to protect the vast oil reserves of Saudi Arabia and Kuwait from global, regional and internal threats. The shift in Western strategic policy to an intrinsic interest in the peninsula which had been heralded by the discovery of oil in Bahrain in 1932 came to fulfilment in the Kuwait War 1990/91. In 1961 it was Britain whose speedy intervention prevented any possible Iraqi designs on Kuwait; three decades later it was an American led force which ejected the Iraqi forces of Saddam Hussein to preserve Western access to oil. As in 1961 pre-positioned equipment and access to facilities in the area played an important role in this military mobilisation. In Oman's case American military commanders recognised the essential role the Sultanate of Oman had played. In the aftermath of the Kuwait War the oil monarchies of the Arabian peninsula came under pressure for political change. In Oman this pressure was particularly acute in that the oil revenues which had been used to buy off traditional elite groups were dwindling: the cake from which all had eaten well, even if the shares of some were vastly unequal, was almost gone. Dissent against nepotism and corruption was expressed in an Islamist plot in 1994. In this context the autocratic Sultan announced first a consultative council in 1991 and then a new constitution - that of a 'hereditary sultanate' – the Basic Law of 1996. Whilst this gave Omanis some codified rights in relation to the state bureaucracy it enshrined the Sultan as the embodiment of the Omani nation. It could be argued that with the economic, political and environmental challenges facing Oman that the fate of Royal Decree which established the Basic Law will be comparable to the 'constitutional' document written in 1920: a stop gap measure which served a limited purpose but was ultimately dispensed with as it became dysfunctional within the state system of the capitalist world market. This would be too economically deterministic. There is no inevitability about the disappearance of monarchy in the Middle East - it may survive or it may not - and if does survive in Oman this decree could be the 'constitution 'of Oman for quite some time.

The key formative process in state formation in Oman has been the conflict between imperialism - external domination or intervention in some form, and anti-imperialism - the internal resistance of the repeated rebellions of the Omanis which took place in the 1860s, 1920s, 1950s and then Dhofar in the 1960s and 1970s. No other Arab Gulf state has such a record of rebellion to external domination or has been so formed by it. These 'external' and 'internal factors' are thus two sides of the same coin rather than opposite ends of a polarity. This study of state formation in Oman has sought to avoid the record of much of the literature where there is either an explanatory stress on external factors – 'imperialism' - or internal factors – 'Islam'. This tendency has either led to the writing of the history of the states of the Middle East as if they are 'driftwood in the sea of international affairs, their destinies shaped by the decisions of others' (Yapp 1996: 3) or on the other hand a stress on the particularism of the Middle East in terms of Islam. A further concern has been to avoid an analysis of state formation in Oman which starts with the discovery of oil: the impact of oil has been set in the context of pre-existing economic and social structures, specifically the forms of political organisation in Oman which existed prior to European expansion and the result of their interaction with informal imperial influence.

The historical narrative found in chapters two to five combines both a strategic approach and a sociological approach based on Simon Bromley's work *Rethinking Middle East Politics*; these are two approaches usually not combined in the discipline of International Relations. Historically this divergence stems from the contention of the dominant realist paradigm in International Relations that the foreign policy and strategic relations of states could not be explained by reference to their societies – this would be a reductionist error. Rather the foreign policy actions of states were explained by the position of that state within the anarchical international system.

One of the key figures in the development of this paradigm, Ken Waltz,[2] maintains that there has been no attempt to develop a theory which combines insights into both the domestic and the international politics of states and the relationship between them; this view is not shared by the present author. One candidate theory that has sought to explicate these connections has been the tradition of historical materialist thought initially developed by Marx. In seeking to relate the development of British and American strategic interests in the Gulf and Oman and how they relate to the development of a global capitalist economy and accompanying state system this thesis is situated in that tradition. It is hoped that this study usefully develops the research programme laid out by Bromley (1986: 187) in providing a case study of one particular society in the Middle East and its economic, political and strategic relationship with the West as part of the expansion of the world capitalist system.

State formation and political development in the GCC states

The second research question asked what is it about state formation in Oman from a comparative perspective that makes Oman different from the other GCC states: Saudi Arabia, Kuwait, Bahrain, Qatar and the United Arab Emirates? It is first necessary to identify the features of similarity in order to identify the differences that pertain to Oman. In his comparative study of the GCC states Gause (1994) identifies a number of similarities that apply to their formation to a greater or lesser extent. He notes that in all the GCC countries, historically, the ruler had to negotiate and deal with rival claims for power and influence from other members of the ruling family, important merchant families and religious figures. The history of state formation in the GCC states is that of the process whereby the ruling families removed themselves from this position. This was facilitated by two external factors: the role of external intervention, that of British imperialism, and then by the possibilities of oil revenue which allowed the centralisation of state power. British support was crucial to the establishment of these rulers even to Ibn Saud who benefited from British subsidies against his Ottoman-backed enemies the Rashidis. The growth of oil revenues after World War Two meant that the state was able to bypass the shaikhs who had traditionally mediated between the ruling families and the tribes. At the same time the state was able to provide the material security which the individual had previously sought in the tribe. Prior to oil rulers had favoured Arab or European expatriates to staff their governments, after oil positions in the government became dominated by members of the ruling families. In this process the ruling families became ruling classes.

Gause (1994: 43) notes that the most distinct aspect of the Arab Gulf monarchies is that due to oil revenues the governments have access to enormous oil wealth without having to tax their relatively small populations. The central question for these states has been how to spend money not how to extract it. These states are, thus, *rentier* states in which the government relies for most of its income on direct transfers from the international economy in the form of oil revenues. A number of direct consequences result from this. Firstly the governments are the dominant players in the local economies. Secondly governments can provide a wide range of free services directly to citizens in the form of free or heavily subsidised education or health. Thirdly governments can build up large civilian and military apparatus which form the bases for patronage, in terms of jobs and contracts. Fourthly the nature of the *rentier* economy has directly and indirectly weakened the economic basis of groups that in the past were sources of political opposition to the state – merchants, tribes and labour organisations. Fifthly, this concentration of revenues in the hands of the state has allowed the ruling families to consolidate power and political positions in their hands to a far greater degree than in previous generations (1994: 43). This has all been accompanied by a legitmization formula based on symbolic ideological appeals to tribalism, Islam and the promotion of heritage (*turath*) (see Gause 1994: 25-27).

A further similarity is that all these 'oil monarchies' are faced by the same challenge. There is now a very different climate to the boom years of 1973 to the mid-1980s. A changed political climate has followed from the reduced oil revenues after the price crash of the mid-1980s coupled with the challenges following the Kuwait War 1990-1991. The immediate response was to draw down on reserves rather than a tightening of belts. Groups which had not pressed demands for political participation under the unofficial social contract of the *rentier* states began to press their demands for political participation (see Crystal 1997). At the same time the rulers faced the demands of their ruling families for positions in government at the same time as a 'commoners' were pressing their claim. A further breach of the *rentier* social contract was that some members of the ruling families seemed to be breaking the unwritten code not to infringe on the business interests which were the preserve of other social groups. Following the Kuwait War

1990-91 all of the GCC states have moved towards some kind of political participation by developing institutions of 'consultation' which may or may not ease the pressures outlined.

State formation in an oil monarchy: the case of Oman

Set in this comparative perspective what makes Oman different in terms of its state formation? A number of differences can be identified in political identity, oil resources and population, the ruling family and the record of conflict in the process of state formation in the modern era. First of all Oman is a very different country to the other Arab Gulf states. Like Yemen it has a history of autonomous political identity stretching back 3000 years based on the solidarity of tribe combined with the solidarity of 'sect', that is, Ibadhism, a form of the Kharijite branch of Islam (Ayubi 1995: 124). This tradition is one of the subnational identities found in the Sultanate today. Having the most diverse geography of the Arab Gulf states it is possible to talk about three Omans in the contemporary Sultanate: the Batinah and Muscat, the interior, and Dhofar, each with their own culture. Each region keeps an eye on the allocation of oil resources and economic benefits accruing to it. To what extent can these three separate areas and other subnational identities be welded into the Omani unitary state and a coherent political identity achieved? In this task Oman has not had access to the vast oil reserves of Saudi Arabia, Kuwait and Abu Dhabi. Like Bahrain and Dubai it has relatively small and dwindling oil reserves, and yet Oman has a greater population than the Gulf Emirates. In 1970 Qabus set himself the task of national unification under his leadership and marked this with the declaration that henceforth the state would be known as the Sultanate of Oman. This was reflected symbolically in the new Omani flag in which the colour red of the sultanate is more pronounced than the white of the Imamate (Riphenburg 1998: 57). It remains to be seen whether the unification of the diverse areas of the interior, coast and Dhofar in an 'hereditary sultanate' will survive the demise of Qabus. Furthermore as oil was discovered in Oman comparatively late (oil exports started in 1967), the economic, social and political processes associated with a rentier economy which took place in Kuwait and Bahrain also took place correspondingly later.

There is a significant difference between the Omani state and the other GCC states at the level of the ruling family. Firstly at the level of size. In Saudi Arabia the state is dominated by the Saudi family which including its collateral branches numbers 20,000 of whom 250 were direct descendants of the founder of the state Abdul al-Aziz. They are all competing for jobs in government and the accompanying power and patronage. Since 1964 the Sudayri clan - the seven sons of Abdul Aziz by a wife from the important Sudayri tribe - has been the leading force in the in the massive Saudi Royal Family. They have managed the succession on the basis of seniority, with the successor and second in line designated in advance by appointment as first and second deputy prime minister (Yapp 1996: 357). A similar dominance of the institutions of the city states gaining independence in 1961 (Kuwait) and 1971was achieved by the al-Sabah of Kuwait, the al-Khalifa of Bahrain and the al-Thani of Qatar. The federal system of the UAE emerged out of the mutual suspicion of the ruling families of the seven shaikhdoms held together by fear and the wealth of Abu Dhabi. Ra's al-Khaima only joined the union when it became apparent that its oil wealth was not as great as hoped. Within the institutions created by the 1971 UAE constitution the supreme council of rulers is dominant and a veto is possessed here by the rulers of Abu Dhabi and Dubai. Abu Dhabi under Sheikh Zaid has generally sought to expand the power of the union but has been opposed by Dubai particularly when Shaikh Rashid assumed the prime ministership (Yapp 1996: 374).

The Al-Sa'id family of Oman, in contrast, is small. It numbers less than one hundred male members; furthermore the provisions for succession outlined in the Basic Law of 1996 restrict succession to the male descendants of Sayyid Turki bin Sa'id bin Sultan to exclude collateral branches of the Al Bu Sa'id (Riphenburg 1998: 113). Additionally, more than anywhere else in the Gulf Sultan Qabus stands alone at the apex of authority. Perhaps the reason for this can be found in the circumstances of his coming to power. Qabus became Sultan during a time of crisis, the Dhofar war, and with a strong candidate as a possible alternative Sultan in his uncle Tariq. In these early days of his rule he sought to grasp the reigns of power and concentrate it in his hands as much as possible. Following the coup of 1970 an expatriate advisory council was established to govern chaired by the Defence Secretary who was a retired British colonel. This council was advisory in name only and made a number of decisions in Sultan Qabus' name, one of which was to appoint Tariq as prime minister who formed his first cabinet in August 1970. Qabus did not share Tariq's ideas on a constitutional monarchy and parliamentary system and preferred the status quo in which power was concentrated in the office of the Sultan (Riphenburg 1998: 51). Qabus' method of rule and his methods of government since 1970 have demonstrated these beliefs. Furthermore he was consolidating his power at the very moment that increased oil revenues became available with the start of oil exports in 1967 and the oil price increases of 1973-4 which meant that the relationships established by the ruler with other important social groups were established at a time when the resources of the *diwan* were exponentially increased. The merchant families of Oman, as well as those of other GCC states, have always been in alliance with the ruling families because of shared mutual interests. Thus, while the Al Bu Sa'id sultans has needed the merchant families in the past to provide them with financial resources to run the state, the latter have sought the sultans' help to ensure their security and protection (al-Haj 1996). In her influential work on the rentier state in Kuwait and Qatar, Crystal argues that merchants have in effect 'renounced their historical claim to participate in decision making. Where economic elites once entered politics to protect their economic interests, after oil, merchants left the realm of formal politics to preserve those interests (Crystal 1990: 1). Allen and Rigsbee argue that Oman has not followed a similar process because during the early years after the coup of 1970 Qaboos was focused on the Dhofar War. The merchant elite consisting of such families as the Zawawis, Harithis, and Shanfaris gained control of economic policy and made sure that the government did not take over their business interests. The result was that by Gulf standards there was very limited participation of government in business and industry and the older established merchant families of Sa'id bin Taimur's era still held sway in business (2000: 62). At the level of the individual Qabus spent his years prior to the coup in isolation in Salalah under virtual house arrest by his father and allowed visits only by people approved of by Sa'id bin Taimur. This has resulted in a tendency to isolate himself and surround himself with advisors. He may be preparing his people for more responsibility and power, as he declares in a recent interview (Miller 1997), but this process is starting from a particularly high degree of concentration of power.[3]

Finally, Oman is different because, as has already been noted, in its formative process the Omani state has a far greater record of conflict than the other GCC states. Oman was a substantial maritime power with overseas dominions and had to be forcibly driven back by the British in order to achieve their aims: first, maritime supremacy and then control of oil resources. The establishment of first a de facto protectorate and then informal empire produced a succession of rebellions against the British and their client Sultans. These rebellions were based in the mountainous interiors of Oman and Dhofar which allowed a space for tribal forces to organise their campaigns under religious or communist ideology against the British-backed Sultans.

Informal empire, collaboration and Oman: Gallagher and Robinson in an Arabian context

The third research question asked to what extent theories of informal empire and collaboration are useful in analysing the relationship between Oman and the West? Gallagher and Robinson originally developed their ideas on the imperialism of free trade in a West African setting. How do they fare when applied in an Arabian context? Informal empire is a term of definition whereas collaboration refers to a process. Under the definition of informal empire employed in this study Oman was the only case of informal empire in Arabia. All the protectorates and protected states, that is, Aden Protectorate, the Trucial States, Bahrain, Qatar and Kuwait were part of Britain's formal empire. Oman was the only country in Arabia which as Doyle puts it was controlled through the 'collaboration of a legally independent (but actually subordinate) government' (1986: 38). It could be questioned as to the extent to which government of the Sultanate was subordinate to the British Political Agent or Consul General – at what point in time did it really fit the category of informal empire as described? To answer this question we can briefly review the periodisation employed in this book and its relationship to the process of collaboration.

Robinson and Gallagher contended that 'without the voluntary or enforced cooperation of their governing elites, economic resources could not be transferred, strategic interests protected or xenophobic reaction and traditional resistance to change contained' (1972). The benefits of collaboration, in the initial stages for the Al Bu Sa'idi rulers of Muscat was to use the alliance with the British to defeat their rivals the Qawasim of Ra's al-Khaima. The crisis of collaboration came when the British expanded British Indian commerce and restricted Arab trade in order to achieve maritime supremacy in the Indian Ocean. The British-mediated separation of the Arabian sultanate from the richer Zanzibar sultanate completely undermined the Sultans in Muscat and they then required ever greater support to prevent tribal forces from ousting them. From 1871 the Sultanate can best be described as a *de facto* protectorate. The British had no programme of imperial development: they were only interested in preventing their Sultan from being removed by tribal forces. This was in order that the British could control the Sultans' external relations and exclude rival European powers from a position on the Arabian littoral which was part of the British strategy for British maritime supremacy in the Indian Ocean. Great power considerations resulting from the 1862 British-French declaration to guarantee the 'independence' of the separate sultanates of Muscat and Zanzibar meant that the 1896 proposal for an official Muscat protectorate was never implemented. However, the British curbs on the trade in slaves and arms struck at the political and economic bases of the Sultan's authority. The change over the 19th century in the Muscat-British relationship from alliance to dominance inevitably changed the relationship of the Sultan of Muscat with his populace from autocratic patrimon to foreign-supported puppet. With growing internal rebellion and instability the British Political Agent (later a Consul-General) backed up by naval gun power, became more involved in defending the increasingly reluctant Sultans culminating in the dispatch of British-Indian troops against the tribes of the interior which besieged Muscat 1913–1920. Following the Treaty of Sib in 1920 the British became increasingly involved in the creation of the administration and even the day-to-day running of the government. This involvement in both internal government and control of foreign relations constituted informal empire. It could be argued that from 1932 the rule of Sa'id bin Taimur saw a lessening of this subordination. However Sa'id achieved this not through the development of independent rule but through withdrawal and isolation: he abolished the Council of Ministers, one of the rudimentary institutions of government, which had been created in the 1920s. By adopting a stance of withdrawal and isolation Sa'id bin Taimur displayed one of the psychological responses of anxiety reduction behaviour which might be expected in such a patron-client relationship as G. Lawrence Timpe has shown in his study (1991) applying clientelism to Oman. Sa'id bin Taimur initially sought to achieve more independence from the British. After the occupation of the interior Sa'id withdrew to Salalah. There were limits to the escape Sa'id bin Taimur could achieve in this manner from British development plans for Oman which were based on their wider Gulf strategic interests relating to oil. Sa'id was clearly a wily character – or 'obstinate' as some of the British in Oman liked to call it. He knew how to play the British officials at their own game; he had the power to stall, and a limited room to manoeuvre and was certainly not a puppet. However the parameters of collaboration meant that in the 1960s while Sa'id could ignore British advice his usefulness was becoming outlived. The British realised they would always bear the burden of military intervention if some form of development was not instituted. The extreme poverty which had resulted from British/Al Bu Sa'idi collaboration provoked resistance from another group - instead of the Imamate forces it was now the role of the Dhofaris who bore the brunt of Sa'id's idiosyncrasies. The violent conflict engendered by the Dhofari struggle against the regime of Sa'id bin Taimur led to a crisis of collaboration. The subordinated nature of the Sultanate's government meant that in 1970 the British replaced Sa'id with a new collaborator - his son Qabus who was keen to institute development. The British domination of Oman which had gradually developed since 1798 and since 1920 had been informal empire finally came to an end with British withdrawal from RAF Salalah and Masirah in 1977.

To understand the nature of British imperialism it is important to recognise that the extent of the British empire was more than those areas of imperial world maps coloured red. It would be hard to find a better case of informal empire than Oman.

However in contrast to other areas in the world where the idea of British informal empire has been applied such as China from 1870 (see Osterhammel 1986) and Argentina in the 1880s (see Lewis 1976:21), British informal empire in Oman was based not on direct economic interests but strategic ones as envisaged by Robinson and Gallagher in their 1953 article: 'imperialism may only be indirectly connected with economic integration in that it sometimes extends beyond areas of economic development, but acts for their strategic protection' (reprinted in Gallagher 1980: 6). In this respect the case of Oman differs from China and Argentina and this thesis adds to the literature by providing a detailed study of informal empire based on strategic interests.

To conclude, the notions of informal empire and collaboration are useful in analysing Oman's relationship with the West and its effect on state formation since 1920 if we recognise certain limitations. Firstly we should confine the category of informal empire to a particular historical period which in Oman's case ended in 1977. Thereafter the relationship between Oman and the West is better understood as the politics of influence between states which occupy a particular place in the international state system. This system has developed with the expansion of capitalism, in which the era of informal and formal empire was a particular historical stage. The contemporary Omani state, while it displays some of the external appearances of a traditional polity is in fact very much a product of modernity: a *rentier* state in the capitalist world system. Secondly, we need to recognise that Robinson and Gallagher's theory of imperialism is a partial theory. It is concerned with the interaction of the metropolitan powers and societies in the periphery - it does not seek to explain the dynamic of expansion from Europe. For attempts at such explanation we must look elsewhere. One candidate is the expansion of capitalism and its state system from a historical materialist perspective. This provides the overall theoretical framework of this study of state formation in Oman.

Endpiece
The author visited the Sultanate of Oman in March 1995. One afternoon we paid a visit to the old town of Muscat and gazed up at the Portuguese forts, reminders of the first European domination. We located the erstwhile British embassy in Muscat and

found it to be deserted; a notice on the door informed us that the British embassy had been moved to the new consulate area outside of the old town. We learnt that the old consulate building was to be demolished to make way for an extension to the Sultan's palace. This is in some ways symbolic of the change in the relationship between Oman and the West which has been surveyed in this study. Britain is now just one of many powers, albeit with a well-established position, competing for influence and business in the Sultanate. The regime of Qabus seeks to define the person of Qabus as the embodiment of Omani unity and independence. This is in contrast to the days of British informal empire in the reign of Said bin Taimur, when, if defined as effective control, 'sovereignty' was not to be found in the Sultan's palace in Muscat but in the adjacent building - the British consulate. Sa'id bin Taimur, the so called 'sovereign ruler' of Muscat and Oman, was in remote isolation in Salalah. Meanwhile, the British Political Agent resided on the seafront at Muscat, the embodiment of the real arbiter of power in the Sultanate - British imperialism, which in this instance had created British informal empire in the Sultanate of Muscat and Oman.

Notes to the Reader

The Harvard system has been used for references to books in the text. The author's name and the date of publication are given in the text, while the full reference is given in the bibliography. A numbered notes system has also been employed - where elaboration is made of points in the text or where the reference is to material in a media source or unpublished primary sources.

Transliteration of Arabic words and names has generally followed that used in the International Journal of Middle East Studies.

Notes

Chapter One

1. Timpe cites Howard Wiarda who defines such theory as 'significant and useful but not necessarily global and all encompassing; theory at [this] level is similarly more modest in its pretensions, concentrating on a single region...rather than encompassing the entire universe of nations' (1985: 6).

2. There is no reference to Wallerstein's work in the bibliography of *Weltmarkt, Stammesgesellschaft und Staatsformation in Suedostarabien (Sultanat Oman)*, (1984).

3. Robinson and Gallagher note (1980: 1) that the term 'informal empire'was first given authority by C.R Fay in the *Cambridge History of the British Empire* (1940: 399). However, in terms of its modern usage W.R. Louis, commenting on their attribution of the term to Fay, notes that 'it is no exaggeration to say that it now has passed into the vocabulary of imperial history as a Robinsonian and Gallagherian concept' (1976: 43).

4. This term is of course, subject to much debate and theoretical contest. For general surveys see Mommsen (1980) and Kemp (1967).

5. Thus Balfour-Paul with reference to the 1960s comments: 'The only counter-observation offered here is that if Muscat and Oman was ever a colony even in Halliday's *de facto* sense, it had certainly ceased to be so by the period we are concerned with. Any British representative (the author was one) who sought in that period to tender advice to Sultan Sa'id bin Taimur on the governing of his country soon found how constitutionally (in both senses of that word) impermeable he was (1991: 199).

6. This definition of the era of modern Middle Eastern politics conforms with Halliday (1996:25), Bromley (1994:4), Owen (1992:9) and Yapp (1996).

7. Owen and Sutcliffe have commented on the way in which case studies of concrete historical situations relate to theories of imperialism thus: 'In the first place theory is seen as suggesting a pattern which events in any area are more or less expected to follow. It provides in other words a paradigm train of events and motives against which an actual situation can be matched. Here, therefore, the concern is with the consistency of the actual set of events and motives with those implied in the paradigm. In the second place, a theory of imperialism provides a way of organising what factual historical material is available; and in this way it gives a pattern to the events. So there are two approaches: on the one hand, facts are being used to test the theory; on the other hand, the theory is being used to organise the facts' (1972: 193) Hence, in this study of Oman and the West theory is being used to define and organise the 'facts' - or in Ngaire Wood's term, theory is being used to 'map' the 'international landscape' (1996: 13).

8. This term is used in Al-Haj (1996) drawing on Linz (1975). Linz (1975: 259) describes 'sultanistic regimes' as those 'based on personal rulership with loyalty

to the ruler based not only on tradition, or on him embodying an ideology, or on a unique personal mission, or on charismatic qualities, but also on a mixture of fear and rewards to his collaborators. The ruler exercises his power without restraint at his own discretion and above all unencumbered by rules or by any commitment to an ideology or value system. The binding norms and relations of bureaucratic administration are constantly subverted by personal arbitrary decisions of the ruler, which he does not feel constrained to justify in ideological terms. In many respects the organization of power and of the staff of the ruler is similar to traditional patrimonialism as described by Weber.'

Chapter Two

1. For a repudiation of this depiction of Arab sea activities see al-Qasimi (1986).

2. Sa'id did manage to persuade the British to get involved with one internal campaign later in his reign. The disastrous 1819 expedition against the Bani Bu Ali of Ja'alan following British accusations of piracy resulted in a near massacre of British troops and necessitated a punitive revenge raid the following year and the court martial of the commanding British officer for having involved British forces unnecessarily in a campaign in the interior of Arabia (Allen 1987: 147).

3. The Maria Theresa dollar was a silver coin first minted in Austria but then reproduced for use in the Arabian Peninsula but always with the date of 1780. At the turn of the twentieth century Sultan Faisal bin Turki adopted the Indian rupee for circulation in the territories under his control although the MT$ remained valid for the territory of the Imamate in the interior of Oman (Peterson 1978: 25).

4. In certain circumstances the usual euphemisms were used for public consumption: Oman was an independent country which Britain 'advises' and 'assists' under treaty obligations (Halliday 1974: 271). However in their private dealings with the Sultans the attitude of the British could be different. For example, in the preamble of the 1937 concession agreement signed by Sa'id bin Taimur with Petroleum Concessions Ltd the word 'Independent' before 'Ruler' was deleted at H.MG's suggestion (Wilkinson 1987: 276). In March 1970 the junior Labour Defence Minister declared to the House of Commons: 'The Sultanate of Muscat and Oman is a fully sovereign and independent state.' Halliday comments: 'The pretence of Omani 'independence', like the 'complexity' of the relationship, is meant to hide the what is in fact a pellucid arrangement. Britain supports the Sultan and has told him what to do when it needed to; otherwise it has allowed him to rule as he likes, provided he keeps Oman tranquil and defends British strategic interests. The Sultans are British collaborators' (1974: 271, 280).

5. In 1891 the Zanzibar sultanate became a British protectorate; following independence in 1964 a nationalist revolution overthrew the Al Bu Sa'id and the ruling Arab caste (Halliday 1974: 298).

NOTES

6. 'The Long Sleep' is the heading of a chapter on Oman in David Holden's *Farewell to Arabia* (1966).

7. For a detailed examination of the geography of Oman and its influence on Oman's social organisation and history see J.C. Wilkinson (1977 and 1987). For an analysis which counters what it sees as Wilkinson's geographical determinism in his work *Water and Tribal Settlement in South-East Arabia* (1977) see Thomas Biershenk (1984), *Weltmarkt, Stammesgesellschaft und Staatsformation in Suedost Arabien*.

8. Wilkinson notes how his through his discussions with Calvin Allen he came to appreciate the importance of overseas links for the society in the interior on which he had hitherto concentrated: 'Increasingly I had become aware that the dichotomy between Muscat and Oman was more apparent than real and that overseas activity was not just the domain of a seafaring merchant class and a few *émigrés* from the Sharqiya, but was fundamental to the whole society in which I was interested' (1987:ix).

9. M. Reda Bhacker cites J.E. Peterson (1978:112) among other Western and Arabic sources.

10. This account of the al-Ya'aribah dynasty is drawn from C.H. Allen, Oman: *The modernisation of the Sultanate* (1987: 35-38). For a detailed study of the dynasty see R.D. Bathurst, *The al-Ya'aribah Dynasty of Oman* (1967). For further studies on the history of the Imamate in Oman see Abdulmalik al_Hinai , 'State Formation in Oman 1861-1970, (PhD thesis, University of London, 2000).

11. Nasir was followed by Sultan bin Saif I (1649-1679) and Balarab bin Sultan (1679-1692). See Allen (1987:37).

12. Bhacker puts it thus: '...the nineteenth century commercial development of Oman owed its genesis, in the final analysis, to the Industrial Revolution of the West. While the Omani economy (together with its East African component) was being increasingly integrated into the international economy, the suppression of the European slave trade gave it an added stimulus as the ensuing surplus slave labour was exploited locally for agricultural and commercial purposes. The demand for commodities such as ivory and cloves from Africa and textiles from Arabia, produced using traditional tribal and communal labour, rose as production was boosted by the increased availability of slave labour. This trend coupled with a corresponding decline in the prices of imported manufactured goods, provided the dynamics of an enormous commercial expansion in both Omani-controlled localities (1992: 195).

13. See Speece (1989: 501). Halliday notes that 'trade fell in 1874-4 to £426,000 - a quarter of its 1830 level' (1974:269).

14. Wilkinson (1987:68)notes that this nomenclature came into use after the Canning Award of 1861 whilst Allen (1978:4) says that the rulers were entitled Sultan after 1865.

15. A protectorate is a formal declaration that a country has responsibility for the conduct of another country's foreign relations (Doyle 1986: 359).

16. Exactly the same change took place with the Zanzibar branch of the Al Bu Sa'id dynasty (Doyle 1986: 359).

17. For a detailed account of the Imamate siege of Muscat and the subsequent signing under British auspices of the Treaty of Sib see J.E.Peterson (1976).

18. The relationship of the expansion of Britain imperial power and capitalism is put by Bromley thus: 'The establishment of British dominance, if not hegemony, within the global system was thus both cause and consequence of the incipient generalization of the capitalist market and the initial breakdown of the great Asian empires (1994: 59).

Chapter Three

1. This is the conclusion of the PGSC, minutes of the 5th meeting, 24 October 1928 quoted in Peterson (1986: 41-42).

2. In 1931 the PRPG assessed the optimal outlines of British policy in the Gulf: 'to maintain the independence of the Arab Shaikhdoms so long as they preserve law and order and maintain a system of administration that will satisfy or at any rate be tolerated by their subjects, to avoid any greater degree of interference in their internal affairs than is forced upon us but at the same time to prevent any other foreign power from dominating them or obtaining any special privileges in the Gulf.' He noted that London was taking an increasing interest in the affairs of the Gulf. This was due to the development of imperial interests - air routes, oil, the Shatt al-Arab and relations with Ibn Saud - as opposed to Indian Government interests, and also due to the fact that with political developments in India it was deemed inevitable the day when the responsibility for the Gulf would pass from the Government of India to H.M.G. in London (Peterson 1986:46).

3. Writing on state formation in Saudi Arabia Simon Bromley argues 'the process of state formation in any recognisable sense only gathered pace when oil was discovered and as oil rents began to enter the kingdom. The need of the oil companies for clear property rights was the occasion for the precise settlement of borders in the region; it was only access to oil wealth that enabled material development and with it the augmenting of state resources; it was only these resources which solved the problems of tribal rivalry and permitted the bedouin and the merchants to be paid off; it was only by means of oil that the economy was linked into the world market; and it was only because of the latter that this small and, therefore, relatively defenceless state attracted the support of an outside power, the United States' (1994: 143).

4. The practice of farming out the customs had ended in 1913 and the collection put in charge of a Director of Customs directly responsible to the Sultan. See J.E. Peterson (1978) p.75.

5. Zubayr b. Ali al-Huti was the only one of the council who could read or

write. In addition the Council found many ways of putting off decisions. The Annual Muscat Administration Report for 1923 stated: 'It functions with delatoriness [sic] and during the absence of His Highness to Dhofar found a new excuse for procrastination by reserving decisions in important matters pending his return. Saiyid Nadir the President when remonstrated with averred that it was impossible for the Council to arrive at a unanimous decision as the second member, the Member for Finance, invariably opposed any suggestion he made and the third member, the Minister of Justice, not being an Arab is treated by the other three as a nonentity, but has to be tolerated by them as he is the only one who can read or write.' See Peterson (1978: 104).

6. See chapter six for details on the attempts to 'Omanise' the armed forces in the 1980s.

7. This section on the functions of Imamate government is drawn from J.C. Wilkinson (1987: 177-190).

Chapter Four

1. Daniel Yergin gives an insight into the views of the experts of the Anglo-Persian Oil Company at the time: 'The company, to be sure, was convinced that there was no oil to be found in Arabia...the geological reports "leave little room for optimism," and one of the company's directors had declared in 1926 that Saudi Arabia appeared "devoid of all prospects" for oil. Albania, the director had added, was the promising oil play.' (1991:281)

2. See Wilkinson (1994: 99). He comments 'legitimacy of government and historic tradition lay at the core of frontier problems in Arabia. Oil was never of any import in western Arabia and scarcely, if at all, entered the frontier dispute with the Imam of Yemen. Interest in eastern Arabia was really only aroused by the discovery of oil in Bahrain in 1932 and it was only then that Britain adopted the Iraq Petroleum Company (IPC) as the sole candidate for concessions in the territories of its proteges. Until after the Second World War the interest of this international conglomerate in Arabia remained essentially pre-emptive. IPC was determined that Standard Oil of California (SOCAL), which held Bahrain and had recently obtained a concession from Ibn Saud, should not get any more.'

3. The Riyadh line 'remained, for the course of the intermittent Anglo-Saudi frontier negotiations, Britain's most generous offer to Saudi Arabia for territorial limits in the region' (Walker 1994: 174). Julian Walker was an official for the Foreign Office and undertook the 'fieldwork' on which many of the boundaries in south-east Arabia are based.

4. This Saudi claim was made following advice on sovereignty rights from international lawyers working for ARAMCO (Wilkinson 1994: 96).

5. In 1937 Fowle categorised the Persian Gulf's strategic importance as the 'Suez Canal of the air' (Peterson 1986: 47)

6. This was replaced by an agreement in 1947 that gave Britain access to the

airfields at Salalah, Masirah and Gwadur for a subsidy to Sa'id bin Taimur of L6000 a year (Skeet 1992: 82).

7. In 1937 a concession was awarded to the Iraq Petroleum Company Group in the name of the local company known as Petroleum Concessions Ltd. This concession was subsequently assigned to the company set up to explore the concession, Petroleum Development (Oman and Dhofar Ltd). Originally the proposed name for the subsidiary was Petroleum Development Muscat but was changed due to Sa'id's insistence that he could sign a concession for the interior (Wilkinson 1987: 276). In 1950 Dhofar was relinquished and the company name was changed to Petroleum Development (Oman) Ltd. In 1960 some of the partners in the IPC group withdrew from the Oman venture but Shell remained as the major shareholder. Oil was discovered in commercial quantities at Fahud in 1964 and exports commenced in 1967 (Hughes 1986: 172).

8. Townsend 1976: 55-56.

9. See US Department of State, 'Information on the Sultan of Muscat and Oman and his Country', February 1938, in Porter (1982: 59).

10. A US State Department document of February 1938 commented: 'As regards oil, the Sultan is known to have been interested in possible American participation in the development of Muscat's resources. Presumably, however, such action could only be undertaken with the approval of the British in view of the Sultan's agreement with the British in which he undertook not to permit the exploitation of his petroleum resources except with the consent of the Government of India.' See 'Information on the Sultan of Muscat and Oman and his country' in Porter (1982: 57).

11. In the subsequent concession documents with P.D.O which were based on the 1925 D'Arcy agreement, the word "independent" before "ruler" was deleted at Her Majesty's Government suggestion (Wilkinson 1987: 276).

12. The *lakh* is an Indian term for one hundred thousand and was used in reference to the Sultanate's budget as the Indian Rupee was the Sultanate's currency in this period.

13. See Petersen 1992 for a detailed account of the US-UK diplomacy over this dispute and its relation to the overall international situation in the Middle East.

14. See Townsend (1976: 168). Conventionally, it is perceived that the Sultan, in cooperation with the Imam, had been the driving force behind the assembling of a tribal force at Sohar to expel the Saudis from Buraimi in 1952. However, a document found by this author in the Foreign Office files in the Public Records Office, London contradicts this view. In 1966 E.F. Henderson produced a report entitled 'Security - Muscat and Oman'. A hand written note on this document by M.S. Weir of the Arabian Department, Foreign and Commonwealth Office, states 'it was not really his action: we had been urging it upon a reluctant Sultan for weeks, until we

suddenly went into reverse' (See, PRO, FO 371/185383; Security - Muscat and Oman, E.F. Henderson, 19 July 1966).

15. For an account of this tour of the interior by a journalist who accompanied Sa'id see James Morris, *Sultan in Oman* (1957).

16. For example, the Imamate began to adopt Western concepts and practices of state in order to play the 'sovereign state game' in the international fora of the Arab League and the UN. It started issuing its own passports, receiving consuls and even issuing its own stamps (the Sultanate's stamps bore the head of Elizabeth II surcharged in rupees and annas - see Innes 1987:63). Indeed the Imamate was more active in this regard than Sultan Sa'id who was not interested in joining international organisations.

17. See Wilkinson 1994 for a synopsis and 1991 for a full exposition of his study on Arabian boundaries.

Chapter Five

1. Darby comments: 'The basic military lesson of the campaign was that air power was no substitute for troops on the ground in maintaining stability in underdeveloped countries. Whatever may have been possible in Iraq and the North-West Frontier before the war, the Oman operation demonstrated that air action alone could no longer quell skirmishes and major uprisings in desert areas (1973: 130).

2. FO 371/149017

3. For a detailed account of Dhofar's cultures and languages, see Miranda Morris, 'Dhofar - What made it different', in Pridham (ed) (1987).

4. FO 371/148934, Telegram, Foreign Office to PRPG, No.863, July 29, 1960.

5. FO 371/179813, Muscat Annual Report for the Year 1964.

6. FO371/185365, Telegram from William Luce, PRPG, to London.

7. See the account of W.C. Carden, Consul General, Muscat in PRO. FO 371/185364.

8. Peter Thwaites, the commander of the Muscat Regiment informs at that these rebels were interrogated by Bob Brown, Sultan Sa'id's Intelligence Officer for Dhofar, and 'eventually ordered to be detained at the Sultan's pleasure'. He comments: 'The Sultan was a merciful man. In obedience to Koranic law, he never took the lives of his prisoners. High on the parched black rock surrounding Muscat harbour was a terrible fort called Jalali, built by the Portuguese in 1589. Here languished the Sultan's enemies, heavily shackled with great iron bars between their ankles; smugglers, murderers, political agitators, adulterers, debtors - and rebels.' See *Muscat Command* (1995: 20).

9. See PRO, FO371/ 185365. The minute is reproduced as an appendix.

10. The account in question is David Arkless (1988), *The Secret War: Dhofar 1971/1972*. The book recounts the author's experiences as an air-drop crew member working with the Skyvans in counter-guerrilla operations in Dhofar between 1971 and 1972.

11. This phrase was used by the Foreign Office official A. Brooke Turnes in July 1966 whilst discussing the possibility of withdrawing from RAF Salalah (FO 371/185375, comment on draft proposal for RAF Salalah, 12.7.66).

12. FO 371/185364, D.A. Roberts to Consul General Carden, 28.11.66.

13. FO 371/185364, Consul General Carden to D.A. Roberts, Political Agency, Dubai, 14.12.66.

14. FO 371/185362, Muscat Annual Report for the Year 1965.

15. FO 371/179814

16. FO 371/179814

17. There is a case of a sheikh who trekked by camel across the desert from northern Oman to Dhofar. When he got there Sa'id refused to see him and gave him enough money to only cover his expenses thus deterring any future missions to Salalah (Eickelman 1985: 18).

18. FO 371/185363, Consul General Carden to PRPG Luce, 15.1.66.

19. The role of another RAF base, that on Masirah Island, is given in another an RAF planning document of 1969 - 'Operational Policy for NEAF Vulcan Squadrons.' This states that two squadrons of Vulcan bombers were to be based at Akrotiri in Cyprus with three operational tasks: to provide the UK nuclear contribution to the Central Treaty Organisation; to provide nuclear support as necessary to meet the requirements of UK war plans; to support UK conventional war plans in the Mediterranean and Gulf areas. In order to meet the first two of these tasks they were to generate 100% of the aircraft within 72 hours which included sending three planes to Maharraq (Bahrain) and six to Masirah island; regular training detachments to Masirah were assessed as six detachments of three aircraft for three weeks each year (Winn 1994: 123).

20. Anthony Parsons informs us that in November 1967 when all the Gulf rulers expected Britain to depart, a Minister was sent out to inform them that Britain was intending to stay. Then two months later the same minister returned to tell them that Britain was in fact going to withdraw; the volte-face was to avoid raising the cost of prescriptions. However, it would seem that money was not the only issue as two of the rulers offered to pay the cost of British protecting forces in the Gulf but the offer was rejected (Balfour-Paul 1991: xvi).

21. In a cable to his superiors just prior to the coup, a British intelligence officer working for the Sultanate's intelligence services 'G2Int' comments that 'he [Sa'id bin Taimur] is fiddling while Rome burns and no one will change him' (Jones and Stone 1997:3).

22. Sheikh Shakhbut of Abu Dhabi, another Gulf ruler who embarrassed Britain with his unsuitableness to the modern world, had been removed from power by the British in 1965 and replaced by his brother Zaid (Halliday 1974: 288).

23. See Halliday (1974:349) for one of these leaflets.

24. See the account of Major General Jeapes of the SAS involvement in Dhofar in *Operation Storm: SAS Secret War*, (1996), or with its original title, *SAS Operation Oman*, (1980).

25. One of the 'perks' in this campaign for some of the members of the SAS was an unofficial bonus derived from the *firqats*. The SAS soldiers in outposts were expected to recruit *firqat* soldiers directly; the payroll of these *firqat* soldiers was adminstered directly by the SAS in the field. Some SAS soldiers issued a rifle to a non-existent firqat soldier and then pocketed the monthly wages. Amounts which could be garnered in this way could amount to 1000 - 2500 pounds in the 1970s. When the whistle was blown on this practice it was kept secret for twenty five years with the knowledge of government Ministers, senior army officers and Whitehall officials (Yvonne Ridley, 'SAS Cash for Arms', *Observer*, 25.10.98.)

26. An account of this battle by one of the soldiers involved is given in the television documentary 'The SAS: The Soldiers' Story. (Carlton, 1996)' See also Geraghty (1980: 124-132) and Ladd (1986: 162-164).

27. Liesl Graz observed that some Dhofari landscapes bore the scars: 'in the Jebel Qamar, around Kazetikayf, napalm killed the trees and the high plateau remains desolate in that otherwise verdant region' (1980: 40).

28. This was the comment of Robert Anderson who admitted he had volunteered information to the CIA but said he had no official responsibilities. Because the CIA was known to run its own show independently of the other channels of government the US Charge d'Affaires, Clifford Quinlan, could vouchsafe 'I discovered that the CIA had connections with Robert Anderson and Omar...I didn't know what representations they were making to His Majesty in the name of the US. They were unofficial representatives of the US government.' See Skeet (1992:59-60).

29. See Crystal (1990: 6) for an analysis of the impact of oil in the Gulf.

30. See J.E. Peterson (1978: 209). A CIA report claims that Tariq was declared *persona non grata* by Shaikh Shakhbut of Abu Dhabi because he had called for the overthrow of Sa'id bin Taimur. According to the same report a constitution for Oman had been prepared and a government-in-exile formed (Skeet 1992: 36).

31. See Bierschenk (1984: 239). Although this assessment of the importance of oil would not have passed comment in the early 1980s at the time of Bierschenk's study on state formation it would now at the end of the 1990s perhaps raise an eyebrow. The significance of water resources in the coming century for the countries of the Middle East is becoming ever more apparent. This will be discussed at greater length in chapter six.

32. Examples of such accounts are Pauline Searle, *Dawn over Oman* (1979) and F.A. Clements, *Oman: The Reborn Land* (1980).

33. The nature of these councils will be discussed in chapter six.

34. With thanks to Fred Halliday for this metaphor.

Chapter Six

1. See Fred Halliday, *Threat from the East? Soviet Policy from Afghanistan and Iran to the Horn of Africa*, (1982). For a summary of the spectrum of contemporary views on Soviet policy in the region in the early 1980s see Peterson, *Defending Arabia* (1986: 122 - 127).

2. For an analysis of the reasons for the collapse of communism in Eastern Europe at this point see Fred Halliday (1994) chapter nine, 'A Singular Collapse: The Soviet Union and Inter-State Competition'.

3. Sultan Qabus was dubbed 'our man in the Middle East' by one American writer. See Allen (1984: 3).

4. Oman's strategic importance had been long apparent to Omanis and the British. It was more Americans, as John Duke Anthony notes, who suddenly became aware in the early 1980's of Oman's strategic location. See John Duke Anthony, ' Oman the Gulf and the United States' in B.R. Pridham (ed), *Oman* (1987: 178).

5. Graz (1982) dubbed the Omanis the 'Sentinels of the Gulf'. Iranian incursions into Omani territorial waters in the early 1980s are listed in Cordesman, *The Gulf and the Search for Strategic Stability*, (1984: 615).

6. See Skeet (1992: 84) for the main text of the letter.

7. See 'US Security Interests in the Gulf - Report of a Staff Study Mission to the Persian Gulf , Middle East and Horn of Africa, October 21-November 13, 1980, to the Committee on Foreign Affairs, US House of Representatives, March 16, 1981. A text of the report is in Graz, *The Omanis: Sentinels of the Gulf*, (1982: 182-189).

8. Kechichian quotes a report in which Qabus explained: 'I would like to reveal one of the reasons behind this agreement. The strategic location of Oman and the possible threats, however remote, made it indispensable that Oman should enlarge its military establishments and airports. Consequently, we asked the GCC brothers to help us in this task, particularly as our oil resources are very limited in comparison to theirs. The required improvements involved about $2 billion, a sum which most brothers declined to spend, while the US showed readiness to finance these projects. That is how we came to agree on the facilities' (1995: 154).

9. See Skeet, *Oman: Politics and Development*, (1992: 85). Public reference to the Presidential letter was made in the Hearings before the Subcommittee on Europe and the Middle East of the Committee on Foreign Affairs, 1980. However the subcommittee took up the matter privately with the executive. See the text in Graz (1982: 191).

10. See Eilts (1988: 34) and Skeet (1992: 88). They both make reference to the article by Jeff Gerth and Judith Miller, 'US Set to Develop Oman as its Major Ally in the Gulf', *The New York Times*, 25 March 1985.

11. For an account of the day-to-day life of a contract officer see Hoskins, *A Contract Officer in Oman*, (1988).

12. See 'Defence' by Roger Matthews in 'Oman: A Special Survey', *The Financial*

Times, 13.1. 83; See also World Development Movement, *Gunrunner's Gold: How the public's money finances arms sales*, (1995: 26) and Skeet (1992: 99).

13. See Rigsbee (1992: 73). For a detailed study of the way in which the British government backed the sale of weapons to, amongst other countries, Oman, see *Gunrunner's Gold: How the public's money finances arms sales*, (London, World Development Movement, 1995).

14. See Bridget Bloom, 'Discreet relationship with the UK', Oman: Special Survey in *The Financial Times*, 11th November 1985.

15. See Bridget Bloom, 'Discreet relationship with the UK', Oman: Special Survey in *The Financial Times*, 11th November 1985. See also Allen, Oman, (1987: 118) and Peterson, Defending Arabia, (1986: 205).

16. This company sized infantry unit, recruited from tribesmen of the Jebel area in Dhofar, is independent of the regular army command structure and is stationed in eastern Oman. See Chris Westhorp, The World's Armies - An illustrated review of the armies of the world (London, Salamander Books, 1991), entry on Oman and The Financial Times, 11th November 1985, Bridget Bloom, Defence, in Oman: A Special Survey. Additionally, there is the Sultan's Royal Guard Brigade under a command independent of the regular army. The *raison d'etre* of the forces can be surmised as to prevent Qabus from being overthrown by the regular army.

17. See *Sunday Times*, 2.11.86, James Adam, 'Hold on, the cavalry's coming' and *Financial Times*, 24.11.86, David Buchan, 'UK practises helping Gulf friends'. See also Kechichian (1995: 133).

18. For details on the development of the Omani economy in this period see Skeet (1992: 100-109), Allen (1987: 94-100), Whelan (1987) and Hughes (1987).

19. 'Cementation not mentioned', *Financial Times*, 1.3.83.

20. 'Thatcher urged to make a full Oman statement', *Financial Times*, 5.3.83.

21. '$148m loan raised for Oman hospital', *Financial Times*, 6.3.83.

22. See *Observer* 16.1.84 and 5.2.84.

23. This phrase is in the title of J.E. Peterson's work, *The Arab Gulf States: Steps Towards Political Participation* (1988).

24. For details on the expansion and composition of the Sultan's Armed Forces in the 1980s see Allen (1987: 86-88), Cordesman (1984: 606-620), and Skeet (1992: 98-100).

25. For details on the evolution of Qabus's foreign policy see Joseph Kechichian, *Oman and the World: the Emergence of an Independent Foreign Policy*, (1995).

26. The Gulf War: Invasion, *BBC Television*, 1995

27. The Gulf War: Invasion, *BBC Television*, 1995

28. General Brent Scowcroft, US National Security Adviser at the time. 'The Gulf War: Invasion', *BBC Television*, 1995.

29. The dual containment policy was set out by Martin Indyk, senior director

for the Near East and South East Asia on the National Security Council, to the Washington Institute for Near East Policy on May 18 1993 (Gause 1994: 190).

30. *Gulf States Newsletter*, No. 503, January 1995.

31. Author's conversation with an expatriate working in the Omani government at the time. Muscat, March 1995.

32. In Oman 15,000 US marines practised three amphibious landings with 18 US landing vessels and 90 fixed wing jets (*The Independent*, 29.10.91).

33. *Gulf States Newsletter*, No. 503, January 1995.

34. *Guardian*, 13.1.03

35. *Guardian*, 9.4.03

36. *Gulf States Newsletter*, No. 503, 30.1.95

37. Oman: Where's Our Sultan, *The Economist*, 9.8.97, p.48.

38. Oman: Where's Our Sultan, *The Economist*, 9.8.97, p.48.

39. *Gulf States Newsletter*, No. 503, 30.1.95.

40. *Qatar News Agency*. Accessed via the internet http://www.ips.org.QNA/Oman

41. See Robin Allen, 'Oman warned: cut spending or face economic upheavals', *Financial Times* 7.11.94.

42. For details on the development of the economic liberalization process in Oman see Nonneman (1993).

43. *Economist Intelligence Unit*, Country Report: Oman, 1st quarter, 1995, p.12-13.

44. *Gulf States Newsletter*, No. 502, 16.1.95.

45. *Economist Intelligence Unit*, Oman, 2nd Quarter, 1995, p.10-11.

46. Conversation at the London School of Economics, 13.12.95.

47. The annual growth rate of the Omani population is 3.5%, with an average fertility rate estimated at seven children per Omani woman. Both these statistics are amongst the highest in the world. See *Economist Intelligence Unit*, Oman, 1st quarter 1994: 12.

48. For an account of the impact of oil on Oman, written by a member of the Omani government, see al-Yousef, *Oil and the transformation of Oman, 1970-1995*, (1995).

49. As late as 1984, Omanis continued to say 'Before Qabus nothing' (Riphenburg 1998: 52).

Conclusion

1. This is the title of J.E. Peterson's overview of political change in Oman: 'Oman's Odessy: from Imamate to Sultanate' in Pridham (ed) *Oman* (1987).

2. See 'Interview with Ken Waltz', Fred Halliday and Justin Rosenberg, *Review of International Studies*, Vol.24, No.1, (July 1998).

3. On the pace of change Qabus explained: 'We're making progress, but quietly. Slowly. I believe in evolution, and not a sudden evolution. But the progress we've made is irreversible.' See Miller (1997: 18).

Bibliography

Acharya, A. 1989: *US Military Strategy in the Gulf: Origins and Evolution under the Carter and Reagan Aministrations.* London: Routledge.

Akehurst, J. 1982: *We won a war: the campaign in Oman 1965 - 1975.* London: Michael Russell .

Al-Abdulkarim, A.A. 1997: *'Political economy and political development in the Arabian Peninsula: the case of the Sultanate of Oman',* PhD thesis, University of Southern California

Allen, C.H. 1978: *Sayyids, Shets and Sultans: Politics and Trade in Masqat Under the Al Bu Sa'id, 1785-1914.* Ph.D Thesis, University of Washington.

Allen, C.H. 1982: The State of Masqat in the Gulf and East Africa, 1785-1829. In *International Journal of Middle East Studies,* vol.14.

Allen, C.H. 1984: The Sultanate of Oman and American Security Interests in the Arabian Gulf. In Stookey, R. (ed).

Allen, C.H. 1987: *Oman: The Modernisation of the Sultanate.* Boulder: Westview Press.

Allen, C.H. and Rigsbee, W.L. 2000: Oman under Qaboos: from coup to constitution (London: Frank Cass)

Allen, C. 1991: *Thunder and Lightning - The RAF in the Gulf.* London: HMSO.

Amire, A. (ed) 1975: *The Persian Gulf and Indian Ocean in International Politics.* Teheran: Institute for International Political and Economic Studies.

Anthony, J.D. 1975: Insurrection and Intervention in Dhofar. In Amire, A (ed).

Anthony, J.D. 1986: Oman, the Gulf and the United States. In Pridham, B.R. (ed) 1986.

Arkless, D. 1988: *The Secret War: Dhofar 1971/1972.* London: Kimber.

Ayubi, N. 1995: *Overstating the Arab State: Politics and Society in the Middle East.* London: I.B Tauris

al-Baharna, H.M. 1968: *The Legal Status of the Arabian Gulf States.* Manchester: Manchester University Press.

al-Baharna, H.M. 1985: *The Consequences of the Britain's Exclusive Treaties: A Gulf View.* In Pridham, B.R. (ed).

Balfour-Paul, G. 1991: *The end of empire in the Middle East: Britain's relinquishment of power in her last three Arab dependencies.* Cambridge: Cambridge University Press.

Bathurst, R.D. 1967: *The Ya'rubi Dynasty of Oman.* D. Phil thesis, Oxford University.

Bathurst, R.D. 1972: Maritime Trade and Imamate Government: Two Principal Themes in the History of Oman to 1728. In Hopwood, D. (ed).

Beckett, I. and Pimlott, J. (eds) 1985: *Armed Forces and Modern Counter-Insurgency.* London: St. Martin's Press.

Behbehani, H. 1981: *China's Foreign Policy in the Arab World 1955 - 1975: Three Case Studies.* London: Keegan Paul International.

Bhacker, M. R. 1992: *Trade and Empire in Muscat and Zanzibar: Roots of British Domination.* London:Routledge.

Bierschenk, T. 1984: *Weltmarkt, Stammesgesellschaft und Staatsformation in Suedostarabien (Sultanat Oman).* Saarbruecken.
Bierschenk, T. 1989: Oil interests and the formation of centralized government in Oman, 1920-1970. In *Orient*, vol.30.
Birks, J.S. and Sinclair, C.A. 1980: *Arab Manpower: The Crisis of Development.* London: Croom Helm.
Bloch, J and Fitxgerald, P. 1983: *British Intelligence and Covert Action.* Dingle: Brandon Book Publishers.
Boxer, C.R. 1969: *The Portuguese Seaborne Empire.* London: Hutchinson.
Bowen-Jones, H. 1987: Geo-Constants in Oman. In Pridham 1987 (ed).
Bradley, C.P. 1982: *Recent United States Policy in the Persian Gulf (1971-1982).* Grantham: Tompson and Rutter.
Brewer, A. 1986: Theories of Imperialism in Perspective. In Mommsen, W. and Osterhammel, J. (eds).
Brittain, V. (ed) 1991: *The Gulf Between Us.* London: Virago.
Bromley, S. 1994: *Rethinking Middle East Politics.* London: Polity Press.
Brown, C. 1997: *Understanding International Relations.* Basingstoke: MacMillan.
Brown, J. 1994: *Modern India: Origins of an Asian Democracy.* Oxford:OUP.
Bulloch, J. and Darwish, A. 1993: *Water Wars: the Coming Conflicts in the Middle East.* London: Victor Gollancz.
Burrows, B. 1990: *Footprints in the Sand: The Gulf in Transition 1953 - 1958.* Salisbury: Michael Russell.
Busch, B.C. 1967: *Britain and the Persian Gulf 1894 -1914.* Berkely: University of California Press.
Chatty, D. 1996: *Mobile Pastoralists: Development Planning and Social Change in Oman.* New York: Columbia University Press.
Chubin, S. and Tripp, C. 1996: *Iran-Saudi Arabia Relations and Regional Order.* Oxford: Oxford University Press.
Chubin, S. and Tripp, C.: *Iran and Iraq at War.* London: I.B. Tauris
Clarke, J.I. (ed) 1981: *Change and Development in the Middle East.* London: Methuen.
Clements, F.A. 1980: *Oman: The Reborn Land.* London: Longman.
Collins Dunn, M. 1996: Oman and Gulf Security - Symposium: Contemporary Oman and U.S.-Relations. *In Middle East Policy*, Vol. IV, No 3, March 1996.
Cooley, J. 1991: *Payback: America's Long War in the Middle East.* New York: Brasseys.
Cordesman, A. 1984: *The Gulf and the Search for Strategic Stability.* Boulder: Westview Press.
Cordesman, A. 1986: *Military Strategy and Regional Security in the Gulf.* In B.R. Pridham (ed) 1986.
Cordesman, A.H. 1997: *Bahrain, Oman, Qatar and the UAE: Challenges of Security.* Boulder: Westview.
Crystal, J. 1990: *Oil and Politics in the Gulf: Rulers and Merchants in Kuwait and Qatar.* Cambridge: Cambridge University Press.
Crystal, J. 1996: Civil Society in the Arabian Gulf. In Norton, A.R. (ed)
Crystal, J. 1998: Social Transformation, Changing Expectations and Gulf Security. In Long, D and Koch, C. (eds).
Darby, P. 1973: *British Defence Policy East of Suez, 1947-1968.* London: Oxford University Press for Royal Institute for International Affairs.

BIBLIOGRAPHY

Darwin, J. 1991: *The End of the British Empire: The Historical Debate.* Oxford: Blackwell.
Davies, C. (ed) 1990: *After the War: Iran, Iraq, and the Arab World.* Chichester: Carden Publications.
De la Billiere, P. 1994: *Looking for Trouble: SAS to Gulf Command.* London: Harper Collins.
Dunn, M.C. 1996: Oman and Gulf Security. In *Middle East Policy,* Vol IV, No. 3.
Dutton, R.W. 1981: A Rural Development Project in Oman. In Clarke, J.I. (ed).
Eickelman, C. 1993: Fertility and Social Change in Oman. In *Middle East Journal*, Vol. 47: No.4.
Eickelman, D. 1986: Ibadhism and the Sectarian Perspective. In B.R. Pridham (ed) 1986
Eickelman, D.F. 1984: Kings and People: Oman's State Consultative Council. *Middle East Journal,* Vol. 38, No. 1.
Eickelman, D.F. 1985: From Theocracy to Monarchy: Authority and Legitimacy in Inner Oman. In *International Journal of Middle East Studies* Vol . 17, No. 1.
Eilts, H.F. 1988: Foreign Policy Perspectives. In Peterson, J. and Sindelar, H.R. (eds).
Faour, M. 1993: *The Arab World After Desert Storm.* Washington: United States Institute of Peace.
Fay, C.R. 1940: *Cambridge History of the British Empire, Vol II.* Cambridge.
Fiennes, R. 1975: *Where Soldiers Fear to Tread.* London: Hodder and Stoughton.
Gaddis, J.L. 1996: History, Science and the Study of International Relations. In Woods, N. (ed).
Gallagher, J. and Robinson, R. 1953: The Imperialism of Free Trade. In *Economic History Review*, 2nd ser. VI, I.
Gallagher, J. and Robinson, R. 1961: *Africa and the Victorians: The Official Mind of Imperialism.* London: MacMillan.
Gallagher, J. 1980: *The Decline, Revival and Fall of the British Empire,* edited by Anil Seal. Cambridge, CUP.
Gause, F.G. 1994: *Oil Monarchies: Domestic and Security Challenges in the Arab Gulf States.* New York: Council on Foreign Relations Press.
Geraghty, T. 1980: *Who Dares Wins.* London: Arms and Armour Press.
Giddens, A. 1985: *The Nation State and Violence.* Cambridge: Polity Press.
Graz, L. 1982: *The Omanis: Sentinels of the Gulf.* London: Longman.
Graz, L. 1992: *The Turbulent Gulf.* London. I.B. Tauris.
Greenstein, F. and Polsby, N. (eds) 1975: *Handbook of Political Science.* Reading, MA: Addison-Wesley.
al-Haj, A.J. 1996: The Politics of Participation in the Gulf Cooperation Council States: The Omani Consultative Council. In *Middle East Journal*, Vol. 50, No. 4.
Hall, J. (ed) 1986: *States in History.* Oxford: Blackwell.
Halliday, F. 1974: *Arabia Without Sultans.* Pelican: Harmondsworth.
Halliday, F. 1977: *Mercenaries: Counter Insurgency in the Gulf.* Nottingham: Spokesman.
Halliday, F. 1980: The Gulf Between Two Revolutions. In T. Niblock (ed).
Halliday, F. 1981: The Arc of Crisis and the New Cold War. In MERIP Reports, Oct.
Halliday, F: 1982: *Threat from the East? Soviet Foreign Policy from Afghanistan and Iran to the Horn of Africa.* Harmondsworth: Penguin.
Halliday, F. 1986: *The Making of the Second Cold War* (2nd edn). London: Verso.

Halliday, 1987a: News Management and Counter Insurgency: The Case of Oman. In Pimlott, B (ed).
Halliday, 1987b: *Beyond Irangate: The Reagan Doctrine and the Third World.* Amsterdam: Transnational Institute.
Halliday, F. 1988: The Gulf in International Affairs: Independence and After. In B.R. Pridham (ed).
Halliday, F. 1990: *Revolution and Foreign Policy - The Case of South Yemen 1967 - 1987.* Cambridge: Cambridge University Press.
Halliday, F. 1994: *Rethinking International Relations.* Basingstoke, MacMillan.
Halliday, F. 1996: *Islam and the Myth of Confrontation.* London, I.B. Tauris.
Halliday, F. 1997: *Arabia Without Sultans Revisited.* MERIP Reports, July/Sept.
Hawley, D. 1977: *Oman and its Renaissance.* London: Stacey International.
Hay, C 1995: 'Structure and Agency' in Marsh and Stoker (eds).
Helms, R.F. 1993: *The Persian Gulf Crisis: Power in the Post-Cold War World.* London: Praegar.
al-Hinai, A.A. 2000: 'State Formation in Oman 1861-1970', PhD thesis, University of London.
Holden, D. 1966: *Farewell to Arabia.* London: Faber and Faber.
Hollis, M. and Smith, S. 1990: *Explaining and Understanding in International Relations.* Oxford: Clarendon Press.
Hoogland, E. 1990: US Policy Towards the Persian Gulf in the 1990s. In Davies, C. (ed).
Hopwood, D. (ed) 1972: *The Arabian Peninsula: Society and Politics.* London: Allen and Unwin.
Hoskins, A. 1988: *A Contract Officer in Oman.* London: Costello.
Hughes, F. 1986: Oil in Oman - A Short Historical Note. In Pridham, B.R. (ed).
Hurewitz, J.C. 1979: *The Middle East and North Africa in World Politics (Volume 2): British-French Supremacy 1914 - 1945.* London: Yale University Press.
Innes, N.M. 1986: *Minister in Oman.* Cambridge: Oleander Press.
Janzen, J. 1982: Dhofar: Vom Weihrauch- zum Erdoelland: Abriss der historischen Entwicklung der politischen und sozio-oekonimischen Verhaeltnisse in einer peripheren Region Arabiens. In Orient (23).
Janzen, J. 1987: *Nomads in the Sultanate of Oman: Tradition and Development in Dhofar.* London: Westview Press.
Jeapes, T. 1980: *SAS Operation Oman.* London: Kimber.
Jeapes, T. 1996: Operation Storm: SAS Secret War. London: HarperCollins.
Janzen, J. 1986: *Nomads in the Sultanate of Oman: Tradition and Development in Dhofar.* Boulder: Westview.
Joffé, G. 1994: Concepts of Soverignty in the Gulf Region in Schofield, R (ed), (1994b).
Jones, C and Stone J. 1997: Britain and the Arabian Gulf: New Perspectives on Strategic Influence . In *International Relations*, vol. XIII, No. 4.
Joyce, M. 1994: Washington and Treaty-Making with the Sultan of Muscat and Oman. In *Middle East Studies*, Vol. 30, No1, January 1994.
Joyce, M. 1995: *The Sultanate of Oman: A Twentieth Century History.* Westport: Praeger.
Katz, M. 1986: *Russia and Arabia: Soviet Foreign Policy Toward the Arabian Peninsula.* Baltimore and London: John Hopkins University Press.
Kaylani, N.M. 1979: Politics and Religion in Oman: A Historical Overview. In *International Journal of Middle East Studies*, vol.10.

Kechichian, J. 1995: *Oman and the World: The Emergence of an Independent Foreign Policy.* Santa Monica: Rand.
Kelly, J.B. 1968: *Britain and the Persian Gulf 1795 - 1880.* Oxford: Clarendon Press.
Kelly, J.B. 1972: A Prevalence of Furies. In Hopwood, D. (ed).
Kelly, J. B. 1976: Hadramhaut, Oman, Dhofar: the Experience of Revolution. *Middle Eastern Studies,* Vol 12. No. 2.
Kemp, T. 1967: *Theories of Imperialism.* London: Dennis Dobson.
Khoury, P. and Kostiner, J. (eds) 1990: *Tribes and State Formation in the Middle East.* London: I.B. Tauris.
Kostiner, J. 1984: *The Struggle for South Yemen.* London: Croom Helm.
Krech, H. 1996: *Bewafnette Konfliket im Sueden der Arabischen Halbinsel: Der Dhofarkrieg im Sultanat Oman und der Buergerkrieg im Jemen 1994.* Berlin: Koester.
Kunniholm, B. 1993a: The US experience in the Persian Gulf. In Helms, R.F. (ed).
Kunniholm, B. 1993b: US Responses to the Persian Gulf Crisis. In Helms, R.F. (ed).
Landen, R.G. 1967: *Oman Since 1856: Disruptive Modernisation in a Traditional Arab Society.* Princeton: Princeton University Press.
Ladd, J.D. 1986: *SAS Operations.*
Lavergne, M. and Dumortier, B. 2002: L'Oman contemporain: état, territoire, identité. Paris, Éditions Karthala
Long, D. and Koch, C. (eds) 1998: *Gulf Security in the Twenty First Century.* Abu Dhabi: Emirates Center for Strategic Studies and Research.
Linz, J.J 1975: Totalitarian and Authoritarian Regimes. In Greenstein, F. and Polsby, N (eds).
Louis, W.R. 1976 (ed): *Imperialism: The Gallagher and Robinson Controversy.* Basingstoke: MacMillan
Louis, W.R. 1977: *Imperialism at Bay: The United States and the Decolonisation of the British Empire, 1941-1945.* Oxford: Clarendon Press.
Louis, W.R. 1984: *The British Empire in the Middle East 1945-1951: Arab Nationalism, The United States, and Postwar Imperialism.* Oxford: Clarendon Press.
Louis, W.M. and Robinson, R. 1994: The Imperialism of Decolonisation. In *Journal of Imperial and Commonwealth History,* Vol. 22, No. 3.
Lunt, J. 1981: *Imperial Sunset: Frontier Solidiering in the 20th Century.* London: MacDonald.
Makallah, R. 1972: Economic Requirements for Development in Oman. In *Middle East Journal,* Vol 26. No.2.
Malek, M.H. 1991: *International Mediation and the Gulf War.* Glasgow: Royston.
Mann, M. 1984: The Autonomous Power of the State. Reprinted in Hall, J. (ed). 1986.
Mann, M. 1994: *The Trucial Oman Scouts.* Norwich: Michael Russell.
Marsh, D and Stoker, G 1995: *Theory and Methods in Political Science* (Basingstoke: MacMillan).
Melamid, A. 1986: Interior Oman. In *Geographical Review,* Vol. 76. No.3.
Miller, J. 1997: Creating Modern Oman: An Interview with Sultan Qabus. In Foreign Affairs 76 (May/June).
Mommsen, W. 1980: *Theories of Imperialism.* London, Weidenfeld and Nicholson.
Mommsen, W. and Osterhammel, J. (eds) 1986: *Imperialism and After: Continuities and Discontinuities.* Basingstoke: MacMillan.
Morris, J. 1957: *Sultan in Oman.* London: Faber and Faber.
Murphy, E. and Niblock, T. (eds) 1993: *Economic and Political Liberalization in*

the Middle East. London: British Academic Press.

Musawi-al, H. 1990: *A History of Omani-British relations, with special reference to the period 1888-1920*. Ph.D thesis, University of Glasgow.

al-Naqeeb, K. 1990: *Society and State in the Gulf and Arab Peninsula: A Different Perspective*. London: Routledge.

Niblock, T. (ed) 1980: *Social and Economic Development in the Arab Gulf.* London: Croom Helm.

Netton, I.R. 1986: *Arabia and the Gulf: Fron Traditional Society to Modern States*. London: Croom Helm.

Norton, A.R. (ed) 1996: *Civil Society in the Middle East*. New York: E.J. Brill.

Nonneman, G. 1993: *Oman and Yemen*. In Murphy, E. and Niblock, T. (eds).

O'Reily, M.J. 1998: Omanibalancing; Oman Confronts an Uncertain Future. In *Middle East Journal*, Vol. 52.

Osterhammel, J. 1986: Semi-Colonialism and Informal Empire in Twentieth Century China: Towards a Framework of Analysis. In Mommsen,W and Osterhammel, J. (eds).

Ovendale, R. 1996: Britain, the United States and the Transfer of Power in the Middle East, 1945-1962. London: Leicester University Press

Owen, R. and Sutcliffe, B. (eds) 1972: *Studies in the Theory of Imperialism*. London: Longman.

Owen, R. 1992: *State, Power and Politics in the Making of the Modern Middle East*. London, Routledge.

Owtram, F.C. 1999: Oman and the West: State Formation in Oman since 1920. PhD thesis, London School of Economics

Owtram, F.C. 2002: L'Oman et L'Occident: le formation de l'État omanaise depuis 1920 in Lavergne, M and Dumortier, B (2002)

Petersen, T.T. 1992: Anglo-American Rivalry in the Middle East: The Struggle for the Buraimi Oasis 1952-1957. In *International History Review* (Canada), Vol. 14, No.1.

Peters, B. Guy 1998: *Comparative Politics: Theory and Method* (Basingstoke: MacMillan)

Peterson, J.E. 1976: The Revival of the Ibadhi Imamate in Oman and the Threat to Muscat, 1913-1920. In *Arabian Studies*, vol.3.

Peterson, J.E. 1977: Tribes and Politics in the Eastern Arabia. In *Middle East Journal*, Vol 3. No. 3.

Peterson, J.E. 1978: *Oman in the Twentieth Century: Political Foundations of an Emerging State*. London: Croom Helm.

Peterson, J.E. 1984: Legitimacy and Political Change in Yemen and Oman. In *Orbis*, Vol. 27. No.4.

Peterson, J.E. 1986: *Defending Arabia*. London: Croom Helm.

Peterson, J.E. 1987: Omans Odyssey: From Imamate to Sultanate. In Pridham, B.R. (ed).

Peterson, J.E. 1988: *The Arab Gulf States: Steps Towards Political Participation*. New York: Praeger.

Peterson, J.E. and Sindelar, H.R. (eds) 1988: Crosscurrents in the Gulf: Arab, Regional and Global Interests. London: Routledge.

Peterson, J.E. 1991: The Arabian Peninsula in Modern Times: A Historiographical Survey. In *American Historical Review*, Vol.96.

Pimlott, B. and Seaton, J. (eds) 1987: The Media in British Politics. Aldershot: Avebury.

Pimlott, J. 1985: The British Army: The Dhofar Campaign, 1970-1975. In Beckett, I. and Pimlott, J. (eds).
Pool, D. et al 1994: *Third World Politics: A Comparative Introduction.* Manchester: Manchester University Press.
Porter, J.D. 1982: *Oman and the Persian Gulf 1835-1949.* Salisbury: Documentary Publications.
Price, D.L. 1975: *Oman: Insurgency and Development.* London: Institute for the Study of Conflict.
Pridham, B.R. 1985: *The Arab Gulf and the West.* Beckenham: Croom Helm.
Pridham, B.R. 1986: Oman: Change or Continuity? in Netton, I (ed).
Pridham. B.R. (ed) 1987: *Oman: Economic, Social and Strategic Developments.* London: Croom Helm.
Pridham, B.R. 1988: *The Arab Gulf and the Arab World.* Beckenham: Croom Helm.
Rashid, Z.M. 1981: *Sa'udi Relations with Eastern Arabia and Oman.* London:Luzac.
Rawlings, J.D. *The History of the RAF.* London: Aerospace Publishing.
Rigsbee, W.L. 1990: *American Foreign Policy toward the Sultanate of Oman 1977-1987.* Ph.D thesis, University of Cincinnati.
Riphenburg, C.J. 1998: *Oman: Political Development in a Changing World.* London: Praeger.
Risso, P. 1986: *Oman and Muscat: An Early Modern History.* London: Croom Helm.
Robinson, R. 1972: Non-European foundations of European imperialism: sketch for a theory of collaboration. In Owen, R. and Sutcliffe, B. (eds).
Robinson, R. 1986: The Excentric Idea of Imperialism, with or without Empire. In Mommsen,W and Osterhammel, J. (eds).
Rosenberg, J. 1994: *The Empire of Civil Society.* London, Verso.
Said Zahlan, R. 1989: *The Making of the Modern Gulf States.* London: Unwin Hyman.
Saify, M.E. 1991: US Military Intervention in the Persian Gulf 1987-1988. In Malek, M.H. (ed).
Schofield, R. (ed) 1994a: *The Middle East and North Africa: World Boundaries* (vol 2). London: Routledge.
Schofield, R. (ed) 1994b: *Territorial Foundations of the Gulf States.* London: UCL Press.
Scholz, F. 1994: Staedtische Armut in den Erdoelforerderlaendern der Golfregion: 'Capital Area' von Oman als Beispeil. In *Geographische Zeitschrift*, Vol. 82 No.1.
Searle, P. 1979: Dawn over Oman. London: Allen and Unwin.
al-Shamlan, A.R. 1987: *The Evolution of National Boundaries in the Southeastern Arabian Peninsula.* Ph.D Thesis, University of Michigan.
Shariff, A. 1994: Indian Ocean Trade. Review of Bhacker, M.R. (1992), *Journal of African History*, Vol. 35.
Siegfried, N. 1998: *Genese und Funktion des omanischen Grundgesetzes vom 6. November 1996.* MA Thesis, Freie Universitaet, Berlin. Accessed via Internet: http://www.rrz.uni-hamburg.de/wst/nas/main.html
Skeet, I. 1974: *Muscat and Oman*: The End of an Era. London: Faber and Faber.
Skeet, I. 1992: *Oman: Politics and Development.* Basingstoke: MacMillan.
Smiley, D. 1975: *Arabian Assignment.* London: Cooper.
Speece, M. 1989: Aspects of Economic Dualism in Oman, 1830-1930. In *International Journal of Middle East Studies*, vol. 21.
Stookey, R. (ed) 1984: *The Arabian Peninsula: Zone of Ferment.* Stanford: Hoover Institution Press.

Stork, J. 1980a: US Targets Persian Gulf for Intervention. In *MERIP* Reports, (85) Feb.
Stork, J. 1980b: The Carter Doctrine and US Bases in the Middle East. In *MERIP* Reports, (90) Sept.
Stork, J. 1980c: Saudi Arabia and the US. In *MERIP* Reports (91).
Stork, J. 1982: Israel as a Strategic Asset. In *MERIP* Reports, (105) May.
Thwaites, P. 1995: *Muscat Command.* London: Leo Cooper.
Timmerman, K. 1992: *The Death Lobby: How the West Armed Iraq.* London: Bantam.
Timpe, L. 1991: *British Foreign Policy Toward the Sultanate of Muscat and Oman 1954-1959.* Ph.D Thesis, University of Exeter.
Townsend, J. 1977: *Oman: The Making of a Modern State.* London: Croom Helm.
Walker, J. 1994: **The United Arab Emirates and Oman Frontiers** in R. Schofield (ed) 1994a.
al-Wasmi, K. 1986: *Oman entre l'indépendance et l'occupation coloniale: recherches sur l'histoire moderne d'Oman dans ses relations régionales et internationales (1789-1904).* Geneva: Labor et Fides.
Warren, B. 1980: *Imperialism: Pioneer of Capitalism.* London, Verso.
Wesseling, H.L. 1986: Imperialism and Empire: An Introduction. In Mommsen,W and Osterhammel, J. (eds).
Westhorpe, C. 1991: *The World's Armies.* London: Salamander.
Whelan, J. 1987: Oman's Development Strategy. In B.R. Pridham (ed).
Wiarda, H. (ed) 1985: *New Directions in Comparative Politics.* Boulder: Westview Press.
Wilkinson, J.C. 1977: *Water and Tribal Settlement in South-east Arabia.* Oxford: OUP.
Wilkinson, J.C. 1972: The Origins of the Omani State. In Hopwood, D. (ed).
Wilkinson, J.C. 1980: Changes in the Structure of Village Life in Oman. In Niblock, T. (ed).
Wilkinson, J.C. 1987: *The Imamate Tradition of Oman.* Oxford: OUP.
Wilkinson, J.C. 1991 Arabia's Frontiers: *The Story of Britain's Boundary Drawing in the Desert.* London: I.B. Tauris
Winn, H. 1994: *The RAF Nuclear Deterrent Forces: Their Origins, Roles and Deployment 1946-1969.* London: HMSO.
Wolf, E. 1982: *Europe and the People Without History.* Berkely: University of California Press.
Woods, N. 1996: The Uses of Theory in the Study of International Relations. In Woods, N. (ed).
Woods, N. (ed) 1996: *Explaining International Relations Since 1945.* Oxford, OUP.
World Development Movement, 1995: *Gunrunners Gold: How the Public's Money Finances Arm Sales.* London: World Development Movement.
Yapp, M.E. 1996: *The Near East since the First World War: A History to 1995.* London: Longman
Yergin, D. 1991: *The Prize: The Epic Quest for Oil, Money and Power.* London: Simon and Schuster.
al-Yousef, M.M. 1995: *Oil and the Transformation of Oman, 1970-1995.* London: Stacey International.
Zubaida, S. 1989: *Islam, the People and the State.* London: Routledge.

Index

Abu Dhabi (UAE) 104, 137, 140, 200, 201, 216, 217
Administration 16, 22, 24, 39,
  under imamate 66-67
  under Qaboos 136-139
  reforms in early 20th century 51, 63, 64, 194, 204, 213
  under Sa'id bin Taimur 82, 121, 116-118
Aflaj. See irrigation
Afonso de Albuquerque 44
Agriculture 10
  ancient development 42, 94
  exports 50
  modernisation 183, 189
  traditional 117
Airforce, see Sultan of Oman's Air Force
Airports 148, 218
Al Bu Shamis 88
Al-Sa'id 141
  Family 137, 164, 165, 201
  Succession 38, 39, 45, 167, 183, 188, 191, 201
America, American, see United States
Anglo-French declaration 18
Anglo-Persian Oil Company 55, 56, 62, 213
Arabian American Oil Company 80, 85, 89, 90, 213
Arabian Peninsula 4, 5, 6, 7, 25, 29, 30, 41, 50, 51, 52, 54, 56, 57, 61, 69 - 72, 74, 84, 93, 94, 97, 98, 100, 115, 124, 142, 193, 194, 196, 210
Arab League 140, 215
Arabs 136, 71
  settlement in Oman 42, 44
Aramco, See Arabian American Oil Company
Armed Forces 6, 59, 65, 69, 103, 111, 112, 124, 130, 145, 150, 153, 156, 157, 161, 162, 213, 219
Arms trade 170
Ayatollah Khomeini (Iran) 143, 146

Baghdad (Iraq) 51, 52, 60, 79, 146, 171, 173
Bahla 106
Bahrain 2, 6, 26, 46, 53, 56 - 57, 59, 60 - 61, 65, 69 - 72, 75-76, 84, 95, 104, 119, 123-124, 128, 132, 139, 145, 147, 172, 179, 194, 196, 200 - 201, 203, 213, 216
Blair, Tony 176-177
Bush, George 155, 168, 170, 171
Bush, George W. 177
Baluchi 63
  in the army 65, 111, 136
Baluchistan 102
Banians 47 See also Hindus
Basra (Iraq) 46, 53
Batinah 30, 43, 44, 45, 53, 58, 60, 65, 76, 79, 88, 90, 96, 106, 118, 200
  Administration 82, 166
  Agriculture 189
Batinah Field Force 91
Buraimi 10, 60, 73, 77, 83, 88, 89, 90-92, 100-101, 140, 214

Central Intelligence Agency 133
Chauncey, Leslie 119
Chamber of Commerce and Industry 187
civil service 185
collaboration 2-3, 10-12, 14-15, 17, 19-21, 49, 96, 122, 203, 204-206
copper 139
Council of Ministers 6, 19, 63, 67, 79, 80, 205

Development Council 138
Dhahirah 76, 81, 88
Dhofar, 30, 58, 59, 61, 76, 79, 88, 96, 98, 108, 114, 118, 122, 138-139, 149, 165
  administration, 109, 121, 181
  war in 7, 97, 105, 109-112, 116, 123-135, 147, 160, 164, 179, 195, 197-203, 213
Dhofar Liberation Front 109, 112, 125

economic development 180, 183-190, 206
  under Sa'id
education 137, 140, 150, 166, 179, 199
  under Sa'id 116, 117, 122
Egypt 14, 32, 83, 85, 93, 97, 126, 153
Empire 1,2, 3, 6, 12, 13, 14, 17, 18-21, 33, 38, 44, 47-67, 83-84, 99, 111, 122, 141-143, 146, 193, 195, 203-207

Fahud 87, 91, 106, 214
Finance Council 138, 139
Finances 62
Firqat 217
Fisheries 152
foreign affairs 147, 159, 164, 167, 179, 191, 218
France 31, 33, 35, 37, 40, 161, 176

Gendarmerie 108
Germany 49
Ghassani, al- 126
Great Britain (Britain) 1-6, 9-10, 12, 14-18, 19, 26, 31-40, 44, 47, 49, 50-55, 60, 64, 69-70, 73, 74, 76, 77, 80, 83, 84-86, 93, 96-106, 112, 114, 116, 118, 120, 125-126, 130-133, 135, 141-142, 146, 150, 157-164, 173, 175, 177, 195, 196, 207
Gulf Co-operation Council 2, 25, 26, 27, 145-146, 151, 153, 158-159, 166-167, 172-173, 177-178, 180, 184, 187, 198, 200-203

Health 116, 137, 179
Henderson, Edward 214
Hindus 137, 138
Hormuz, Straits of 125, 143, 145, 146, 147, 155, 161, 175
Housing 179

Ibadhism 41, 42, 46, 200
Ibri 91, 127
imam, imamate 12, 14, 34, 42, 43 - 49, 59, 66 - 67, 77, 81- 83, 86 -87, 90, 91- 92, 95, 100 - 101, 115, 140, 213, 214
imperialism 1, 2, 8, 12, 13, 14, 15, 16, 17, 20, 21, 23, 25, 41, 43, 47-50, 55, 57, 100, 112, 124, 169, 193-198, 203, 205, 206, 207, 209
India 6, 29, 30, 31, 32, 33, 35, 36, 38, 39, 44, 47, 50, 51, 52, 53, 57, 59, 60, 62, 63, 64, 65, 67, 76, 79, 80, 82, 83, 86, 94, 98, 114, 142, 193, 194, 212, 214
industry, 26, 73, 169, 189, 202,
Iran 56, 70, 75, 86, 93, 123-125, 134, 143, 145-147, 151, 154-155, 168-169, 171, 175, 188,
Iraq 7, 49, 57, 70-71, 75, 85, 93, 109, 114, 145, 146, 154, 161, 168, 169, 170, 171, 172, 173, 174, 175, 177, 215,
irrigation 42, 117, 119
Israel 126, 147

Jebal Akhdar 88, 90, 105, 106, 107, 117, 119, 129, 195
Japan 79, 187
Jordan 85, 135, 171

Khalili, al- 67, 87, 90, 140
Kuwait 2, 5, 7, 25, 26, 53, 56, 60, 63, 97, 100, 102, 116, 119-120, 138, 139, 145, 146, 151, 161, 168-171, 172-175, 177, 178, 179, 185, 196, 198-203

Landon, Tim 128, 176

Majlis al-Shura 179
Musandam 30, 58, 79, 117, 118, 125, 130, 164, 166, 175
Masirah Island 7, 76, 77, 84, 103, 132, 133, 148, 150, 151, 155, 156, 161, 216
Matrah 30, 39, 63, 65, 96, 118, 138, 148
Muscat 6, 7, 12, 15, 16, 18, 29-47, 49-54, 58-65, 67, 69, 72-83, 86-87, 92, 96
Muscat and Oman Field Force 91
Muscat Mafia 164

Nabhani, see Sulaiman bin Himyar
Nizwa 6, 30, 67, 69, 91, 92, 93, 100, 106, 117, 127, 190
Northern Frontier Regiment 111

INDEX

oil 2, 4, 5, 6, 7, 11, 12, 25-27, 50-51, 55-62, 65, 67, 69-76, 78, 80-81, 84, 85, 87, 88, 89, 91-96, 98, 100-101, 105, 110, 113-114, 118, 119, 121, 123, 125, 130, 133, 136-138, 144-147, 154, 161, 163, 169, 170-172, 177, 180, 183, 184-190, 192-203, 205
Omar bin Abd al-Mu'nim al-Zawawi 138
Omanisation 137, 138, 150, 168, 175
OPEC 171,
Operation Swift Sword 161, 176

Pakistan 102, 117, 138
Petroleum 54, 60
Petroleum Development Oman (PDO) 69, 76, 86, 89, 91, 96, 127, 137
Philips, Wendell 118
police 61, 108, 138, 139, 141, 156, 157, 190
Popular Front for the Liberation of Oman 131
Popular Front for the Liberation of Oman and the Arabian Gulf 129, 131

Qabus bin Sa'id Al Sa'id 2, 7, 98, 123, 126-128, 132-136, 140-141, 149, 151-153, 156-158, 160, 162-168, 175, 178-180, 182, 187, 190, 195, 200-202, 205, 207
Qais bin Abd al-Mu'nim al-Zawawi 138, 148, 152, 164
Qara 109
Qatar 2, 25, 26, 53, 60, 72, 124, 145, 179, 198, 201, 202, 203

Ras al-Hadd 30, 44
Royal Air Force (RAF) (Great Britain) 52, 53, 77, 86, 87, 91, 103, 110, 130, 135, 142, 161, 176, 205
royal family 7, 63, 119, 120, 158, 165, 167, 191
Russia, see Soviet Union
Rustaq 30, 45, 46, 82

Sa'id b. Taimur Al-Sa'id 6-7, 9-10, 19, 39, 64, 69-70, 78-79, 86-87, 90, 96, 98, 104, 112-113, 115-116, 119, 121-123, 195, 203, 205, 207
Sa'id bin Ahmad al-Shanfari 165
Salalah 160, 174, 189, 202, 207
  Dhofar war 3, 7, 110, 111, 130, 131, 134, 135, 142
  under Sa'id 7, 52, 54, 76, 78, 79, 82, 92, 103, 108, 109, 119, 122, 126, 128, 205
Saudi Arabia 2, 4, 5, 12, 26, 56, 72, 75, 85-86, 89, 92, 93, 100-101, 106-107, 109, 114-116, 119, 123-125, 134, 135-138, 140-141, 145-147, 153, 158, 169, 171-173, 184, 196, 198, 201
September 11th 176
Sharjah 53, 106
Shell Oil Company 127
Soviet Union 124, 130
State Consultative Council 165-168, 179, 182
Sultan of Oman's Air Force 108
Sultan of Oman's Land Forces 155
Sulaiman bin Himyar 90, 91, 106

Thatcher, Margaret 146, 157, 162
Thumrait 131, 148, 149, 172, 174
Treaty of Sib 6, 50, 58, 62, 65, 66, 81, 90, 194, 204, 212
Tribes 37, 42, 43, 45, 48, 49, 65, 76
  under Sai'id bin Taimur 76, 81, 86, 87, 88, 89, 93, 119, 179, 198, 199, 204
Trucial Oman Scouts 91, 106

United Arab Emirates 2, 26, 30, 198
United Nations 10, 106, 112, 115, 116
United States 1, 4, 5, 7, 26, 40, 55, 77, 79, 83, 84-86, 97, 107, 112-115, 123, 125, 133, 142, 144, 147-149, 153, 168, 170-173, 177-178, 180, 212

Walis 58, 63, 66, 82, 111, 128
Waterfield, Pat 111, 127
water resources 152, 183, 188-189, 193
Watts, John 126, 135, 153, 156, 157
World Bank 178, 184-186, 189

Yemen 95, 114, 115, 124, 175, 188
 People's Democratic Republic 97,
  111, 124, 125, 126, 132, 140, 144

Zakat 63
Zanzibar 16, 17, 18, 19, 29, 38, 39, 40,
 47, 63, 117, 204, 210
Zawawi 138, 139, 148, 152, 164, 190